What people are saying about

Where Airy Voices Lead

The best book currently available on the meaning of immortality and its interpreters through the ages. Learned, wide-ranging and wise, this is essential reading for the Hamlets among us!
Geoffrey Scarre, Professor of Philosophy, Department of Philosophy, Durham University, UK, author of *Death*, published by Acumen, 2007.

Where Airy Voices Lead is impressively global in scope, yet exceedingly nuanced in its appraisal and strikingly dispassionate in tone. Bienkowski's history demonstrates that any culture's afterlife beliefs reflect the values of that society. He challenges the reader by arguing that, although none of these types of immortality can be proved, equally none can be dismissed and are deserving of respect and investigation. He concludes that our attitude toward immortality is an ethical choice.
Brian Schmidt, Professor of Hebrew Bible and Ancient Mediterranean West Asian Cultures, The University of Michigan, author of *Israel's Beneficent Dead: Ancestor Cult and Necromancy in Ancient Israelite Religion and Tradition* and numerous articles on death, memory and immortality.

Where Airy Voices Lead

A Short History of Immortality

Where Airy Voices Lead

A Short History of Immortality

Piotr Bienkowski

BOOKS

Winchester, UK
Washington, USA

JOHN HUNT PUBLISHING

First published by O-Books, 2020
O-Books is an imprint of John Hunt Publishing Ltd., 3 East St., Alresford,
Hampshire SO24 9EE, UK
office@jhpbooks.com
www.johnhuntpublishing.com
www.o-books.com

For distributor details and how to order please visit the 'Ordering' section on our website.

Design: Stuart Davies

UK: Printed and bound by CPI Group (UK) Ltd, Croydon, CR0 4YY
US: Printed and bound by Thomson-Shore, 7300 West Joy Road, Dexter, MI 48130

We operate a distinctive and ethical publishing philosophy in
all areas of our business, from our global network of authors to
production and worldwide distribution.

Contents

Previous titles

Gifts of the Nile. ISBN 0 11 290538 2
The British Museum Dictionary of the Ancient Near East.
ISBN 0 7141 1141 4
Treasures from an Ancient Land: The Art of Jordan.
ISBN 0 86299 729 1
Umm al-Biyara: Excavations by Crystal-M. Bennett in Petra 1960-1965. ISBN 978 1 84217 439 5
Studies on Iron Age Moab and Neighbouring Areas in Honour of Michèle Daviau. ISBN 978 90 429 2180 1
Crossing the Rift: Resources, Routes, Settlement Patterns and Interaction in the Wadi Arabah. ISBN 978 1 84217 209 4
Writing and Ancient Near Eastern Society. ISBN 0 567 02691 4
Busayra: Excavations by Crystal-M. Bennett 1971-1980.
ISBN 0 19 727012 3
The Archaeology of Jordan. ISBN 1 84127 136 5
Excavations at Tawilan in Southern Jordan. ISBN 0 19 727007 7
Early Edom and Moab. ISBN 0 906090 45 8
Jericho in the Late Bronze Age. ISBN 0 85668 320 5

He ne'er is crown'd
With immortality, who fears to follow
Where airy voices lead: so through the hollow,
The silent mysteries of earth, descend!
John Keats, *Endymion*

Preface

Immortality is a theme that, in one way or another, runs through most, if not all, of the world's cultures, ancient and modern. But there are different ways to achieve immortality. There is belief in 'real' immortality in an afterlife of some kind, and this might be achieved in various ways, through resurrection, an immortal soul, reincarnation or transformation. Many have pursued, and continue to pursue, real immortality by seeking to prolong their lives on this earth. There is also symbolic or proxy immortality, through children, fame or being part of something long-lasting that outlives the individual. One can imagine these different forms of immortality as a menu of options of how to live forever: you click the one that appeals to you most and best fits your beliefs, hopes, values and worldview.

This book is a history of those options, and is divided into four parts:

Part 1 concerns the history of resurrection from the ancient Near East and Egypt to Jesus, ideas about the immortal soul in different cultures and religions from ancient to modern times, and the origins and development of variant visions of heaven and hell.

Part 2 tracks the history of belief in reincarnation from its beginnings in India and its development in all the major Eastern religions, as well as in the classical world, in Christianity, Judaism and Islam, and in the modern theosophical movement. A separate chapter covers reincarnation and other types of transformation in animist societies, in which ancestors have a role preserving the traditional social structures of communities.

Part 3 follows the search for everlasting life on this earth, and the pursuit of an immortal legacy through fame and children, from ancient legends to the present day.

Part 4 takes a step back to reflect on immortality: it considers the pros and cons of the scientific evidence, as well as speculation across the centuries in myth, fiction and philosophy about whether immortality is worth having and what its impact might be on the individual and society.

It seems rather ironic to produce a 'short' history of immortality, which by its very definition is endless. Nevertheless, the word 'short' in this book's subtitle – *A Short History of Immortality* – is crucial. Not only every chapter, but every subsection, and sometimes individual paragraphs, could be (and in some cases have been) expanded into a book-length study, and more often than not several books. The present book is, necessarily, selective, and should be treated as no more than an introduction. Its focus is on exploring the history and development of belief in immortality as a key part of many cultures. Inevitably, it is also a history of borrowings from other cultures, of adaptations, of interpretations, and of disputes between different and sometimes incompatible interpretations concerning the afterlife and immortality. At every step, I have tried to clarify what the evidence and sources are, and how they are interpreted in different ways, so that we can be clear about how we know something, and what the limitations of the evidence might be. I have also tried to explain the contemporary context of the various beliefs and practices, as this impacts how we understand and assess them today.

Like many people, consciously or unconsciously, the idea of immortality has been with me my whole (short...) life. I was brought up as a Roman Catholic, with its promise of eternal life in heaven. As a young boy, my head span and I came close to panic when trying to imagine what living for ever and ever would really be like: millions and millions of years, and then millions more, never ending... It was scary. I suspect I feared not so much death, as the prospect of eternal life.

Many years later, as a professional archaeologist, museum curator and director, and university professor, not only was

I responsible for a large ancient Egyptian collection with its echoes of immortality, but I worked with different indigenous groups from Australia, New Zealand and North America on the repatriation of the human remains of their ancestors from British museums. This brought me into direct contact with different, living perspectives on death, immortality and time. In these cultures, the dead – even the long dead – continue to be regarded as persons, and their consciousness remains as an animating force in the dead body, in the landscape, and in the community. None of this is theoretical – the dead are experienced viscerally on a daily basis. This impressed upon me the limitations of a theoretical scientific perspective that dismisses such experiences as 'constructs' that cannot be supported by objective evidence. Consequently, this book is not only a history of immortality, but a key theme is that worldviews, cultural norms, goals and values directly impact on how the afterlife and immortality are understood. The threads of uncertain evidence, variant interpretations and choices weave their way through every chapter.

This book developed from a Master's module I taught while Professor of Archaeology and Museology at the University of Manchester, entitled 'Immortality: from Gilgamesh to the Postmodern'. However, it is not intended as a referenced academic study, but as a general introduction to the history of immortality. Because of the large number of sources and reference works consulted, I have limited notes mostly to sources of direct quotations and specific points which I feel require reference or additional elucidation, and these are grouped by chapters at the end of the book. A simplified timeline shows the relationship of key people and events mentioned in the book across four geographical areas: the Near East and Egypt, the classical world, the Far East, and Europe. There are suggestions for further reading, also arranged by chapters at the end of the book, together with a full bibliography, including original sources, translations and key reference works.

A note on dating: this book uses the notations BCE (Before the Common Era) and CE (Common Era), instead of BC (Before Christ) and AD (Anno Domini, 'Year of the Lord'). Since 2002, these have been part of the official school curriculum in England and Wales, and are now standard in many academic disciplines. As my approach has been historical, each chapter or subsection, where possible and appropriate, tries to follow a chronological path.

Acknowledgments

I wish to thank friends and colleagues who read all or part of the draft manuscript, made useful comments and suggestions, and provided references I had missed: Sally Francis, Geoffrey Scarre and Brian Schmidt. Thanks too to Ewa Ochman and Malcolm Chapman for checking references in libraries I was unable to get to.

Prologue

An urge to immortality?

Mortal nature does all it can to achieve immortality and live for ever.
– Plato, *Symposium*

Is immortality important, and does the pursuit of it, and the attempt to defeat death, provide meaning to life?

The French writer and philosopher Albert Camus thought that life was meaningless. The search for the meaning of human existence could never be satisfied, he concluded, as there could be no answer. For him, life was a continuous revolt against meaninglessness. Despite this, he felt it was an issue that constantly needed to be raised:

The meaning of life is the most urgent of questions.[1]

Human beings, in general, do more than just survive. As well as eating, drinking and putting a roof over our heads to keep us warm and dry – and working in order to provide those essentials – we read, write, compose, play and listen to music, take part in sports, go to the theatre, cinema and on holiday, dance, sculpt, draw and paint. It is what makes life worth living. A fulfilled human life, then, is not just about survival. Yet, Camus might respond, none of this is about the real meaning of life: these activities are about enjoying life and getting through it as best you can, but they are not what life is essentially *about* or *for*.

So why do we do all those things? As human animals, why are we not satisfied with mere survival? A growing number of philosophers, psychologists and sociologists are proposing that the fundamental driver for all these human activities is an innate urge or impulse to immortality. The perpetuation of life – or perhaps the awareness of and attempt to overcome death and fear of it – is what gives life its meaning, and lies at the core of all human culture.

Put simply, we humans find it extremely difficult to imagine our own death and non-existence. According to Sigmund Freud,

> Our Unconscious does not believe in our own death; it conducts itself as if immortal.[2]

As a result, much (or arguably all) of what we do and create is a way of overcoming death and becoming 'immortal' in some way. This remains true whether immortality is envisaged as an eternal afterlife offered by the monotheistic religions in return for living a virtuous life, or the search to extend individual human life by defeating ageing and death, or the leaving of a lasting legacy and perpetuating one's name through children, great works or fame. If we were not mortal, and if death did not put a stop to our short lives, there would be no urgency to do anything at all. There would be no need to strive or create anything, beyond mere survival, and no culture or civilisation. The philosopher Arthur Schopenhauer, who did not believe in God or in a personal survival of death, concluded that all religions and philosophies were created as an antidote to the certainty and fear of death, and in hope of a future existence after death.[3]

This theory that the fear of death and the urge to immortality lie at the root of all human culture has been growing in popularity particularly since the late nineteenth century until the present. Its development and influence can be attributed to several interconnected strands: Darwin's theory of evolution and the consequent realisation that humans might not be a special creation made in the image of God or have particular value compared with the rest of nature, making the ultimate purpose of their lives unclear; the demise of the certainties of traditional religions; and growing understanding about the relative recency of life – and even more recent human life – on the planet. The universe is so immense, and humans are so very tiny and short-lived: what possible importance or impact can individual lives have in so short a time? Hence the questions: what does it all mean and why am I here?

The writing on this topic involves two subtly different, though linked, arguments. One stresses the presence of death, and consequent fear and anxiety about it, as a constraint on human endeavour, while the second stresses the urge to overcome death. In the first, the certainty of death makes human lives brief, precarious and precious, and so we need to get as much done as we can before our time runs out; in the second, it is our (often subconscious) wish either to achieve immortality ourselves or, failing that, to create and take part in things that will outlive us and give meaning to our short existence on this planet.

However, the idea that the impulse to immortality is a fundamental motivator for humans and human culture did not originate in the nineteenth century, but has ancient antecedents in Greek philosophy. In his *Symposium*, Plato (427-347 BCE) imagined a high-society dinner party in Athens in 416 BCE (to discuss love), during which his mentor, Socrates, describes how the prophetess Diotima taught him that human creativity is powered by the urge for immortality:

> I'm not sure that the prospect of undying virtue and fame of this kind isn't what motivates people to do anything, and that the better they are, the more this is their motivation. The point is, they're in love with immortality.[4]

Diotima's argument is that creative people long for their work to have a lasting reputation. She compares the products of creativity to children:

We'd all prefer to have children of this sort rather than the human kind, and we cast envious glances at good poets like Homer and Hesiod because the kind of children they leave behind are those which earn their parents renown and 'fame immortal', since the children themselves are immortal.[5]

Born a few years after Plato's death, Epicurus (341-270 BCE) had a different slant on overcoming death. For him, the goal of life was pleasure (and the absence of pain), and the biggest threat to this pleasure was fear, especially of death. The whole purpose of his philosophy was to understand the universe in such a way that these fears, including that of death, were dispelled. This philosophy was most extensively described about two centuries later by the Roman philosopher Lucretius (c. 95-c. 54 BCE) in his *De Rerum Natura* (On the Nature of Things). Here, Lucretius argued that death was insignificant, and was at pains to stress that one should not be concerned about death or pursue immortality:

Death then to us is nothing and concerns us not a whit... Why do you groan and weep at death? ... why not retire, O foolish one, from life's feast like a well filled guest, and take resignedly the rest that cannot be disturbed? But, if your joys have all been lost and squandered, and if life is an offence to you, why seek to add a longer span, that it again may come to a bad ending and all thanklessly be lost? Why not prefer to make an end of life and labour?[6]

Let us attempt to track the development into modern times of this ancient idea regarding the fear of death and the urge to immortality. Until the mid-nineteenth century, philosophy did not concern itself unduly with questions about the meaning of life – in more religious ages and societies, that had been rather taken for granted, with divine purpose guiding human lives, and the promise of eternal life as a reward for virtuous behaviour. The human condition now came to the fore, and many philosophers in the European or Continental tradition integrated the Epicurean fear of death into their thinking: for example, Schopenhauer, Søren Kierkegaard, William James (who was American, but educated in Europe), and later the existentialists Jean-Paul Sartre, Karl Jaspers, Simone de Beauvoir, and particularly Martin Heidegger, for whom death, and anxiety about it, was central to his thinking.[7] Indeed, much of Heidegger's philosophical project was not dissimilar to that of Epicurus: to face death and dispel anxiety about it. For Heidegger, the sense of ourselves as individuals is based on awareness and acceptance of our inevitable mortality and finitude, which frees us to make the most of the possibilities of life without being ground down by the anxiety and fear of death. He calls this 'freedom towards death', through which

> ... one is liberated in such a way that for the first time one can authentically understand and choose among the factical possibilities lying ahead...[8]

In short, and massively generalising the whole central part of Heidegger's *Being and Time*, acknowledgment of death, which is typically denied and repressed, allows for fulfilment in life.[9]

As for the contemporary psychoanalysts, Sigmund Freud did not write so much about the fear of death, although he recognised that humans try to escape the thought of their own death, but instead developed his controversial theory of a death drive, a built-in urge towards death that explained human aggression and violence. His psychoanalyst colleague, Otto Rank, however, did think that fear and consciousness of death were a prime motivator for human actions, and he was a primary influence on the writing of the cultural anthropologist Ernest Becker. While Heidegger's philosophy of death was largely applied to individuals and how they respond and behave, Becker explored the wider cultural implications of the fear of death and the urge to immortality, albeit from a psychoanalytical perspective.

The basic theme of Ernest Becker's Pulitzer Prize-winning book, *The Denial of Death*, first published in 1973, is that refusal to acknowledge the terror of death is a fundamental and universal fact of existence and the mainspring of human activity, achievement and civilisation:

> ... the idea of death, the fear of it, haunts the human animal like nothing else; it is a mainspring of human activity – activity designed largely to avoid the fatality of death, to overcome it by denying in some way that it is the final destiny for man.[10]

The Denial of Death is, essentially, a dense psychoanalytical critique of Freud, which reworks his death drive into an existential fear of death that results in an urge to immortality. That key starting point is borrowed from Plato and the Epicureans. According to Becker, humans try to transcend mortality through 'heroic' acts to achieve a form of immortality – what he calls 'immortality projects' – which allow them to believe they are participating in something of lasting worth that gives meaning to their lives (which is more or less what Diotima said in Plato's *Symposium*). This can be creating an empire, writing a book, having a family, becoming an Olympic champion, or supporting a winning football team. But different immortality projects can conflict with each other to produce tension and conflicts between religions, nations, ideologies, families and football clubs.

After Becker's death, Terror Management Theory (TMT) was introduced in 1984 by three psychologists who were hugely influenced by his work.[11] It continues Becker's core theme: that death is one of the primary driving forces of human action, and our attitude to it shapes our lives and everyday decisions. Its originators follow Schopenhauer in arguing that religion and myth were created by humans to cope with their own mortality. Today, the fear of death continues to affect us, manifested through what they call 'symbolic' immortality, such as religious, national, ethnic, tribal or group identity, which are forms of immortality by proxy that offer us a chance to be part of something enduring, something greater than the individual that outlives us and thus gives meaning to our lives. In their view, the fear of death creates a sort of self-preservation instinct that, perhaps paradoxically, also explains everyday actions like driving fast, eating unhealthily and spending too much. Mostly, TMT has been practised therapeutically to understand how the fear of death affects health, well-being and behaviour, especially in mental illness, and it has been used to analyse psychological and emotional reactions to the terror attacks of 11 September 2001 in the United States.[12]

In some ways, Zygmunt Bauman's *Mortality, Immortality and Other Life Strategies*, first published in 1992, makes the same point as Becker's *The Denial of Death* and TMT, but using the language of sociology instead of psychology.[13] Bauman argues that death and the pursuit of immortality are central to culture, and in particular that death is repressed in human institutions, rituals and beliefs that seem on the surface to have nothing to do with death. His claim is that death is most powerful where it does not appear under its own name, and that human cultures subconsciously design elaborate subterfuges to try to avoid it:

> There would probably be no culture were humans unaware of their mortality; culture is an elaborate counter-mnemotechnic device to forget what they are aware of... Thus the constant risk of death – the risk always *knowable* even if flushed down into the murky depths of the subconscious – is, arguably, the very foundation of culture.[14]

So the whole purpose of culture, in a phrase borrowed from

Freud, is prosthetic – culture artificially pushes away death. Bauman concludes that the fact of death empties life of meaning, leaving humans to create meaning to fill the void, knowing that they are not immortal and that every moment is precious and must be used purposefully. Social life and culture depend on death and its consequences, and all human achievements across different civilisations make sense only in the context of culture as prosthetics:

> Immortality is not a mere absence of death; it is *defiance* and denial of death. It is 'meaningful' only because there is death, that implacable reality which is to be defied. There would be no immortality without mortality. Without mortality, no history, no culture – no humanity.[15]

Most recently, Stephen Cave has drawn on all these ideas for his book *Immortality*, first published in 2012, in which he calls the will to immortality the foundation of human achievement, responsible for all religion, philosophy, architecture and the arts.[16] He defines four 'paths' to immortality: Staying Alive, Resurrection, Soul, and Legacy. However, his main purpose is to critique them from a materialist perspective – the theory that matter alone exists, denying the existence of souls and minds – to show that they are all mistaken and futile and that there can be nothing beyond bodily death. Although he may well be right, Chapter 8 will show that other possibilities and explanations cannot be excluded, and materialism itself is not without faults and gaps: the issue of immortality is more about competing worldviews and interpretations than about measurable fact and proof.

As we have seen, the idea that fear of death and an urge to immortality lie at the heart of human culture, and are, in a sense, the real meaning of life, has had a long and distinguished history for nearly two and half thousand years. But is the theory right? The concern is that it sometimes comes across as a dogma that explains everything, reminiscent of Edward Casaubon's misguided Key to All Mythologies in George Eliot's *Middlemarch*, in which he claims to have found a comprehensive explanation for the whole of mythology; or, more comically, in Douglas Adams' *The Hitchhiker's Guide to the Galaxy*, in which the answer to the great question of life, the universe and everything is 42. As an archaeologist and historian, I tend to be suspicious of single, universal explanations for human culture and what underlies and motivates it. The history of human societies is always more complex than any single explanation can support, with interplay between many competing threads and tensions, which ebb and flow at different times and in different circumstances.

For example, while one hesitates to disagree with the great Schopenhauer about the origins and meaning of religion, we now know considerably more about the earliest documented religion in ancient Mesopotamia, where written records of religious practice date to c. 3500 BCE. While humans sought immortality (and that search will be documented later in this book), the main lesson of the ancient Near Eastern myths is that it was unachievable. Humans were confined to earth, and, after death, to the underworld. Heaven was for the gods. Religion had a much wider remit than immortality. Mostly, it recognised that there were super-human controlling powers – the gods – who demanded obedience and worship. Religion and ritual attempted to influence them and their decisions, particularly concerning the natural forces that impacted life, fertility and growth: primarily the sun, rain and wind. So, yes, it was about survival, but not necessarily as a bid for immortality.

Of course, this refers to documented religion. There is plenty of archaeological evidence of what appears to be religious behaviour that precedes writing by thousands of years, but the problem is how to interpret it. To take a particularly tricky example, the Neanderthals may have been the first to bury their dead intentionally, although this is disputed. Their burials included stone tools and animal bones. It is possible to interpret this as some sort of belief in an afterlife, as tools and sustenance required either in the journey to the afterlife, or in the afterlife itself, or both, and therefore perhaps as evidence for some sort of belief in immortality. But there are other more secular and mundane explanations: burial, with or without grave goods, does not necessarily imply belief in a soul or an afterlife.[17] It is simply not possible to know for certain how to interpret such evidence. When it comes to certainty about belief in immortality, we are completely reliant on the written record. We cannot necessarily discount belief in immortality before humans wrote about it – it is highly likely that they had the same fear of death and therefore some hope or sense of an afterlife – but we do not know and will never know for certain. Moreover, there is evidence of special treatment of the recently dead in chimpanzee communities, suggesting that awareness of death is not limited to humans.[18]

The philosopher Geoffrey Scarre thinks it is far from evident that humans have any innate desire for immortality, as opposed to an instinct for self-preservation, though of course TMT suggests that an urge to symbolic or proxy immortality is exactly that: a self-preservation instinct. Moreover, Scarre and others are puzzled by the mass of books that tell us we are denying and suppressing death, and that it is somehow a taboo subject that motivates us from our subconscious. The sheer number of books on the topic strongly suggests the opposite, and at no time in history has there been so much attention paid to death and its impact on human nature and culture.[19] One might, conversely, argue that we have been talking about the fear of death quite openly ever since Epicurus, if not before. The increasing popularity of the idea that humans have an innate urge to immortality, which we see across different disciplines such as philosophy, sociology and psychology, might be explained as a product of our age, in which there is a deep social need for universal explanations of what it all means – as Douglas Adams satirically highlighted.

It may well be that awareness of mortality creates no more than a desire to make the best of the time we have available, to make it as interesting as possible, and the idea of immortality creeps in because we want to try to enjoy it for longer. One of the oldest quotes on the subject, probably written soon after the death of Epicurus, like Camus later on characterises life as utter futility:

> For the living know that they will die, but the dead know nothing and they have no more reward, for the memory of them is forgotten.[20]

But, as the following chapters demonstrate, we cannot dismiss the reality that the pursuit of immortality of one kind or another is an element – though not the only element – in many cultures and religions, is clearly of great significance to some individuals, and looms large in myth, legend and literature. Whether it is more than that, and is the wellspring of all human culture, remains a question of interpretation and is up to the reader to decide. Perhaps more importantly, our attitude to death and immortality says much about our values and how we treat others with different perspectives, and about the worldviews that fuel those attitudes, and that theme will be taken up again in the Epilogue.

Part 1

Resurrection and the Immortal Soul

Chapter 1

Resurrection from the ancient Near East to Jesus

Rise again, yes, you will rise again, my dust, after a short rest!
– Friedrich Klopstock, *Die Auferstehung* (*Resurrection Hymn*)

The word 'resurrection' means the act of restoring a dead being to life. The use of the vague term 'dead being' is deliberate, because in different traditions, and at different times, exactly what was believed to resurrect or live on after death varied. It could be the body, the 'soul' (we'll get to the soul in Chapter 2), both together, and sometimes it was a mythical god who resurrected annually according to a seasonal cycle.

In religion, its most influential form is the resurrection of Jesus, the Christian New Testament reporting that he died, was buried, then rose from the dead, to live forever in heaven. But long before Jesus, ancient traditions, religions, myths and rituals involved some aspect of resurrection. Usually, these were based on observation of nature and the cycle of the seasons: death in winter and new life in spring, endlessly repeating.

The earliest recorded accounts of resurrection are in myths from the ancient Near East. Should we pay any attention to myths? Nowadays, myth is equated with something untrue or fictitious ('an urban myth'), but the dictionary definition also describes myth as a traditional narrative which embodies popular ideas about natural or social phenomena. We can learn a lot about the deepest beliefs, hopes and fears of societies from their myths, even if they are not necessarily related to reality. Myths are important statements about a society, how it understands itself, what is important and fundamental to it, or what it believes about its shared origins. Especially in ancient and traditional societies, myths were played out in rituals at regular intervals, creating significant moments in which members of those societies came together to reaffirm shared beliefs about their world.

Dying and rising gods in the ancient Near East

Sir James Frazer (1854-1941) popularised the idea of gods who died and rose again. In his book *The Golden Bough*, first published in 1890 and still in print and widely read today in an abridged version, he argued that at the core of all religions was a myth of a god incarnating the power of fertility, who was ritually killed every year, and then, like the grain, was resurrected. Frazer regarded this as true of all religions, and looked for traces of it all over the world, including Africa and the Americas. Controversially, he saw it as the basis of the story of Jesus' death and resurrection, which he argued was ritual and symbolic, just like his other examples.

Many historians and anthropologists have since dismissed the whole category of dying and rising gods as a simplistic generalisation. In particular, Frazer's work was criticised because many of the myths he used as examples simply did not have clear themes of rebirth or resurrection – Frazer was seeing things he wanted to see, to fit his hypothesis. Also, the primary sources that Frazer used have been criticised as biased, and had sometimes been deliberately manipulated by Christian theologians in order to show that Jesus' own death and resurrection were logical and inevitable. From that perspective, the widespread category of 'dying and rising gods' created by Frazer can only exist within a Christian frame of reference, culminating logically in the death and resurrection of Jesus.[1]

Nevertheless, more recently it has been shown that, at least in the ancient Near East and Mediterranean, there are definite recorded examples of gods who died and returned to life, but they are very diverse and cannot be lumped together simplistically. A list typically includes (in alphabetical order) Adonis, Attis,

Baal, Dionysos, Dumuzi/Tammuz, Jesus, Osiris and Persephone. Many of these had associations with the seasons, agriculture and fertility.

These ancient societies depended completely on agriculture to survive. In an agricultural society, it is crucial to be able to mark the passage of the seasons, to know when the rain is likely to come, or a period of drought, or when the grain is ready to be harvested, or when the soil is ready for planting. These were polytheistic societies, with particular gods identified with rains or storms or the fertility of the soil and of women. Their actions were often erratic, so they needed to be appeased and asked for help, and showered with gifts and prayers through rituals.

In practice, in the ancient Near East, a god's 'resurrection' was enacted in ritual. The timing of the god's reappearance was linked to the re-emergence of vegetation, crops and the changing seasons. At such times, a divine image of the god would 'appear' to the people in processions at a particular temple, and this might be linked to ritual celebrations, feasting and public holidays – much as today Christians still celebrate the birth of Jesus at Christmas, and his death and resurrection at Easter, with particular rituals, appearances of statues of the god, and feasts (such as nativity plays, cribs in churches, Christmas dinner, Easter vigils and Easter eggs). Of course, the timing of Christmas was originally chosen by the early Christians in the fourth century to coincide with the winter solstice, which was already widely celebrated by other religions; so Christmas as an annual midwinter celebration continues that ancient link between the changing seasons, the fallow earth ready for rebirth, and the (re)birth of a god.

The Baal Cycle

From the ancient Near East, the prime example of a dying and rising god is Baal. This is the one we know most about. The name Baal means 'lord', 'master' or 'owner'. He was a storm and warrior god, the association with rain also making him a god of fertility. He is best known from the Baal Cycle, recorded on six clay tablets plus fragments excavated between 1930 and 1933 at the modern site of Ras Shamra in north-west Syria, the ancient city of Ugarit. They were written in the local Ugaritic alphabetic cuneiform script and composed in the first half of the fourteenth century BCE.

Ugarit was a major city on the Syrian coast at that time, with a royal palace and temples (including one to Baal). Around the palace were houses of all sizes, palatial and poor, arranged along narrow, winding streets – similar to traditional towns and villages across the modern Middle East.

The Cycle concerns the exploits of Baal as he establishes himself as king over the land, but the overt symbolism is all about linking fertility, agriculture and the changing seasons to his death and resurrection. Baal announces himself as king to Mot (Death). Mot then invites him to a feast, but it is Baal himself who is eaten by Mot. Baal's death is announced, and the gods go into formal mourning and bury his corpse. But the goddess Anat urges Mot to return Baal, and eventually she kills him. The way Anat kills Mot emphasises the agricultural and fertility aspects. Essentially she treats him as if he were corn: she splits him with a sword, winnows him with a sieve, burns him with fire, grinds him with a millstone, and sows the fields with him. The death of Mot precipitates the return of Baal – the death of Death (Mot) and the reappearance of the god of rain and fertility are a prime metaphor for resurrection.

The Baal Cycle is full of links between death, resurrection, fertility and the agricultural cycle. Baal's death coincides with the summer drought:[2]

... the furrows of the fields are parched.

But when he is resurrected,

… the heavens rain oil, the wadis flow with honey.

On his way to face Mot, Baal mates ('77 times, 88 times…') with a cow, producing a bull. He proclaims:

I alone fatten gods and men, I alone satisfy earth's masses.

This same link between fertility and a dying and rising god is seen in the Mesopotamian myth of Dumuzi and the Greek myth of Persephone. Both Dumuzi and Persephone are forced to return to the underworld for part of every year, during which time the earth is barren. When they return to life, the grain grows. This, too, was re-enacted in ritual. Persephone's ascent and reunion with her mother, Demeter, were the main theme of the famous, though still obscure, Eleusinian mysteries, annually celebrated in the city of Eleusis from the sixth century BCE. The initiates in this ritual were offered a form of immortality, a promise of a better fate in the underworld after death. As with Baal, the myth and ritual stress the links between fertility and rebirth.

The cult of Baal was certainly known later on in the time of Jesus. Many passages in the Hebrew Bible – the Christian Old Testament – refer to Baal, recording a long-term, intense animosity towards him and those who worshipped him. This is not surprising, since the Israelites had settled among the Canaanites, who worshipped Baal, and so the Baal cult was regarded as a threat to the exclusive worship of the Israelite god, Yahweh, the sole god of the ancient Israelites. There were even times when the Israelites themselves are recorded as worshipping Baal, and some key aspects of Baal were borrowed for Yahweh, for example riding the clouds or creating storms.

Osiris, mummification and the Egyptian afterlife
In many ways, the Egyptian god Osiris is not so much a dying and rising god, as a dead god who was once resurrected. His

dominion is the underworld, and dead Egyptians were identified with him in their own resurrection. In art, he is usually portrayed as a mummy, wearing a tall crown and holding the royal insignia of crook and flail.

Yet, like Baal, there is a connection between the cult of Osiris, fertility and the growth of corn. Spells on coffins equated the resurrection of the dead person with the sprouting of barley from the body of Osiris; and in later periods miniature corn mummies in the shape of Osiris were buried in tombs and pits.

It is not easy to pin down the role and significance of Osiris, as it changes and develops through three thousand years of ancient Egyptian history. There are scraps of myths and stories about him from different periods, from the earliest mentions in the Old Kingdom (the 'Pyramid Age') to the Graeco-Roman period. The Greek historian Plutarch (c. 45-125 CE) compiled the most coherent, though not necessarily the most accurate, account in his essay 'On Isis and Osiris', some of which matches ancient Egyptian sources.

In Plutarch's account, Osiris was an earthly ruler, sealed into a coffin and cast into the Nile by his jealous brother Seth, who eventually dismembered his body and scattered the parts throughout Egypt. The goddess Isis, the wife of Osiris, searched for the pieces and buried each one, with the exception of the phallus which had been eaten by the Nile carp, so that an artificial penis had to be made (and an erect phallus was often a distinctive feature on depictions of Osiris – underlining that continuing link between resurrection and fertility). In the ancient Egyptian accounts, at this stage the dismembered body was reassembled into the form of the first mummy, with which Isis conceived their son Horus. Horus then avenged his father's death in a series of contests with Seth. Finally, Osiris was declared ruler of the underworld, Horus the ruler of the living, with Seth confined to the deserts as god of chaos and evil.

The great annual festival at Abydos celebrated the resurrection of Osiris, with a procession of the god in his bark, enacting scenes of his triumph over his enemies. The timing of the festival, at the rising of the river Nile in late summer, linked the myth and ritual to the fertility of the land.

The myth of Osiris and his resurrection is really the key to Egyptian ideas of mummification and the afterlife. The entire funerary process was designed to substitute the dead person for Osiris, so that the deceased could re-enact the myth of resurrection and achieve eternal life.

Egyptologists disagree on whether resurrection was available for everyone right from the beginning. It has long been argued that, during the Old Kingdom, it was only the dead king who was identified with Osiris, while the living ruler was identified with his son Horus, so that, in this period, any sort of afterlife was the sole prerogative of the king. Court officials tried to build their tombs as close as possible to the royal tomb, so that they too could benefit from his funerary rituals and attain at least some sort of afterlife. With the collapse of the old, traditional structures of the Old Kingdom, many things loosened up, including access to resurrection and the afterlife. What some Egyptologists rather misleadingly call 'the democratisation of the afterlife' meant that it became possible for private individuals to be identified at death with Osiris and to be resurrected.

However, others disagree with this interpretation, and cite evidence that at least some non-royal individuals were already identified with Osiris during the Old Kingdom, and could share in the benefits and privileges of the afterlife. If this is correct, there was no 'democratisation' of the afterlife of any kind, the only difference being that non-royals now had specific funerary texts – the so-called Coffin Texts – inscribed in their tombs, which were similar but not identical to the royal Pyramid Texts of the Old Kingdom.

We must always bear in mind, however, that the evidence we have about ancient Egyptian beliefs concerning resurrection and the afterlife comes from the tombs of the elite: members of the royal family, officials, priests, senior army officers (and sometimes one person could be all four). As we will see below, they were the only ones who could afford the meticulous preparations necessary to ensure a successful transition to the afterlife – and it is their tombs, monuments and texts that have survived and that provide all our information. We know virtually nothing about the beliefs of the vast majority of ancient Egyptians, the ordinary peasants who worked in the fields. We do not know what they really believed about the afterlife, and whether they thought it was accessible to them.

The sources paint the ancient Egyptian afterlife mostly as a continuation of earthly life, but there was no single understanding of what that afterlife was like (see Chapter 3). Many of the sources show that the Egyptians aimed to continue their bodily existence and believed that life after death was the same as life in Egypt, but funerary texts also demonstrate that this afterlife was essentially the same as the world of the gods. In this sense, as the Egyptologist Jan Assmann has pointed out, the ancient Egyptian belief in bodily resurrection was not dissimilar to the later Christian belief in resurrection,[3] although some Egyptian funerary texts refer to the transformation of humans into stars after death. The earliest burials contain food, implying that from earliest times the Egyptians believed in some sort of bodily existence and need for sustenance after death.

The dead also had the ability to intercede in the affairs of the living: letters to the dead show that people could communicate with deceased family members and ask for their help. They indicate that the dead were considered not really much different from the living, and that a continuation of life was expected as the norm.

But all of this was only available if elaborate, and expensive, preparations and precautions were taken. The Egyptians believed that each human comprised not only a physical body, but three other crucial elements, which are not completely understood and are virtually impossible to translate: the *ka* (a sort of life force), the *ba* (something like the personality or manifestation of one's identity), and the *akh* (the part of the individual that, at death, is freed and becomes immortal). These were further complemented by one's name and shadow. Each of these was essential to human survival before and after death. Ensuring immortality and the afterlife was a matter of sustaining and protecting all these elements. This could be achieved by various means: the preservation of the body through mummification; funerary equipment, spells and rituals to sustain the deceased, keep their name alive and guide them to the afterlife; and a virtuous life.

The first step was to ensure the deceased was buried in Egypt. Egyptian texts allow for the dreadful possibility of disappearing into nothingness after death, which might happen in the event of drowning, or not being buried in Egypt – essentially, if you were not buried in the actual land of Egypt. The popular story of Sinuhe voices this fear. Sinuhe was a courtier who fled Egypt during turmoil after the king's death and lived in exile in Syria. As he grows old, he worries that he will die abroad, outside Egypt. The new pharaoh hears of his plight and invites him back to die and be buried in Egypt:

You shall not die abroad... think of your corpse, come back![4]

Sinuhe replies that returning to Egypt saves him from death. The message is clear: survival after death was only possible in Egypt.

The full paraphernalia of Egyptian funerary ritual are effectively a comprehensive belt-and-braces job to ensure survival into the afterlife. If one method failed, there were backup plans. Preservation of the body through mummification was only one element.

The idea of mummification – and of the mythical appearance

of Osiris as a mummy – may have developed after the earliest burials in the desert, in the Predynastic period, were naturally preserved by the hot, desiccating sand. The skin dried naturally, accidentally preserving the lifelike appearance of the corpse. Attempts to provide better security for the body by building proper tombs resulted in the decay of the tissues, because they were no longer in contact with the sand. Artificial methods of preserving the body therefore had to be developed.

In the classic Egyptian funerary ritual, in order to gain eternal life, it was essential that the mummified body imitate the appearance of Osiris as closely as possible. But, at first, mummification comprised little more than wrapping the body and limbs tightly in lengths of linen bandaging, probably in the misguided belief that covering the skin would prevent decay. Eventually, the means to preserve the body tissues were perfected, as well as the skill of wrapping the finished mummy. In later periods, though, mummification reverted to the art of elaborate wrapping, culminating in individually wrapped fingers and toes and intricate patterns in the bandaging. Little attention was paid to preserving the tissues.

Should the corpse decay, despite all these efforts, there were other safeguards, only one of which needed to work for resurrection to be achieved. A statue of the deceased's *ka* acted as a substitute body and guaranteed survival. The function of the other offerings left inside the tomb, and the texts inscribed or painted on the tomb or coffin or on papyrus, was to become real and active through magic. The primary purpose of the texts – known variously as Pyramid Texts, Coffin Texts or the Book of the Dead – was to preserve the name of the deceased and provide them with the knowledge necessary for the afterlife, primarily what to do and what not to do to get there.

In order to be assimilated with Osiris and achieve immortality, the deceased had to prove that they had lived a good and virtuous life. The Egyptians regarded the heart as the seat of their intelligence and personality, and so the judgment scene painted on the Book of the Dead papyri shows the heart being weighed against the feather of the goddess Maat, symbol of harmony and truth. The Book of the Dead helpfully includes a long, detailed list of the infractions one must avoid in order to pass this test – the so-called negative confession. But in the catastrophic event that the heart weighed heavier than Maat's feather, standing by and waiting to devour it was a demon, part hippo, part lion, part crocodile. This awful fate was another route to unimaginable nothingness. It is the first manifestation of a theme that is treated in different ways by the world's later great religions – immortality is conditional on living a good life, and the punishment for bad behaviour is either nothingness or something quite unpleasant.

The afterlife in ancient Near Eastern, Mediterranean and early Jewish traditions

Ancient Near Eastern and Mediterranean cultures did not have such a developed sense of the afterlife and immortality as the Egyptians. Generally, they shared a belief that some aspect of the human person (the 'soul') persisted in some way after death, usually after a journey from the grave to the underworld. How that underworld was conceived was strikingly similar in Mesopotamia, Canaan, ancient Israel, Greece and Rome: in all those cultures, it was a bleak and dreary place.

In Mesopotamian cultures, there was no resurrection of the body, and no concept of heaven or hell. Provided that burial and mourning rites were properly carried out, the spirits of everyone who died journeyed to the underworld, which was understood as being located underground at the bottom of a stairway. It was often represented as a dark, dusty and gloomy place,

On the road where travelling is one-way only,
To the house where those who enter are deprived of light,

Where dust is their food, clay their bread,
They see no light, they dwell in darkness.[5]

But in some accounts it is slightly less bleak, and more like a shadowy imitation of life on earth. The deceased ate bread, drank water, and had a similar state structure including a palace with seven or 14 gates, a full court system and a royal couple, the gods of the underworld Nergal and Ereshkigal.

On the other hand, people who were not properly buried and denied mourning rites were regarded more or less as ghosts, living a bleak, peripheral existence, who could at times turn into vicious demons. The earliest Sumerian poems contrast the relative ease of an underworld existence for those with sons who made offerings on their behalf, with those who have no one to make funerary offerings. The worst fate of all was burning to death: those people disappeared in smoke and did not go down to the underworld. This belief that proper burial and ritual are essential to attain the afterlife was echoed by the Greeks and Romans later on, most notably in Sophocles' *Antigone*, whose brother Polynices is denied burial by the tyrant Creon as a punishment; in both Homer's *Odyssey* and Virgil's *Aeneid*, too, when Odysseus and Aeneas journey to the underworld, they find unburied comrades who cannot enter the underworld without proper burial. In the *Aeneid*, the unburied dead wait on the other side of the river and cannot be ferried across to the underworld

... until their bones are buried, and they rest in peace...
A hundred years they wander, hovering round these shores...[6]

That this was more than just poetic licence, but popular belief, is suggested in a report by the Roman lawyer and administrator Pliny the Younger (c. 61/2-113 CE) in one of his numerous letters. He recounts that a manacled ghost haunting an Athenian house led the prospective buyer, the philosopher Athenodorus, to the courtyard, where it disappeared. In that exact spot a chained skeleton was excavated, and once given a proper funeral the hauntings stopped.[7] Roman law forbade the disturbance of burials.

The Hebrew Bible portrays the underworld of the ancient Israelites, called Sheol, as a similarly subterranean and gloomy afterlife, where the dead are forgotten and cut off from God. That the ancient Hebrews believed in some sort of dismal existence of the dead is suggested by the passage in 1 Samuel 28, in which the 'witch' of Endor – a medium or shaman similar to those referred to in Chapter 5 – summons the dead prophet Samuel's spirit, to which he responds:

Why have you disturbed me by bringing me up?

There are great similarities between the Mesopotamian underworld, Sheol, and the Greek Hades. In fact, in the Septuagint (the ancient translation of the Hebrew Bible into Greek) and in the New Testament, the Greek word *hades* is often used to describe the abode of the dead. In Greek culture, after death one's 'soul', or shadow, or image journeyed to Hades, the bleak underworld realm, although some who died heroically went to the Isles of the Blessed, an earthly paradise located by the Classical writers in the Atlantic. This basic idea was also adopted by the Romans, whose religion and mythology were heavily influenced by the Greeks. The Roman poet Horace likened death to an 'everlasting exile'.

So the ancient Near Eastern and Mediterranean conceptions of the afterlife did not appear to involve bodily resurrection. As far as we can understand the ancient texts, they believed that some sort of 'soul' journeyed to the dismal underworld.

Around the third and second centuries BCE, strikingly different ideas started to appear in Jewish writings, in response to religious persecution by the Seleucid kings, the successors of Alexander the Great. They were inspired by a belief in the imminent arrival of a new age of righteousness, the expectation of the end of the world, a final judgment and the punishment of the wicked, and they spawned new speculation about the resurrection of the dead. This is what historians call apocalypticism – and the individual writings are called apocalypses – from the Greek word meaning 'revelation'.

It was not a single movement, more like a scattered ferment of speculative ideas thrown out by a motley variety of apocalyptic Jewish sects and thinkers. Jon Davies rather poetically calls this flood of radical ideas

> the return of the repressed, as the martyr-heroes of a defeated and ground-down world sought, in and through their victorious martyrdom, to proclaim the terrible risen glory of the world that was to come.[8]

Among the ideas in the apocalypses were the notions of a blessed afterlife for the righteous in heaven; punishment for the wicked in hell; resurrection of the dead (including a brief mention in a fragment of one of the Dead Sea Scrolls); and the immortality of the soul.

Some of the Jewish apocalypses envisaged resurrection as a reward reserved specifically for the righteous, or even exclusively for their own sect, but others believed that all humans would be raised bodily to be judged. For example, in the Hebrew Bible's Book of Daniel, part of which is regarded as apocalyptic literature and was composed later, during the persecutions of the second century BCE, there is a clear reference to resurrection for the righteous and damnation for the wicked:

> And many of those who sleep in the dust of the earth shall awake, some to everlasting life, and some to shame and everlasting contempt.

This was not necessarily a universal resurrection, available to all; principally it was focused on persecuted, pious Jews.

Some of the apocalypses refer specifically to a resurrection of the body – for example, that the souls of the dead in Sheol will be raised in their original bodies so that they will be recognised by the living – while others are concerned only with the immortality of the soul (perhaps influenced by Plato, see Chapter 2). It has been suggested that the apocalyptic Jewish community of the Essenes – the probable writers of the Dead Sea Scrolls – expected to be transformed into angels after death, and perhaps even before.

Resurrection as an idea – and indeed any proper description of an afterlife – had not been part of the early Israelite traditions and texts, recorded in the early books of the Hebrew Bible. Some Jewish priestly communities, such as the conservative Sadducees, continued to deny it. There is a passage in the biblical Book of Ezekiel, chapter 37, which at first glance appears to be about bodily resurrection:

> I will lay sinews upon you, and will cause flesh to come upon you, and cover you with skin, and put breath in you, and you shall live.

But this is actually a metaphor for the national rebirth of ancient Israel, returning from exile in Babylon at about the same time as this passage was written in the mid-late sixth century BCE.

It is possible, but not certain, that the new ideas about resurrection were influenced by contact with the Zoroastrian religion of Persia, during the period when the Jews were assimilated into the Persian empire (539-331 BCE). The early Zoroastrian texts are difficult to date, and they were mainly transmitted orally until the fourth or fifth centuries CE. But they were based on much older traditions, pre-dating the Persian empire, of which Zoroastrianism became the official religion. The

Zoroastrian texts refer to a bodily resurrection which includes everyone, including the wicked who have been punished and their sins expiated. Some scholars argue that this idea of bodily resurrection was borrowed and adapted particularly by Jewish apocalyptic sects so that it could justify the persecutions and martyrdoms that they were suffering under Seleucid and then Roman rule.

However, we cannot be certain that Zoroastrian ideas of resurrection were already sufficiently developed by that time in order to have such a direct influence. We can have more certainty about the continuing influence of Jewish apocalyptic ideas of resurrection, as many of them were woven into the new religion of Christianity, which grew out of Judaism in the same geographical region.

The resurrection of Jesus

The resurrection of Jesus became the foundation of Christianity: it is through his resurrection that Christianity claims eternal salvation will come. More than two thousand years later, there are an estimated 2.3 billion Christians, making up 32 per cent of the world's population. Jesus' death and resurrection continue to be celebrated every Easter as the Christian church's most important festival.

Jesus was born into the Jewish society of Palestine at the beginning of the first century CE, a society under Roman rule, rocked by apocalyptic movements with revolutionary ideas about resurrection. He can be variously described as a teacher, a healer, a prophet and a social reformer, who proclaimed the coming of God's kingdom, effectively led a new apocalyptic movement within Judaism focused on repentance and salvation that spawned a new religion, and was crucified by the Roman authorities who regarded him as a subversive. The title 'Christ' was appended to his name in the early years of Christianity, from the Greek *Christos*, which means 'anointed', the same meaning as the word 'messiah', derived from Hebrew. During his lifetime, he was more commonly referred to as Jesus of Nazareth. The best estimate for the date of his death is around 30 CE.

All of the sources on the life, death and resurrection of Jesus are problematic and continue to be reinterpreted and disputed. The only scholarly consensus on the historical person of Jesus is an acknowledgment that there is no consensus. It really comes down to faith: if you are a Christian and believe in the actions, sayings, teachings and resurrection of Jesus, then you may be more inclined to ignore the problems and contradictions and accept the sources as a record of what actually happened. If you are not, then it may be easier to dismiss many of the sources as unreliable, and biased, historical records.

The critical reaction to the most comprehensive scholarly exploration of the resurrection in recent times, Tom Wright's monumental *The Resurrection of the Son of God*, running to over 800 pages, underlines this point. Wright forensically dissects every single aspect in detail, to conclude that there really was a bodily resurrection. But, as an Anglican bishop as well as a scholar, he has been charged by his critics with too easily dismissing or sidelining evidence that undermines the historicity and originality of Jesus' resurrection, and that it was bodily rather than spiritual. Yet, as a bishop, we cannot really expect him to come to any other conclusion (although one of his predecessors as Bishop of Durham, David Jenkins, famously rejected a literally physical interpretation of the resurrection). A belief in a bodily resurrection is fundamental to his beliefs, and those of his whole established church, so he always tends to that interpretation and provides a traditional Christian view – he interprets the evidence through orthodox-tinted glasses, if you like. But other interpretations are possible, depending on your worldview. There is no right answer: the sources do not allow for any certainty.

The problem is that none of the sources on the life and death of Jesus are eyewitness accounts. In fact, as has been pointed out countless times, all the primary sources were written many years later by people who believed that Jesus had resurrected and was the messiah, so these are not disinterested accounts. Moreover, the actual resurrection of Jesus is not described anywhere: there appear to have been no witnesses to the moment of his resurrection.

The earliest mention of the resurrection, in any text, is in Paul's first letter to the Corinthians, chapter 15:

> ... that he was buried, that he was raised on the third day in accordance with the scriptures, and that he appeared to Cephas, then to the twelve. Then he appeared to more than five hundred brethren at one time...

The dating of this text is difficult, but it was probably written in the mid-50s CE, 25 years or so after Jesus' death. It was written in Greek, and the earliest surviving example of the whole letter is on papyri dating to c. 200 CE.

This letter is the bedrock of Christianity's understanding of the resurrection. Paul – originally called Saul – was a Jew from Tarsus in Cilicia, who had persecuted the followers of Jesus. After a vision of Jesus on the road to Damascus, he changed his perspective (and his name), becoming the most influential missionary in spreading the message about Jesus. He undertook several long missionary journeys across the Mediterranean and Asia Minor, and wrote letters to various Christian communities, including this one to the community at Corinth in Greece. Eventually, Paul was taken to Rome where he was executed.

1 Corinthians 15 as a whole is not just the earliest mention of Jesus' resurrection, but is Paul's statement on the nature of resurrection and the transformation of the resurrected dead. Because of its date, it is the earliest Christian discussion about resurrection, and remains fundamental to Christian beliefs. Paul

writes that, just as Jesus has resurrected, so all those who have died can be resurrected:

All shall be made alive.

This is Christianity's first offer of eternal life for everyone.

Needless to say, each word and nuance has been analysed and interpreted countless times over the last two thousand years. Paul is categorical that the dead will be wholly transformed by resurrection:

... we shall all be changed.

He is clear that life in the hereafter would differ radically from present life. He is asked two hypothetical questions:

How are the dead raised? With what kind of body do they come?

He rejects them as foolish, responding:

... it is raised a spiritual body... flesh and blood cannot inherit the kingdom of God... this mortal nature must put on immortality.

Scholars have discussed endlessly whether this rather mystical statement really means just a spiritual resurrection or if a bodily one can be inferred: no consensus is possible. Paul often refers to his own visions, revelations and ecstatic experiences – not dissimilar to those seen in Jewish apocalyptic writings – so what he writes needs to be interpreted through that veil of mysticism. All we can really conclude is that Paul refers to resurrection as transformational – as something *different* from what we are now.

The Christian gospels, all dating later than Paul's letter, do not describe the moment of Jesus' resurrection, but they do provide more detail about the resurrected Jesus' appearances to his followers. The word 'gospel' is used for the title of many early Christian books. Four gospels were accepted by the early Christian church as 'canonical', that is, recognised and authorised as reliable teachings, while others were rejected and are referred to as apocryphal. The canonical gospels – Mark, Matthew, Luke and John – are essentially biographies of Jesus, from his birth or baptism to his death and resurrection. They are not eyewitness accounts, and they were not concerned with historical accuracy – they frequently contradict each other.

Their primary purpose was to inform the emerging Christian communities about Jesus' life, teachings and resurrection, and shape their understandings and practices. They are more objective and narrative accounts compared with Paul's personal, spiritual visions. They were written in Greek, and much of their intended readership were Greek-speaking communities outside Palestine. They were all written 40 to 60 years after Jesus' death, based on other written sources which have not survived, and oral traditions.

The dating of the different gospels is notoriously difficult, but Mark was the earliest around 70 CE (already 40 or so years after the death of Jesus; although the ending, which includes the resurrected Jesus' appearance to his followers, may be later and may not have been written by Mark); then Matthew after 70 CE; Luke between 80 and 85 CE or slightly later; John is most often dated 90-95 CE but may have been a decade earlier. The earliest fragments of the gospels are preserved on papyri dating to the early second century CE.

The different gospels give varying detail about the discovery of Jesus' empty tomb and his post-resurrection appearances, and end with Jesus commissioning his disciples to spread his word to all nations: an action that was, essentially, the beginning of the Christian church. Luke and John are particularly insistent on providing details as proof that this was a bodily resurrection. Jesus asks them to feel the marks of the nails and the cut in his side that were a result of his crucifixion, and insists he is here in body:

... for a spirit has not flesh and bones as you see that I have.[9]

But many scholars find the stories of Jesus' post-resurrection appearances problematic. They are certainly highly stylised and stereotyped, following the same pattern: Jesus appears just to a closed circle of followers, not to everyone; his followers express fear and doubt; they see the tangibility of his body; they worship him; Jesus commissions his disciples to spread the word. Despite the insistence on Jesus' bodily presence, there are elements that undermine this simple explanation: Jesus materialises but then suddenly disappears; he is mistaken for a stranger; he is thought to be a spirit or a ghost; the disciples do not believe it is really him.

Some scholars suggest that these stories deliberately overemphasise the bodily aspects of Jesus' resurrection, because the gospel writers were aware of other stories circulating which emphasised the precise opposite – a more spiritual resurrection which denied that Jesus had resurrected bodily. Such stories are known from second-century CE gnostic sources, that is, strands of early Christianity which did not accept the beliefs and practices of what was becoming the established church, but pursued their own interpretations. For example, a more spiritual and rather unearthly resurrection is presented in the non-canonical gospel of Thomas, a collection of sometimes puzzling sayings ascribed to Jesus, which was written between the end of the first and mid-second century CE.

In some ways, Paul's 'spiritual body' and the canonical gospels' literally physical body suggest different perspectives and interpretations of the resurrection in these earliest accounts.

So did Jesus' resurrection really happen? If it did, was it a bodily or a spiritual resurrection? Is the Christian promise of a resurrection of all the dead a bodily or a spiritual one, and how will we be transformed after death? There are no clear answers: it all depends on how you interpret the sources, which sources' accounts you prioritise, and what worldview, beliefs and hopes you bring to that interpretation.

Of course, today's 2.3 billion Christians are testament to the continuing power of the story and efficacy of the church it inspired. Yet not all Christians believe in the resurrection, not even the clergy. Different surveys carried out between 1994 and 2017 by Harris, Ipsos MORI, Christian Research and ComRes found that a third of Church of England clergy and between a quarter and a third of Christians in the United Kingdom did not believe in the resurrection – but this compared with over 85 per cent of American adults who did (though not necessarily in a physical, bodily resurrection).

Paul and the gospel writers are the primary evidence for Jesus' resurrection, although they were not eyewitnesses. There is endless debate and speculation among scholars around how much the accounts of Jesus' resurrection, and especially Paul's account, were directly influenced by Jewish apocalyptic ideas of resurrection. There are lots of individual parallels, but it is impossible to be certain of the scale of influence, and in any case such ideas were part of the intellectual and religious climate of Jesus' world, part of its response to Roman repression.

But, just as Paul and the gospel writers were themselves interpreting earlier written and oral sources, so early Christian thinkers continued to ponder whether the resurrection was bodily or spiritual – or perhaps both? The question of the immortality of the soul was about to become central to the idea of resurrection and to have a huge influence on Christianity.

Chapter 2

The immortal soul

Oh, who shall me deliver whole
From bonds of this tyrannic soul?
– Andrew Marvell, *A Dialogue between the Soul and Body*

The idea of the 'soul' permeates the English language (and, similarly, other languages). Its widespread use seems unconnected to any religious belief: 'body and soul'; 'soul mate'; 'soul music'; 'to sell one's soul'; 'soul searching'; 'soul destroying' ... Surveys report that most people believe they have souls: 70 per cent in the United Kingdom and 96 per cent of adults in the USA.[1]

But what exactly is the soul, and does it really exist? A dictionary definition includes the following: the spiritual or immaterial part of humans; the moral and emotional part of humans; the intellectual part of humans; an animating or essential part. Some, but not all, of these definitions extend the idea of possession of a soul beyond humans to animals.

The idea that humans, in particular, consist of not only a physical body, but also an immaterial soul, is an ancient one. It is one of the earliest examples of what philosophers call dualism: that there are two kinds of reality, matter and spirit ('body and soul'). The Greek philosophers, particularly Plato, were the first to speculate seriously about this dualism, and about the possibility that the soul does not die with the body but is immortal. Plato's understanding of the immortal soul had a huge influence on Christianity, and continues to reverberate in the modern world.

But we saw in Chapter 1 that earlier Egyptian and Near Eastern cultures had some notion of a soul that survived death. It is not always clear what they understood this soul to be, as they have not left any philosophical speculation about it in the way that the later Greeks did. So we have to piece together their ideas about the soul from the context in which the word or concept of soul is used in texts that are sometimes obscure; and we often come up against problems of translation – is 'soul' always the right English word to use?

The soul from ancient Egypt to the early Greeks

Chapter 1 introduced the three immaterial aspects that ancient Egyptians understood were part of a complete person: the *ka*, the *ba* and the *akh*. These are difficult to translate, and their meanings seem to have varied at different times and places (we must remain aware that ancient Egyptian culture lasted for about three thousand years, with discontinuities, developments and regional variations, so we cannot expect consistency over such a long period). It is not uncommon for one or even all three to be translated as 'soul', but this is misleading as each had a specific function. Essentially, it seems that it was necessary for the *ba* and *ka* to unite to enable the *akh* to become the immortal and unchanging form in which the deceased inhabited the afterlife, but no one really knows how these were understood to interact. The best explanation seems to be that, to transform into an immortal *akh*, the deceased had to rejoin his *ka* (life force); since the physical body was unable to do this, the job was done by the *ba* (a sort of personality).

In Mesopotamian cultures, the closest equivalent to what we call 'soul' was the *zaqiqu*, portrayed as a sort of mobile but shadowy phantom which could not interfere in human affairs. There was also the *etemmu*, the ghost associated with the corpse, or spirit of the deceased. Both the *zaqiqu* and the *etemmu* descended to the underworld after death, but it was the *etemmu* from which help was requested through prayers and offerings.

In the Hebrew Bible, the word *nephesh* is often translated as 'soul', but is probably more like 'personality', 'living being', or even 'appetite'. It was restricted to humans, and there is no evidence that the ancient Hebrews conceived of an immortal soul.

To the east of Mesopotamia, the Zoroastrians were strict dualists and had quite a different understanding: humans were composed of body and an immortal soul. We noted in Chapter 1 the difficulty of dating Zoroastrian texts, although it was the official religion of the Persian empire. The Zoroastrian soul is variously described as a permanent pre-existing spirit, or as a more individualised existence. After death, the soul was judged and went to heaven or hell, although at the end of the world everyone would undergo purification, and perfection would be established for all eternity.

Homer's epics, the *Iliad* and the *Odyssey*, give an insight into the early Greek understanding of the word *psyche*, which is usually translated as 'soul', though some prefer the less religiously loaded term 'mind'. The date of composition of the epics is not certain – probably somewhere between 750 and 650 BCE, with later redactions – although they are ostensibly set within the Mycenaean age, c. 1400-1100 BCE. It is also one of the enduring debates of literary history whether 'Homer' was a single author or many, a sort of brand.

Homer's *psyche* or soul/mind is that part of the person which gives life, is often represented as the seat of the emotions, and leaves the body after death. It is the individual being after death, living in the underworld, Hades, and able occasionally to communicate with the living. Odysseus visits the underworld in Book 11 of the *Odyssey*, and among others meets his mother, Anticleia. He finds that he cannot touch her, as she is a soul: she is recognisable but intangible. She explains:

Our muscles cease
to hold the flesh and skeleton together

as soon as life departs from our white bones,
the force of blazing fire destroys the corpse.
The spirit flies away and soon is gone,
just like a dream.[2]

A similar scene occurs centuries later in Virgil's *Aeneid*, when Aeneas tries to embrace the ghost of his dead wife:

... her phantom
sifting through my fingers,
light as wind, quick as a dream in flight.[3]

The nature of the soul and the question of its survival after death was much discussed by later Greek philosophers, and they reached a variety of conclusions. Some of them, like Pythagoras (c. 570-495 BCE) and the contemporary Orphics (and, indeed, Plato), believed in an immortal soul that was reincarnated into other bodies, and we will return to them in Chapter 4.

The first philosopher to write systematically about a soul was Heraclitus (c. 540-480 BCE), a great critic of Pythagoras. Like Homer, he used the word *psyche* and saw it as endowed with rationality and virtue. For Heraclitus, there was only one universal substance, fire, which was transformed into other substances in a constant process of change that maintains the world as we know it. The soul was part of this process, part of the oneness of the world:

The soul is a spark of the substance of the stars... the soul is immortal and returns upon death to the all-soul to which it is related.[4]

Plato and the immortal soul

In his belief in reincarnation, Plato (427-347 BCE) may have been influenced by Pythagoras, but his exposition of the immortality of the soul became the most influential philosophy for Western religions until the modern period. For the philosopher Alfred North Whitehead (1861-1947), he was such a giant that the subsequent history of European philosophy

> ... consists of a series of footnotes to Plato.[5]

Plato was born into an aristocratic family in Athens. After hearing lectures from Cratylus, a follower of Heraclitus, he became a follower of Socrates, who himself wrote nothing but established a systematic method of philosophical enquiry. After Socrates' death, Plato began to write Socratic dialogues – fictional give-and-take philosophical conversations in which Socrates is the main protagonist – partly to defend Socrates' memory. In these dialogues, the figure of Socrates changes from representing the arguments, methods and views of the real Socrates in the early dialogues, to being more or less a mouthpiece for Plato later on.

The main text in which Plato lays out his understanding of the nature of the soul (presented as Socrates' understanding, but almost certainly reflecting Plato's own views) is the *Phaedo*. This describes Socrates' last hours and ends with his suicide by drinking hemlock.

For Plato, body and soul are distinctly separate. The soul (*psyche*) governs and moves the body, but is contaminated by it, and is therefore unable to attain pure knowledge. Such pure knowledge is only possible after death, when the soul is separated from the body. Plato also argued that souls had a previous existence, independent of bodies, that they had intelligence, and continued to exist after death:

> The soul is most like that which is divine, immortal, intelligible, uniform, indissoluble, and ever self-consistent and invariable, whereas the body is most like that which is human, mortal, multiform, unintelligible, dissoluble, and

never self-consistent.[6]

After death, the soul is invisible, divine, immortal and wise, and happiness awaits it, free from human bodily burdens:

So it appears that when death comes to a man, the mortal part of him dies, but the immortal part retires at the approach of death and escapes unharmed and indestructible... then it is as certain as anything can be that the soul is immortal and imperishable, and that our souls will really exist in the next world.[7]

Plato also linked the immortal soul to his theory of Forms, which are ideal realities, absolute and changeless objects of knowledge. The soul was connected to the Form of Life, and was therefore immortal. In *The Republic*, Plato extended his definition and argued for a tripartite soul consisting of Reason, Spirit and Desire. When these three function properly and in balance, the individual is virtuous and just; but when Reason is subordinated to another part, there is moral failure.

Although Plato's understanding of the immortal soul became hugely influential in the long term – and may have been borrowed by some of the Jewish apocalyptic sects described in Chapter 1, especially those comprising the richer elite who were conversant with Greek thinking – later Greek philosophers did not all let him have it his own way. For them, the soul was not necessarily distinct from the body, nor was it necessarily immaterial or immortal.

Plato's own pupil, Aristotle (384-322 BCE), sought to integrate body and soul, distancing himself from his teacher's strict dualism and grounding himself in the material world. In his *De Anima* ('On the Soul'), Aristotle writes that the soul is the form of the body, and the body is the matter of the soul. It is the soul that gives life to the body. But parts of *De Anima* are obscure and notoriously difficult to interpret. On the one hand, it seems that Aristotle did not believe in personal immortality: the soul might survive, but not as an individual. On the other hand, he throws in the strange concept of the 'active mind' or 'active intellect', which may be immortal and individual. But how, and if, it is linked to his conception of the soul is uncertain and remains controversial.

Democritus (c. 460-371 CE), an older contemporary of Plato, developed an atomic theory of the universe, in which the universe is formed of an infinite number of indestructible atoms that move and combine to form many different objects. He explained all natural events as the products of these mechanical forces, the earliest version of the modern materialist philosophy that matter alone exists. Democritus believed that the soul was a life force, but that it too was composed of atoms: fine, spherical, fire atoms, from the association of life with heat.

This theory was followed later by Epicurus (c. 341-270 BCE) and the Stoics (founded by Zeno of Citium c. 300 BCE), who believed in only one substance, matter, rather than strictly separate bodies and souls. Both the Epicureans and the Stoics regarded the soul as corporeal and explicitly denied its immortality. For Epicurus, fear of death was therefore pointless:

> The most terrifying of evils, death, is nothing to us, since when we exist, death is not present. But when death is present, then we do not exist.[8]

Epicureanism – especially through the writings of the Roman philosopher Lucretius (c. 95-c. 54 BCE), the most extensive source on this philosophical school – became an influential philosophy through which these atomist ideas became the basis of theories during the Renaissance and Enlightenment from which the modern theory of matter developed. This was to have huge implications for the modern understanding of whether or not the soul exists, which we will come back to at the end of this chapter.

The early Church: the battle between physical resurrection and the immortal soul

We left the early Christians, at the end of Chapter 1, divided on whether Jesus' resurrection – and their own future resurrections after death – were bodily or spiritual, with different groups stressing different aspects, including some who claimed that Jesus only seemed to die and therefore only seemed to be resurrected. What became the mainstream, or 'orthodox', view believed strongly that a physical resurrection was the bedrock of the new Church.

Through the second and third centuries CE, the early Christian Church continued to fight for its existence (and self-respect) against attacks from opponents well-versed in Greek philosophy, who were determined to show that its teachings and doctrines were ridiculous and simple-minded. One of these was Celsus, a second-century CE Platonist, who criticised all aspects of Christianity in his wide-ranging *True Doctrine*, including what he regarded as its absurd and rather revolting notion of physical resurrection.

In response, Origen of Alexandria (c. 185-254 CE), himself educated in Greek literature and the philosophy of Plato, attempted to fight the critics on their own philosophical ground. He was the first to try to systematise Christian theology, incorporating aspects of Greek philosophy to give it a more sophisticated intellectual basis. Origen ostensibly went back to Paul's account by stressing the spiritual resurrected body (see Chapter 1). But in fact he went a lot further, trying to reconcile Christian doctrine with Greek philosophy, and getting the balance between them wrong was what got him into trouble.

For Origen, souls were pre-existing rational creatures who had become corporeal, and their earthly experience allowed them to choose freely to return to God. The fact that such a resurrection was not about the resurrection of ordinary flesh betrayed the fact that Origen had essentially adopted Plato's notion of a pre-existing immortal soul, albeit a soul judged and saved by God.

This effective rejection of a physical resurrection was a step too far for many of the Church's orthodox bishops, staunch supporters of a real bodily resurrection: if immortality of the soul were available to everyone, then what had been the point of Jesus' suffering and death, which were the very basis of Christianity? Tertullian (c. 160-220 CE), the first major Church father to write in Latin rather than Greek, began his treatise on the resurrection of the flesh with:

> The resurrection of the dead is the Christian's trust. By it we are believers.[9]

For him and the other early Church fathers, immortality of the soul was a dangerous and subversive idea. Bodily resurrection was what made Jesus, and Christianity, unique.

Not surprisingly, they rejected Origen's solution and condemned him as a heretic, despite having devoted himself to a life of Christian teaching and rigorous self-mortification, which almost certainly included voluntary castration. Later, the emperor Justinian (483-565 CE) formally declared Origen a heretic and had most of his works destroyed. Fortunately, enough survived, mostly in Latin translations, to give a good idea of his thinking, but the loss of so much of his writing means there are difficulties of interpretation, and sometimes widely divergent estimates of his views. Ironically, what has survived includes the only excerpts of his opponent Celsus' otherwise lost polemic against Christianity, *True Doctrine*, which Origen had embedded in his response *Against Celsus*.

There were other attempts to reconcile the orthodox Christian belief in a physical resurrection with Greek philosophy, until the problem was finally solved by Augustine. His solution became the new orthodoxy and remains one of the fundamental beliefs of many Christian denominations.

Augustine (354-430 CE) was born in North Africa and had a classical education. For someone who became the most influential Christian theologian until the Middle Ages, his early life was remarkable for its changes of belief. He moved from Christianity to paganism to heresy and back to Christianity, eventually becoming bishop of the coastal town of Hippo in North Africa. He wrote a huge series of works in which he used philosophy to attack opposing doctrines and to systematise the Christian faith. In fact, more of Augustine's writings have been preserved than of any other ancient author.

In his later writings, Augustine's starting point was the complete opposite of Origen's: he was firm in his belief in a physical resurrection (having earlier been more inclined to a spiritual resurrection). In some ways, he borrowed Plato's notion of an immortal soul that is rational and intellectual. He distanced himself from Plato by seeing the body and soul not as antagonistic to each other, but interdependent. He defined the soul as an immaterial substance that is the life force and gives the body movement, but does not have its own independent immortality. At death, the soul is separated and exists on its own until the resurrection of the dead, when it is reunited with the body. The soul must be reunited with the body, as on its own it is not fully an individual.

But death, for Augustine, is also the moment for judgment of the soul. At the end of time, only the virtuous and repentant would go to heaven, while the sinners would be punished, in their bodies, in hell. The virtuous would be reunited with their bodies: but these would be transformed, perfected bodies, free from all human desires and bodily needs including eating, drinking and sex. Purified body and soul together would become like angels or stars in heaven.

This approach essentially found a way around the difficulty of reconciling a physical resurrection with Plato's notion of an immortal soul, while staying true to orthodox beliefs in the primacy of a bodily resurrection. Augustine's view became Christian orthodoxy: that humans are both corporeal and have an immaterial soul that are reunited at the resurrection. It also neatly solved another of the early Church's problems: what happens to the soul between death and the end of time? Augustine's solution remains enshrined in the catechism of the Catholic Church to this day:

> In death, the separation of the soul from the body, the human body decays and the soul goes to meet God, while awaiting its reunion with its glorified body. God, in his almighty power, will definitively grant incorruptible life to our bodies by reuniting them with our souls.[10]

Aquinas and Descartes

About 800 years after Augustine, the issue of bodily resurrection and the immortality of the soul came to the fore again, partly as a result of the new availability of Latin translations of Aristotle and a renewed interest in the Greek philosophers. Thomas Aquinas built on what Augustine had written and tried to avoid contradicting him, while at the same time attempting to create a more robust synthesis between Christian scripture and philosophy. In practical terms, he arrived at a similar solution to Augustine regarding resurrection and immortality, but he got there in different ways, relying more on Aristotle than on Plato.

Thomas Aquinas (c. 1225-1274) was born in Italy, studied Aristotle, and became a Dominican friar. His best known work is the *Summa Theologiae* (1266-1273), also known as the *Summa Theologica*, an attempt to create the standard textbook of theology. His thinking was deeply influenced by Aristotle, and he also wrote commentaries on his works, including one on *De*

Anima. In his writings, he does not even need to name Aristotle, but refers to him as 'the Philosopher'.

Aquinas' views on resurrection and immortality are essentially a blend of Christian orthodoxy with Aristotle (in contrast to Augustine, who had followed Plato). He accepted Aristotle's view that body and soul are not separate substances, as in Plato and Augustine, but are a unity. The soul is an immaterial and integral part of a human being, and it is incomplete without the body, although it is capable of existing without the body at death. In his view, the soul was rational, explicitly following Aristotle's 'active mind' or 'active intellect'. Aquinas regarded rationality as characteristically human. Although the soul cannot see, hear or smell except through the body, it can think without the body.

Aquinas disagreed with Plato on the pre-existence and reincarnation of souls. For him, the soul is created by God as the soul of a particular human being, and cannot pre-exist that human being whose soul it is, although it can survive the death of the human being. He was quite definite that the soul on its own was not the complete human being:

> However, the soul, since it is part of man's body, it is not the whole man, and I am not my soul.[11]

For Aquinas, body and soul together constituted a person. Some modern philosophers and theologians are puzzled why he did not take what seems to them a logical step to equate the soul with individual identity, so that an individual soul is, effectively, the whole person, an individual human being. But this modern view misunderstands Aquinas' medieval religious context. Had he done so, he would have been in the same position as Origen a thousand years earlier, arguing for an immortal soul that was the complete person and that had no need of a bodily resurrection. In that case, from Aquinas' orthodox Christian perspective, there would have been no need for Jesus' death and physical resurrection, which he explicitly states is heresy. Aquinas needed to stress the importance of a bodily resurrection and that body and soul together constituted a human being.

His argument for bodily resurrection and the soul's immortality was subtly different from Augustine's, but basically came to a similar conclusion. For a human to be immortal, both body and soul must be immortal, not just the soul. If the soul really did gain salvation in a life after death, then it could not do so without its body. Since he regarded bodily resurrection as a central tenet of his belief, he argued that the soul rejoined the body when the latter rose from the dead, thus resurrecting the complete person. Explicitly rejecting reincarnation, he wrote:

> For we cannot call it resurrection unless the soul return to the same body...[12]

According to Aquinas, the soul receives its reward or punishment immediately after death, although the reward may be delayed by the need for cleansing from sin. The soul is either 'plunged into hell or sent to heaven', unless its flight is delayed. This, too, followed the orthodox view that heaven was for the virtuous and cleansed, and Aquinas explicitly stated that any other view was heretical. Like Paul (see Chapter 1) and Augustine, Aquinas believed the resurrected body would be a transformed body, without any defect of human nature. Like Augustine, he imagined the resurrected body as sexless and lacking all desires, and was quite specific about its age. It would be brought to its ultimate perfection in its prime, before any effects of ageing.

It was partly Aquinas' reliance on Aristotle that led to condemnations and attacks on him, even before his death: the introduction of Aristotle was regarded by some as a threat to the purity of Christianity. Christian denominations and theologians divided into adherents of his views, called Thomists, and opponents, called non-Thomists. Serious study and reappraisal of his work burgeoned after Pope Leo XIII called for a renewal of the study of Aquinas in 1879. His work remains an important theological source for the Catholic Church.

The Church continued to discuss issues of whether the resurrection is soul on its own or soul with its body, and especially whether dead souls went straight to heaven or had to await reunion with their bodies on the last day – a vital consideration for medieval Christians. But, more than 350 years after Aquinas, the longstanding link between physical resurrection and immortality of the soul was fundamentally challenged by René Descartes. Although Descartes was very interested in proving the existence of God, he approached his task from a systematic perspective rather than citing Christian orthodoxy, and his conclusions excluded the idea of bodily resurrection. More than any other philosopher, Descartes is responsible for the modern conception of the mind and the popular understanding of the immortal soul.

Descartes (1596-1650) was born in France and educated by the Jesuits. At the age of 23, he explicitly set out on a philosophical mission to produce

> an absolutely new science enabling one to resolve all questions proposed on any order of continuous or discontinuous quantities.[13]

He approached the problem of how to acquire certain and reliable knowledge through a methodology of systematic doubt: treat all your beliefs as if they were false, and only accept something if there is no doubt that it is true. He was the quintessential dualist, concluding that matter and mind were different substances and exist separately. Material substances had extension, while mental substances think. All observed phenomena, that is, all the world around us, are explained by interactions of matter which can be described solely in terms of measurability: length, depth, breadth, shape and motion.

Descartes concluded that he himself was simply a thinking being: his body, though attached in some way to his soul, was not a part of his thinking self, but a distinct physical mechanism:

> ... because... I have a distinct idea of the body in so far as it is only an extended thing but which does not think, it is certain that I, that is to say my mind, by which I am what I am, is entirely and truly distinct from my body, and may exist without it.[14]

Descartes made clear that his terms 'soul' and 'mind' were interchangeable. He rejected the ancient idea that the soul gives life to the body: the body was its own substance, a mechanism or machine. Contrary to Aquinas, he maintained that the soul is the human individual, it is identical to the self, the 'I'. The human soul is immaterial, indivisible, and rational. Although the soul is joined to the whole body, and not just a part of it, Descartes identified the pineal gland in the brain as the place in which the soul exercised its functions more particularly than in other parts, and in this way the soul was able to interact with the body. So the soul, or mind, could set the body in motion: willing an action moved the pineal gland, which eventually led to movement in other parts of the body. That the pineal gland functions in this way has long been disproved, and even in his own lifetime there were objections to his understanding of how exactly the immaterial soul interacts with the physical body. The problem of soul-body causal interaction remains a much debated issue among dualist philosophers today.

For Descartes, death was the breakdown of the body, at which point the soul left the corpse. Since the body was not the individual person, but just a mechanism, the possibility of physical resurrection did not even arise for him.

Given his rigorous methodology elsewhere, his proof of the

immortality of the soul is a little disappointing, although to his credit he did not simply refer to Christian scripture to back him up. Essentially, he argues that the soul does not derive from matter, but is specially created, and is

> of a nature entirely independent of the body, and that, consequently, it is not subject to die with it; then, since one cannot see other causes for its destruction, one is naturally led to judge from this that it is immortal.[15]

There are some indications that Descartes had originally hoped to do better.[16] The title page of the first edition of his *Meditations* in 1641 includes the words (translated from Latin) 'in which the existence of God and the immortality of the soul are demonstrated'. By the time of the second edition, the title page made no reference to the immortality of the soul, instead promising to prove the distinction between body and soul. Many philosophers since have concluded that Descartes himself recognised that he had failed to provide a robust proof for the immortality of the soul, and consequently appealed to faith rather than reason. Some, like Immanuel Kant (1724-1804), felt that there were no rational arguments for the immortality of the soul, only religious ones, and saw the issue, at the very least, as philosophically undemonstrated and undemonstrable; while David Hume (1711-1776) regarded what he called the 'religious theory' of an immortal soul as rash and daring.[17]

From now on, largely inspired by Descartes' insights, philosophers showed more interest in other aspects of the soul, such as the causal interaction between soul and body – for example Gottfried Leibniz (1646-1716) – or the soul or mind as the locus of personal identity – for example John Locke (1632-1704), Hume and Kant. Locke explicitly linked personal identity and responsibility to rewards and punishments at the time of resurrection in his *An Essay Concerning Human Understanding* of 1689, but his views on the immortal soul and on physical resurrection are less explicit.

The discussion of the immortal soul had gone about as far as it could. For Christianity, Augustine and Aquinas, basing themselves on Plato and Aristotle respectively, had provided adequate syntheses between physical resurrection and the immortality of the soul that were compatible with scriptures, Christian orthodoxy and philosophy. For the emerging scientific world of the Enlightenment, Descartes had provided a usable and influential theory of matter and an argument for the immortality of the soul unencumbered by the resurrection of a body that was no more than a physical mechanism. The next big step in the story of the immortal soul would be the denial that the soul even exists, let alone that it is immortal, and we will return to that in the last section of this chapter.

The immortal soul and bodily resurrection in later Judaism

We have followed the story of the immortal soul through the prism of its impact on Christianity. Meanwhile, we left the early Jews, at the end of Chapter 1, divided between the ancient ideas of Sheol as the abode of the dead and apocalyptic visions of physical resurrection and the immortality of the soul. It is time to pick up their story.

The Jews in first-century CE Palestine were divided into antagonistic factions that seethed under Roman rule. Eventually, Jewish revolts led to the Roman destruction of the temple in Jerusalem in 70 CE and the expulsion of the Jews. Although it is likely that the majority of Jews were already living outside Palestine by that point, in what is called the Diaspora, the destruction of the temple meant a loss of central religious authority.

This had a significant impact on the development of Judaism. Worship could no longer be organised around the temple, but instead was reconfigured around rabbis who acted as teachers, leaders, judges and authorities on the interpretation of scripture in individual communities across the Diaspora. This is what is referred to as rabbinic Judaism, which developed in the Diaspora between the second and sixth centuries CE and since has become the mainstream form of Judaism.

It did not function in the same hierarchical and centralised way as Christianity, which tried to fix a single orthodox interpretation of belief and practice. Instead, interpretation was left to individual rabbis, who were free to emphasise different aspects for different audiences. Although the rabbis dealt mostly with legal issues, not theological ones, they did provide some explanations and debates about the afterlife.

They certainly believed in a life after death, but at no point does rabbinic literature provide a unified conception of the afterlife. Rabbinic texts show a remarkable range of views, flexibility and ambiguity, which was almost certainly a deliberate strategy to ensure they were tolerated by the varied cultures within which they lived. Rabbinic Judaism therefore happily incorporated both the resurrection of the body and the immortality of the soul into its thinking and debates, usually leaving the details quite ambiguous, and without coming to definitive conclusions – although there was a little more scepticism concerning bodily as opposed to spiritual resurrection.

This ambiguity was deliberate:

> The Rabbis do not seem to care much whether resurrection is as literal, fleshly body, or as a perfected, spiritual body. Evidently, they believed that the nature of the resurrection was for God to define.[18]

In the early rabbinic literature, there was no mention of hell or punishment, and disagreement about whether only righteous Jews would be saved or righteous gentiles too; but occasionally there is mention of Sheol – the biblical abode of the dead – as the place where the wicked will go.

Some of this was very similar to Christian notions of resurrection and the reunification of body and soul. One tradition related that the dead buried outside Israel would return to Israel through an underground tunnel to be resurrected:

> The Holy One, blessed be He, will burrow the earth before them, and their bodies will roll through the excavation like bottles, and when they arrive at the land of Israel, their souls will be reunited with them.[19]

Much like Christian philosophers were influenced primarily either by Plato or Aristotle, so it was with Jewish philosophers. The first rabbi to attempt to integrate the Jewish philosophy of the afterlife with Greek philosophy was Saadia ben Yosef (882-942), usually known as Saadia Gaon (Gaon is a title, 'head of the academy' – he was appointed Gaon of Sura in Iraq in 928). His ideas were explicitly based on Plato. On death, the soul is released from the body and is stored until the last judgment, when it is reunited with its body and lives for eternity, which Saadia Gaon envisaged as like this world only better. The wicked would be sent to Sheol.

The first Jewish philosopher to base himself on Aristotle was Moses ben Maimon, known as Maimonides (1135-1204), who worked within the rabbinic tradition. Developing Aristotle's idea of the 'active intellect', he regarded the soul as seeking the pure intelligence of God. The righteous soul which attains knowledge of God becomes immortal, while the wicked cease to exist. Maimonides regarded belief in a physical resurrection as foolish, but rather oddly suggested that any dead who resurrected must eventually die again, as the afterlife was purely spiritual.

Jewish intellectual life in the Diaspora was isolated from the great philosophical debates of the Enlightenment following Descartes, until it began to flourish again with Moses Mendelssohn (1729-1786). Born in Germany, he engaged in debates with other leading philosophers like Kant and did much to introduce philosophy to a wider public. His *Phädon* (*Phaedo or On the Immortality of Souls*) was a Socratic dialogue modelled on Plato's *Phaedo*, which gave Platonic arguments for the indivisibility, indestructibility and immortality of the soul.

But there were also strands of Judaism which developed in mystical ways, emphasising inner wisdom. The document known as the *Tanya*, a systematic exposition of Hasidic Jewish philosophy, published in 1814 (allegedly after the first edition was lost), has quite a lot to say about the immortal soul. According to the *Tanya*, every Jew has two distinct souls: one animates the body with its desires and needs; the second is part of God. Before it descends to earth, the second soul is taken on a tour of heaven, shown the various sections of the Garden of Eden, and also hell (called Gehinom), and has to take an oath to remain righteous.

In Kabbalah, another mystical strand that probably originated in the twelfth and thirteenth centuries CE in southern France and Spain among the Jewish Diaspora, and remains popular today, there are also multiple levels of soul and a belief that they will return to their bodies at the final resurrection.

In many ways, all these ambiguities and inconsistencies have survived in the various modern strands of Judaism. Today, Jews believe in different, often irreconcilable theories, from a belief in a soul that survives after death, with judgment, reward and punishment in the afterlife, to a belief in a literal resurrection of the body. Some appear to have similar attitudes to the early rabbis, happy hardly to discuss the subject but leave it in God's hands.

The immortal soul and resurrection in Islam

Islamic ideas of the immortal soul and resurrection had a similar history of influences from Plato and Aristotle. There were debates and conflicting positions about whether humans were body or soul or both, whether the soul was corporeal, and attempts to reconcile Greek philosophy with religious orthodoxy.

Islam built on Judaism and Christianity, acknowledging Moses and Jesus as true prophets, but Muhammad (c. 570-632 CE) as the last and perfect prophet. The life of Muhammad is known almost entirely from early Muslim sources, the historicity of which is disputed. There are no primary sources from his lifetime: the earliest extant ones date from a century or so after his death, and those are not straightforward historical accounts. However, the majority of scholars agree on the basic outlines of his life.

Muhammad was born in Mecca, a flourishing commercial city in the sixth century. He regularly made retreats into the mountains to meditate and pray. During one, in the year 610 CE, he received the first of many divine revelations from the angel Gabriel. After several years, he began to preach these revelations and gathered a following. This made him unwelcome in Mecca, so he fled to the city of Yathrib (later renamed Madina, from the Arabic *madinat al-nabi*, 'the city of the Prophet'). This flight – in Arabic *hijra* – marks the beginning of the Islamic tradition (and of the Islamic calendar, whose years are marked AH, for *anno hijra*, 'the year of the flight').

Muhammad and his followers took up arms to spread their new religion, and within years had unified the whole Arabian peninsula and extended into Syria. After Muhammad's death, his successors expanded further, into North Africa, parts of Asia and as far as Spain.

The earliest Islamic doctrine on the soul and resurrection is in the Quran, which contains the collected revelations of Muhammad. He regarded these as the piecemeal revelations, over 22 years, of a divine book on the proper worship of God (Allah) and moral behaviour, sent down from heaven through the intermediary of an angel.

Muhammad's companions committed these oral revelations to memory and wrote at least some of them down. After his death, they were collected, from separate, scattered sources, and it is this that forms the Quran. An authorised version in Arabic was edited some years after Muhammad's death – exactly when is a matter of discussion – and all other versions were reportedly destroyed, as they were thought likely to cause disagreement and quarrels among believers.

Despite the existence of a canonical version, there is nevertheless lots of room for interpretation of the Quran, as parts of it can be confusing: its verses are not ordered chronologically, and there is disagreement whether some should apply literally or were just responses to particular problems in Muhammad's time. Islam, like Judaism but unlike the Catholic Church, has no hierarchical structures which impose a definitive, authorised view. Instead, Islamic scholars make rulings according to their interpretation of the Quran, Islamic tradition, and their own reasoning. Not surprisingly, understanding of the soul was a topic ripe for interpretation.

The word *nafs* (from the same root as the Hebrew *nephesh*, see above) was used in early Arabic poetry to refer to self or person. In the Quran, it also means 'soul'. Later on, the word *ruh* – breath or wind – could also apply to the human soul or spirit, and both words were used interchangeably. In the Quran, the soul has three characteristics: it means appetite, especially in the sense of an evil desire; it censures; and it is tranquil.

Most of the influences from Christianity, Plato and Aristotle about the understanding of the soul are post-Quranic. Al-Kindi (801-873 CE) introduced the Platonic doctrine of the soul into the earliest Islamic philosophy. Like Plato, he regarded the soul as an immaterial but intelligent substance, and salvation consisted of freeing the soul from the corrupt body and returning to the world of spiritual substances. Although his ideas did not become mainstream Islamic doctrine, this theory of the soul's origin, nature and destiny did influence later Muslim mysticism – for example, Ibn Al-Arabi's (1165-1240) definition that a man's animal spirit comes from the blowing of the divine breath, his reasoning soul from the universal soul, and his body from the earthly elements.

Many of the earliest Islamic philosophers argued that the soul was incorporeal. The theologian and poet Ibn Hazm (994-1064) taught that Allah created all human spirits, and that they exist in heaven until an angel blows them into embryos. Al-Ghazzali (1058-1111), regarded as Islam's greatest theologian, explicitly followed Aristotle's *De Anima* with little modification and defined the soul as a spiritual substance, not confined in a body or separated from it, which possesses knowledge and perception. For Al-Baidawi (1226-1260), too, the soul was incorporeal, created when the body was complete. He poetically defined the soul as not embodied, and not close to the body, but attached to the body as the lover is attached to the beloved.

But these positions were unable to reconcile Greek philosophy with orthodox Islam, and were not destined to dominate Islamic thought, which tended towards the traditional Quranic view that the soul is a direct creation of Allah and has various qualities. The dominant Muslim doctrine on the soul was provided most fully by Ibn Kaiyim al-Jawziya (1292-1350) in his *Book of the Soul*, published in 1324. Of its 21 chapters, the nineteenth is on the specific nature of the soul. He affirms that man is both body and spirit. The soul is itself a body, but different from the corporeal body: poetically, it is living, moving and interpenetrates the bodily members as water in the rose. Created by Allah, it is immortal, and departs temporarily from the body in sleep. When the body dies, it leaves the body for the first judgment, then returns and remains in the grave until the last day and the resurrection.

This is regarded as an intermediate state, sometimes with the soul in a place called *barzakh*. This word, found in the Quran, means 'obstacle', 'hindrance' or 'separation', but is often used to describe the boundary between the human world and spiritual world of Allah, and is where the soul waits after death and before resurrection. However, within Islam there are different interpretations of *barzakh*. In some traditions, it is largely ignored, whereas in others the dead souls in *barzakh* are given temporary light or dark bodies, depending on whether they are destined for heaven or hell.

The Quran is full of references to the final resurrection. Muhammad preached the need for repentance and self-surrender to Allah in order to achieve salvation in heaven. In the Quran, on the last day, all living things will die and then will be brought to life again for the final judgment by Allah, and consigned to heaven or hell, or, according to some Islamic theologians, limbo. The Quran is not explicit whether this is a bodily resurrection, but most Islamic scholars interpret the passages as meaning that the soul and the physical body together are brought to life at the resurrection for reward or punishment.

Materialism and the death of the soul

At the beginning of this chapter, we posed the question: does the soul really exist? We have followed ideas about the nature of the soul from the ancient Near East and Egypt, through the Greek, medieval and early modern philosophers, to its continuing importance in modern Christianity, Judaism and Islam. But modern science is based on a philosophy of materialism: that nothing exists except matter. This position denies the existence of soul or spirit.

Like many of the key ideas we have encountered, materialism too goes back to the ancient Greeks, especially Democritus and Epicurus, mentioned above, although the word itself was not used before the 1660s. In the early seventeenth century, Descartes had developed a dualist philosophy of soul (or mind) and body, but bequeathed the tricky problem of how a mind or soul that has no mass and occupies no space could interact with matter (body) which has mass and occupies space. Even Descartes' contemporary, Thomas Hobbes (1588-1679), published an objection to his dualism. Later, in his treatise *De corpore* ('On the Body', 1655), Hobbes presented a strong mechanistic alternative. For him, the only thing that existed was matter in motion, and humans too were composed of matter in motion, and nothing else. There was no immortal soul.

This materialism had become the modern scientific and philosophical orthodoxy by the 1960s, if not earlier – it was referred to pejoratively as 'the mechanistic dogma' already in the early twentieth century. The term materialism – often used more or less interchangeably with the terms physicalism and naturalism – means that all that exists are the material entities recognised and measurable by physics. It denies the existence of anything mental, psychological or spiritual: everything mental or spiritual is really physical. All mental life is caused by brain processes and not by a separate mind or soul.

Modern neuroscience associates most of the activities once thought to have been carried out by a separate mind or soul with the functioning of specific parts or systems of the brain. It concludes that the brain itself performs these functions. This orthodox scientific view leaves no room for the soul, which has been replaced by the activity of electrochemical impulses and neurons in the brain.

Where does that leave the immortal soul? In Chapter 8, we will look at how this orthodox scientific view – which recognises only material entities and rejects the existence of the soul – is used to deny all forms of immortality. However, we will also consider arguments and objections against the materialist position which, despite being the prevailing orthodoxy, is not universally accepted and has many explanatory gaps.

As in most things to do with the subject of immortality,

what any one person believes depends on their worldview, what assumptions they bring with them, and how they choose to prioritise and evaluate the evidence. As regards materialism, and the existence of the soul, there is no definitive proof either way. If evidence for the materialist position falls short of proof, then it opens up the possibility of considering other explanations and worldviews in which the existence of the soul – and its immortality – cannot be excluded.

Chapter 3

Journeys to heaven and hell

I write of hell; I sing (and ever shall)
Of heaven, and hope to have it after all.
– Robert Herrick, *The Argument of His Book*

To introduce this chapter, imagine you have died and been resurrected. Where are you? What is this place or state of being? Or, to put it more accurately, if during life you had expectations of resurrection, where did you expect to find yourself after death?

Different people will answer in different ways, depending on their worldviews, beliefs and hopes. One might wake up in a sexless body amidst choirs of angels; another might be in a pleasure garden, with family and friends, surrounded by willing virgins; yet another will be in a place very much like the world they lived in. Of course, you may have deluded yourself, and where you end up may not be heaven at all, but hell.

Many people today believe in an eternal heaven and hell. A 2014 survey by the Pew Research Center found that 72 per cent of US adults believe in heaven and 58 per cent in hell; those figures rise to 82 per cent and 67 per cent respectively of those with a religious affiliation. Strangely, too, 5 per cent of atheists believe in heaven and 3 per cent in hell.[1] A 2016 YouGov poll reported markedly lower figures across the same categories in the United Kingdom, with 44 per cent of UK Christians believing in heaven and 27 per cent in hell.[2]

Yet there are no single agreed descriptions of heaven and hell. Just the Christian view of heaven alone has been endlessly imagined over two thousand years with little consensus: as a heavenly Jerusalem; a garden paradise; a place where angels sing eternal praises to God; where we meet our loved ones and remember everything; a place with hierarchies and grades of reward, where our bodies are perfected and purified and we have no desires; or as a state of perfection and love outside time and space, which is not a 'place' at all – and sometimes a mix of these. If you do end up in heaven, which heaven will it be? Different religions, cultures and individuals have imagined myriad possible heavens and hells, although there are overlaps and common motifs. To properly represent the vast spectrum of how heaven and hell have been imagined across the ages would take several books.[3] This chapter addresses the question through the prism of journeys to heaven and hell, an approach that allows us to follow how the notions of heaven and hell first developed, and provides a reasonably balanced perspective of how different cultures conceived and adapted them. It also demonstrates succinctly how visions of heaven and hell were constantly shifting in line with social, religious and scientific developments.

The journeys included here are necessarily selective, because many of them essentially repeated motifs – for example, that of a temple or palace, a heavenly city or a garden paradise – which had become traditional, especially in Christian journeys, or adapted motifs first encountered in classical journeys, for example the idea of Elysium. Cultural borrowing permeates ideas about the afterlife, and it can be difficult to untangle and judge which idea came first. The word 'paradise' itself comes from the Greek *paradeisos*, used in the Septuagint, the Greek translation of the Old Testament, for the Garden of Eden, and the Greek word in its turn was borrowed from Old Persian *pairadaeza*, which means 'enclosure', 'park' or 'garden'. The shift to the meaning of paradise as a heavenly pleasure garden, or heaven itself, and the abode of the righteous dead in the afterlife, was secondary, possibly inspired by the Greek idea of Elysium, at a time when Greek ideas were influential on early Jewish and

Christian thought.

Traditions of journeys to heaven, hell, or an otherworld within different religions and cultures address the question of what the afterlife is like, and who can go there. In these, typically, a prophet or seer journeys to the realms of the afterlife, often has a guided tour, then returns transformed and reports back on what he has seen. Some of these journeys are described as dreams, some are explicitly drug-induced altered states of consciousness, while others seem similar to what today we call near-death experiences. The aim of many of them was to exhort people to lead a moral life. Accounts of these journeys were therefore one of the key ways in which understandings of the afterlife – and, eventually, ideas of reward or punishment in the hereafter – were transmitted within cultures and religious groups, some of which, of course, believed that entry to heaven was restricted to their own group.

We start our own journey with heaven, then descend into hell.

Ancient Near Eastern and Egyptian ascents to heaven

In the ancient Near East and early Greece, the cosmos was understood as being in three layers: earth, the underworld and heaven. Earth was for humans. Under the earth was the bleak underworld, the abode of the dead and the gods of the underworld, where all who died were destined to go, regardless of virtue or lack of it. Above the earth was heaven, populated solely by the gods. Heaven was not for humans, and a theme of some of the early journeys is that humans might visit heaven temporarily, but they cannot stay there, nor do they have any hope of immortality.

The story of Adapa concerns a man's squandered opportunity to gain immortality. Adapa was the first of seven antediluvian sages sent by the god Ea to bring civilisation to mankind. The story is known from second-millennium BCE tablets in Akkadian from Amarna in Egypt and Assur in modern Iraq.

Adapa is summoned to heaven to explain why he cursed the South Wind and stopped it blowing. We get a picture of heaven as a city or a palace with gates:

> ... when you go up to heaven,
> When you approach the Gate of Anu,
> Dumuzi and Gizzida will be standing in the Gate of Anu.[4]

The god Ea instructs Adapa what to say to the gods:

> They will hold out for you bread of death, so you must not eat.
> They will hold out for you water of death, so you must not drink.

But Adapa has either been deliberately tricked or he has misunderstood – the precise implications are unclear from the fragmentary story. The gods actually offer him the bread and water of eternal life, which he rejects, according to his understanding of Ea's instructions. The god Anu then laughs at him:

> Didn't you want to be immortal? ...
> Take him and send him back to his earth.

Adapa gains wisdom, but not eternal life. The message is that, one way or another, immortality will elude humans.

The story of Etana concerns a legendary king of the city of Kish after the Flood. It is known from various Akkadian tablets of different dates. Its central motif of a man's ascent to heaven on an eagle's back was incorporated into the Greek myth of the abducted Ganymede, the Alexander Romance (dating between the third and sixteenth centuries CE), and into Iranian stories and Islamic legends. It was a popular story in ancient Mesopotamia, and the motif of Etana on an eagle's back is depicted on ancient cylinder seals, which were rolled on to clay as a mark of ownership.[5]

Etana has been chosen by the gods to provide mankind with the security of kingship, but he needs an heir in order to establish a dynasty. He plans to ascend to heaven to obtain the only remedy, the 'plant of birth' that will provide him with an heir. Etana rescues an eagle from a pit, and, as a reward, is carried up to heaven on its back. On their first trip, Etana is overcome by fear and they return to Kish. But then Etana has a series of dreams, including one about heaven, its gates, and a girl on a throne beneath which are snarling lions. Inspired by this dream, Etana and the eagle make a second attempt, during which they arrive at the heaven of Anu and go through two gates, the gate of Anu, Ellil and Ea, and the gate of Sin, Shamash, Adad and Ishtar. Unfortunately, the rest of the text is missing, but, according to the Sumerian king list, Etana was succeeded by his son, so presumably the story had a happy ending. But the lesson is clear: there is a chasm separating heaven from earth, it is difficult and perilous to get to, and only gods live there permanently.

The eternal afterlife that is recorded in ancient Egyptian texts was quite different, and surprisingly diverse. There was no canonical portrayal of the Egyptian hereafter. Sometimes, the dead worked in the Field of Offerings (also known as the Field of Reeds) producing offerings for Osiris. This was a place of green, watered fields and orchards, synonymous with fertility and abundance. Later on, this developed into a sort of paradise, with the deceased relaxing and enjoying mansions, gardens and boats. An alternative was to spend eternity sailing with the sun-god in his bark on his cyclical journey from day to night back to day. A few texts refer to flying to heaven in the form of a hawk, or ascending on a ladder made by the gods.

Classical journeys to Elysium and heaven

In the classical world, the underworld was understood much the same as in the ancient Near East, offering a bleak continued existence for all dead souls. But something better was reserved for heroes, the distinguished and the privileged: a paradise called Elysium (alternatively the Elysian Fields or Plain). This is first mentioned in Book 4 of Homer's *Odyssey* as the destination of Menelaus, Helen of Troy's husband:

> Gods will carry you
> off to the world's end, to Elysium...
> There is no snow, no heavy storms or rain,
> but Ocean always sends up gentle breezes
> of Zephyr to refresh the people there.[6]

This description is remarkably like that of Olympus, the home of the gods, in Book 6:

> The place is never shaken by the wind,
> or wet with rain or blanketed by snow.
> A cloudless sky is spread above the mountain,
> white radiance all round. The blessed gods
> live there in happiness forevermore.[7]

By the fifth century BCE, in the writings of the poet Pindar (c. 518-c. 446 BCE), entry to Elysium had broadened to include the righteous. A similar place originally reserved for the privileged few were the Isles of the Blessed, a mythical, winterless home of the happy dead, which some classical writers in fact identified with Elysium. In Plato's *Gorgias*, a little after Pindar, Socrates described a myth, which he said he believed, concerning the reward of virtuous and the punishment of unrighteous souls. At a crossroads, the virtuous were sent one way to the Isles of the Blessed, the unrighteous the other way to Tartarus to undergo punishment: here, some of the wicked could be cured, an idea adapted later into the Christian notion of purgatory.

A more detailed description of the underworld and of Elysium is found in the *Aeneid*. The *Aeneid* was unfinished when Publius Vergilius Maro, known in English as Virgil (or Vergil), died in 19 BCE. It tells the story of Aeneas, a Trojan, who travels to Italy and becomes the ancestor of the Romans. Borrowing themes from the Homeric epics, Virgil deliberately set out to write a Roman national epic, linking Rome to the Trojan War and making the hero, Aeneas, an ancestor of the emperor Augustus.

In Book 6 of the *Aeneid*, Aeneas journeys to visit his dead father, Anchises, in Elysium. Virgil locates Elysium in part of the underworld, which was itself in a real place, north-west of Naples, where volcanic activity had supposedly created an entrance to the underworld. Nearby was the town of Cumae, and it was the Cumaean Sibyl, an aged virgin prophetess, who led Aeneas on his journey.

The entrance to the underworld is a miserable place:

Grief and the pangs of Conscience make their beds,
and fatal pale Disease lives there, and bleak Old Age,
Dread and Hunger, seductress to crime, and grinding Poverty,
all, terrible shapes to see – and Death and deadly Struggle…
… and mad, raging Strife
whose blood-stained headbands knot her snaky locks.[8]

This entrance is guarded by monstrous creatures: Centaurs, the man-eating dog-women Scyllas, the hundred-armed Briareus, a fiercely hissing seven-headed serpent Hydra, the Chimaera breathing fire, snake-haired Gorgons and winged-demon Harpies. Once ferried across the River Acheron, guarded by the three-headed dog Cerberus with serpents writhing round his neck, there are places for dead infants (an idea later echoed by the Christian limbo), those condemned innocently and suicides.

As in Plato's *Gorgias*, the path divides: left to Tartarus, right to Elysium (instead of to Plato's Isles of the Blessed, demonstrating that the two were essentially interchangeable).

After a description of Tartarus (see below, when we look at journeys to the underworld and hell), Virgil describes their entry into Elysium,

> the land of joy, the fresh green fields,
> the Fortunate Groves where the blessed make their homes.[9]

Some of the privileged dead here take part in sport, or dance and sing, or feast:

> We live in shady groves,
> we settle on pillowed banks and meadows washed with brooks.[10]

This is not dissimilar to some descriptions of the ancient Egyptian afterlife. The Egyptologist Jan Assmann has suggested that there may have been direct cultural borrowing between the Egyptian Field of Reeds and Greek Elysium – indeed, the ancient Greeks themselves recognised the similarity, and explained that the mythical Orpheus brought the idea over from Egypt to Greece.[11] If there is any truth at all in this, then, given the huge influence that the bucolic images of Elysium were to wield over future descriptions of heaven, we can credit the ancient Egyptians with inventing the idea of the afterlife as a restful paradise.

The heaven of the *Aeneid* is reserved for the gods: Jupiter's palace on Olympus is among the stars, from which he looks down on earth, while gods often sit on clouds. A very different journey to heaven is found in the Roman orator and politician Cicero's 'Dream of Scipio', from Book 6 of his *De republica*, written in 52 BCE. Although this predates the *Aeneid*, its vision of heaven departs from the traditional classical depiction of a tripartite cosmos, with an underworld and an Elysium, as in Homer and Virgil. Cicero's heaven is informed both by Plato's philosophy of the soul and by the discoveries of Greek and Roman astronomy. From the sixth century BCE onwards, astronomical observation had become more accurate, and the Greeks developed the idea of a spherical, as opposed to a flat, earth, with the seven planetary spheres above: the moon, sun, Venus, Mercury, Mars, Jupiter and Saturn, as well as the fixed stars. Later, Claudius Ptolemy (c. 100-170 CE) synthesised this into a new structure of the cosmos and explained the motions of the heavenly bodies. These discoveries had a huge impact on how the afterlife was understood: rather than being located in an underworld, or somewhere at the world's end, 'heaven' came to be conceived as being beyond the known planetary bodies.

In a dream, Scipio's dead grandfather tells him that a special place in heaven is assigned to loyal subjects, where they may enjoy an eternal life of happiness. Scipio's dead father and grandfather are in fact still alive, but their souls have been released from the bonds of the body. At death, the souls of loyal subjects are released from the body and dwell in the Milky Way. Scipio is elevated above the earth and shown the structure of the cosmos. His grandfather shows him nine concentric circles, the outermost of which is heaven, containing all the rest. The other eight circles are the planetary bodies known to Greek and Roman astronomy: the stars, planets, sun and moon, which revolve in the opposite direction to heaven. Below the moon, everything is mortal and doomed to decay, while above the moon everything is eternal.

This vision of heaven is a reward for good and loyal behaviour. But the souls of those who indulge in sensual pleasure fly close to the earth and only return to heaven after many ages of torture. Scipio hears the music of the celestial spheres as they move, producing sweet harmonies – a sound mortal men are deaf to.

Jewish, early Christian and Zoroastrian ascents to heaven

The new ideas of resurrection and the immortal soul in early Judaism and Christianity that we encountered in Chapters 1 and 2, possibly influenced by Zoroastrianism, inevitably led to the development of the concepts of heaven and hell as places of reward and punishment. The persecuted Jewish sects came to believe that their reward for righteous behaviour would come in the afterlife, as recompense and explanation for their earthly sufferings. But, if everyone was destined to end up in the bleak Jewish underworld of Sheol – similar to the ancient Near Eastern and early Greek underworlds – irrespective of their virtue, then what was the point of leading a righteous life? Putting it rather simplistically, there had to be a heaven, a place of eternal reward, at least for their own group, and a hell for everyone else.

Some of the early Jewish and Christian writings about heaven were based on the traditional tripartite system of the cosmos – underworld, earth, heaven – with a single heaven now reinterpreted as the abode of the one God and a destination for the righteous. The earliest ascent to heaven known in Jewish literature is that of Enoch, in the apocalyptic First Book of Enoch (henceforth 1 Enoch). 1 Enoch is not a single book, but a collection of five apocalypses of different dates, attributed to Enoch, a patriarch mentioned briefly in the Book of Genesis who lived for 365 years before the Flood and was taken by God while still alive because of his exceptional piety. A huge amount of material was later attributed to him – what scholars call pseudepigrapha, or falsely attributed writings – mostly concerned with secrets he learned while in the heavenly realm.

Chapters 1-36 of 1 Enoch form the separate Book of the Watchers, concerning the fate of the fallen angels, dated between the late third and early second centuries BCE. Enoch is lifted up to heaven in his sleep by strong winds, amidst lightning, clouds and fog. Passing through a wall of hailstones surrounded by fire, he enters a house made of fire and ice, with a floor like snow, and a ceiling like water with lightning, stars and cherubim. A larger, inner building has open doors and is built of fire. Inside, God sits on a shining throne, with wheels like a chariot, wearing a brilliant white garment. The throne has rivers of fire flowing below it and a sea of fire surrounding it. A multitude of angels stands before God, singing his praises.

This description of heaven as a building, with doors, a throne, and angels singing praises, indicates that heaven here is understood as a temple (as well as a palace, since it is God's house). It is likely that this was influenced by the ideology of the temple in Jerusalem, which was central to Jewish worship and identity. The original temple had been destroyed by the Babylonians and rebuilt under the Persians. The rebuilt temple, in its turn, was to be irrevocably destroyed later by the Romans, with a deep, long-lasting effect on Jewish worship and psychology. As a result, later apocalypses, as we shall see, also imagined heaven as a temple, inspired by the fall of Jerusalem and the final destruction of the temple.

Heaven in 1 Enoch, then, is a single heaven, imagined as a temple/palace, in some ways recalling the ancient Near Eastern image of heaven as a palace or city, with gates and a throne, of the stories of Adapa and Etana. The later Book of Revelation, the only apocalypse in the Christian New Testament (which gave its name to the whole genre of apocalypses, from its opening words, 'The revelation [apokalypsis] of Jesus Christ'), dating to the first century CE, though not describing an ascent to heaven, also imagines heaven as a city. Its New Jerusalem is a future heaven on earth, sent down by God from heaven. Its description treats it as a temple, built of gold with jewelled walls and gates of pearl, and this image of pearly gates survives to the present as a popular motif of heaven.

But, just as with Cicero's 'Dream of Scipio', astronomical observations had a profound impact on early Jewish and

Christian ideas of what heaven might be like. Once the nature of the cosmos was understood as being more complex than the old tripartite system, heaven too developed from a single to multiple levels, although not all scholars accept that Greek cosmology was the source of multiple heavens, and to a great extent the two schema coexisted. Many of the journeys to heaven envisaged an ascent not to a single heaven, but through several levels, sometimes roughly corresponding to the planetary spheres. Seven levels were common (the likely origin of the phrase 'in seventh heaven', i.e. the ultimate joy, since the seventh and final level is where God resides), but sometimes there were three, five or 10 levels, and later rabbinic speculation concluded that there could be more than 955 heavens. Multiple levels of heaven became common in early Jewish, Christian and Islamic thought, culminating in the nine levels of Dante's heaven in his *Divine Comedy*, which he derived from Ptolemy's system.

The most influential of the apocalypses was that of Paul, dating between the fourth and fifth centuries CE, which continued to be popular into the Middle Ages. Although this mentions seven heavens, Paul ascends only as far as the third heaven. It is the apocalypses of 3 Baruch and 2 Enoch that provide two examples of detailed descriptions of the different levels of multiple heavens. In both, heaven is again imagined as a temple, as in 1 Enoch. Like many of the apocalypses, it is not always clear if they were originally Jewish or Christian, and it is possible that both of these were first written for Jewish audiences but were gradually Christianised.

The Greek apocalypse of Baruch, known as 3 Baruch, falsely attributed to the prophet Jeremiah's scribe, and probably dating to the early second century CE, describes how an angel leads Baruch through five heavens. The angel and Baruch first cross a vast ocean at the farthest reaches of the earth – an image adapted from classical mythology, recalling the crossing of the River Acheron to reach the underworld, or the location of

Elysium and the Isles of the Blessed at the world's end. They arrive at an enormous gateway leading to the first heaven. A group of grotesque people lives on a wide plain, which is a place of punishment for sinners.

The same pattern is repeated for the different levels of heaven: the angel leads Baruch; they travel far and pass through a gateway; Baruch sees a wide plain inhabited by different kinds of people. The second and third heavens are also places of punishment, the third with images of chariots drawn by horses and angels, and the movements of the sun and moon used as a metaphor for the punishment of sins. The fourth heaven is a lake with birds, the destination of righteous souls after death, the equivalent of the classical image of the Isles of the Blessed at the ends of the earth.[12]

Finally, in the fifth heaven, the archangel Michael opens the gate and takes prayers to God as an offering. This is the sort of activity undertaken in a temple, and J. Edward Wright notes that this is the heavenly counterpart of the now destroyed temple in Jerusalem.[13] Baruch himself is not allowed in, perhaps because this is the level where God resides. Some scholars suggest that there were two more levels in 3 Baruch's heaven, now lost, making the total seven, but this is disputed.

The apocalypse of 2 Enoch, preserved only in Slavonic manuscripts in different versions, the earliest of which dates to the fourteenth century CE, is difficult to date, but the original Greek version is likely to be close to the first centuries BCE/CE. Here there are 10 heavens, but similar themes and motifs to 3 Baruch.

Two angels carry Enoch to the first heaven, where he sees a vast ocean, angels, and the storehouses of snow, ice, clouds and dew. In the second heaven is darkness and rebellious angels awaiting punishment. In the third heaven, Enoch sees paradise, the tree of life, and angels singing praises to God: this is a place reserved for the righteous, but elsewhere the wicked are being tortured and punished. In the fourth heaven, the angels show Enoch the movement of the celestial bodies. The fifth heaven is a place of punishment for fallen angels. In the sixth heaven, Enoch sees seven groups of angels who oversee the cosmos, supervise other angels, and keep records of all human deeds. In the seventh heaven, heavenly beings praise God, and Enoch is able to see God sitting on his throne in the tenth heaven.

One version mentions only seven heavens, with God on his throne in the seventh, but another continues the journey through the eighth, ninth and tenth heavens. The angel Gabriel takes Enoch to the tenth heaven, and on the way he sees, fleetingly, the eighth and ninth heavens, with the regulation of the seasons and the zodiacs. In the tenth heaven, Enoch sees God and is initiated into the heavenly assembly. The face of God is

like iron made burning hot in a fire and brought out, and it emits sparks and is incandescent.[14]

The multiple heavens in these texts are not only a place of reward, imagined as a temple or palace, with angels singing praises, and God seated on his throne, but some levels are also places of punishment, of both humans and fallen angels. As in both these examples, apocalypses often refer to astronomical data and the movements of the celestial bodies, which can be observed and understood from different levels of heaven. Some of the images of paradise, lakes and birds have their roots in the classical mythology of Elysium and the Isles of the Blessed. This is almost certainly direct borrowing from classical sources, as evidenced by the paraphrasing of words from the *Aeneid* by the popular apocalypse of Paul, albeit in the context of a description of hell rather than heaven.[15]

In the hekhalot texts – Jewish mystical works in Hebrew dating from around the seventh century CE to the early Middle Ages – the heavenly realm contains five palaces ('hekhalot'), one inside the other, with God seated on his chariot-throne in the innermost palace. There are five of these compositions, which record the ascent through the seven palaces of a fictive sage, typically rabbis Aqiba or Ishmael. Angels guard the entrance to each palace, and the sage joins the angels in singing praises to God. The texts also contain instructions on how to reach God's chariot-throne. We find, once more, the now familiar motifs of heaven as a palace or temple, angels singing praises, and God on a chariot-throne, as these texts built on a tradition going back many hundreds of years to the earliest apocalypses and ascents.

We saw in Chapter 1 that the original inspiration for ideas of resurrection behind these Jewish and early Christian texts may have come from Zoroastrianism in Persia, although the Zoroastrian texts are difficult to date and so the influence is not certain. However, later Zoroastrian texts exhibit similar themes, with some differences, to the apocalypses and hekhalot texts. In a text dated to the ninth century CE or later, Arda Viraz Namag (alternatively Arda Viraf – the reading is uncertain) is elected to travel to heaven and hell to solve the crisis caused by the arrival of Alexander the Great. After taking a drug to ease his passage – evidence that his journey was undertaken in some altered state of consciousness – he is led to heaven by two guides, one an angel. First they pass through the stars, moon and sun, areas reserved for righteous non-Zoroastrians, an echo of the astronomical motifs of the apocalypses and the Dream of Scipio. In heaven (single rather than multiple), he encounters men and women of different earthly occupations, all of whom are living luxurious and sublime afterlives, with mention of golden thrones, fine carpets and cushions. There are also trees, fountains and streams, reminiscent of the motifs of Elysium which permeate many visions of heaven. These motifs are also found in Islamic understandings of heaven.

Muhammad's journey to heaven and other Islamic ascents

Muhammad's night journey from Mecca to Jerusalem and ascent to heaven are implied very briefly – and enigmatically – in the Quran (Sura 17). Jerusalem is not in fact named, though it may be implied, nor does the text explicitly state that Muhammad ascended to heaven (though seven heavens are mentioned later in that chapter, and elsewhere in the Quran). The Quran also does not mention his winged horse, Buraq. It was later Islamic tradition which expanded this story, with some variations of detail.

In some accounts, Muhammad ascended to heaven on a ladder. Most versions agree that he was accompanied by the angel Gabriel, who led him through the gates of each of seven heavens. In each heaven, they meet earlier prophets – including Adam, Enoch (called Idris in Arabic), Jesus and Moses. In the seventh heaven, Abraham sits on a throne at the gate, through which 70,000 angels pass each day. Muhammad appears before Allah's throne in the seventh heaven and has a conversation about the number of obligatory daily prayers for Muslims.

These traditions follow the patterns of the earlier Jewish and Christian ascents – with, possibly, some influence too from the Zoroastrian journey of Arda Viraz. There are many common motifs: multiple heavens (seven being the most popular number in the earlier apocalypses), an angelic guide, meeting the righteous dead, angels in heaven, heaven imagined as a temple or palace with gates, and God (Allah) seated on a throne.

In later Islamic tradition, a popular theme was dreams in which a person ascends to heaven. Unlike the rather sparse Quranic account, or even the later traditions of Muhammad's ascent, these focus specifically, and in great detail, on the rewards available in heaven for the righteous, and include instructions on proper moral conduct. This Islamic heaven – called *janna* in Arabic, and often *jannat 'adn*, 'the gardens of Eden' – consists of elaborate mansions, gardens with shady trees, rivers of milk, honey and wine, delicious food and fruits. The pious resurrected dead rest on couches adorned with gold and precious stones, attended by eternally young youths.

The aspect of the Islamic heaven that is probably best known to non-Muslims are the *hur* (often rendered as 'houris' in English), the chaste maidens of paradise. The word *hur* probably derives from the plural of the word 'white', and literally means 'the white ones', maidens whose eyes have a black iris in strong contrast to the whiteness around it. But what exactly the houris are remains obscure and continues to be debated. In the Quran, they are referred to as purified or modest wives, and sex is not mentioned. In the year 2000, the scholar Christoph Luxenberg suggested controversially that the word *hur* was Syriac in origin, not Arabic, and referred not to women at all but to a white raisin, which he concluded fitted into the context of the Quranic passages in which it is found.[16] This provoked much ridicule in the media, who pounced on the image of Islamist suicide bombers expecting virgins in heaven as a reward for martyrdom but getting a bowl of raisins instead (*The Guardian* newspaper printed a column entitled 'Virgins? What virgins?')[17], but in general this translation has been rejected by scholars. The dream ascents of Islamic tradition assume that the houris are concubines. In one such account, the believer lives in a heavenly mansion with 70 bedrooms, each bedroom with 70 sleeping mats, and on every mat a woman.[18]

In later tradition, the houris seem not to be earthly women at all, but a distinct, almost spiritual class of being. They are described as created of saffron, musk, amber and camphor, in four colours, and so transparent that the marrow of their bones is visible through between 70 and 70,000 silk garments. They have no bodily defects, do not sleep, get pregnant, or menstruate, or do annoying things like spit or blow their noses (actions which, presumably, were not regarded as acceptably sensual). When the pious Muslim enters paradise, he is welcomed by one of these. A large number are at his disposal and, though he sleeps with each of them, they always remain virgins.

Scholars have long pointed out that such images of the *hur* may have been directly inspired by Christian miniatures or mosaics representing the gardens of paradise, and that the multitudes of angels depicted there were mistakenly thought to be young, ethereal and virginal women. It is also popularly believed that there are 72 such virgins awaiting pious Muslims in heaven. However, the Quran is not specific about numbers, and although 72 appears in some later texts, others offer varying numbers or are also not specific.

We saw in Chapter 2 that, for most Muslims, on death, the body remains in the grave until the last day and the resurrection, while the soul is in an intermediate state called *barzakh*. There are exceptions. According to Muslim tradition, those who die in battle against unbelievers will go immediately to paradise and receive its full rewards, without having to wait in an intermediate state or to be judged in the grave. This tradition began with the battle of Badr in the Hejaz in 624 CE: although the battle is mentioned in the Quran, it provides no details, but in later tradition Muhammad is reported as saying that the soul of anyone killed would be transported immediately to paradise. It is a tradition that continues to have profound reverberations today, through the motivations of Islamic fundamentalists who carry out suicide attacks on people they regard as infidels. Alan Segal has analysed the direct link between the sensuous and sexual rewards of the Islamic heaven and the present-day concept of martyrdom, suicide bombing and suicide attacks in Islamic fundamentalism.[19] The heavenly rewards, and especially the anticipation of 72 virgins, are mentioned in recruitment tapes and are reported to be an important motivation to violence, alongside heavenly dispensation for family and friends and substantial payments to families of the martyr. As Segal points out, the 'alluring portrait' of a paradise of sensual pleasures is a key part of Islam's 'efficient organization for conversion and conquest', and has been throughout its history. The pleasure garden motif, ultimately derived from classical Elysium, is still central today for those who seek martyrdom.

In contrast to the Jewish and Christian apocalypses and hekhalot texts, God (Allah) is conspicuously absent from the descriptions of paradise in the Islamic dream ascents – and there are varying explanations in the Islamic tradition concerning which level of the seven heavens the garden paradise is located in. Explicit rewards for women are also absent, and there is no doubt that the traditional imagery of the sensual rewards of heaven is largely, if not entirely, male-oriented; in a very few texts, women are even rewarded in heaven only according to their husbands' virtue, and not their own. Jane Smith and Yvonne Haddad have reviewed the evidence concerning women in the Islamic afterlife, and conclude that, according to the Quran and most later Islamic tradition, women do have souls, are individually accountable, and do go to heaven, but there is little specifically about their individual rewards.[20] Although some texts are clear that houris are created as a specific reward for pious males, some Islamic scholars maintain that the word *hur* is neither female nor male, and that houris will be available to both men and women.

Celtic and medieval journeys to the Otherworld and heaven

The influence of Elysium as the Blessed Isles of the West is clearly seen in the Celtic tradition of the Otherworld. This is always depicted as located across water, to the west: so, for the Celts, it was usually imagined to be across the Atlantic.

The earliest of the Irish stories of voyages to the Otherworld – known as *immrama*, 'mystical voyages' – is that of Bran, dating to the seventh or eighth century CE. A mysterious woman sings to

Bran of the delights of the Otherworld, where it is eternal spring, with flowery meadows, birds, music, drinking wine, playing games and happiness:

> Unknown is wailing or treachery
> In the familiar cultivated land,
> There is nothing rough or harsh,
> But sweet music striking on the ear.[21]

She urges him to sail to the land of women, across the ocean. So, the next day, Bran sets out over the sea with 27 companions. They encounter a man driving a chariot across the sea: this is the sea-god Manannan mac Lir (whose name is associated with the Isle of Man). He describes the sea as a vision of the Otherworld – as a flowery plain, with salmon 'leaping from the womb of the white sea' imagined as calves, and his boat as floating over an orchard of fruit trees.

Bran reaches the island of women, a common theme in the *immrama*. In Celtic tradition, these women, who had great magical power and usually attempted to detain travellers, were known as *bean-sidhe*, later corrupted to 'banshees', and later stories talk of the overwhelming impact of their keenings for the dead. The women lead Bran and his companions to a large house, with a bed for every couple. They remain many years there until, homesick, they sail back to Ireland, where they find they have been forgotten, except in legend. A common theme in stories about the Otherworld is that time passes differently, either considerably longer or shorter than earthly time. The first of the band to set foot ashore becomes a heap of ashes,

> as though he had been in the earth for many hundreds of years.[22]

The voyage of Mael Duin – probably eighth century, although the extant version dates to the tenth century – contains more details about the Otherworld. The voyage, in a magical curragh or skin boat constructed under the instructions of a druid, is ostensibly to avenge his father's murder, but becomes an exploration of the fantastical islands of the Otherworld. There are 33 of these islands, which include wonders like swarms of giant ants, fiery pigs, many other strange beasts, one island where black and white are reversed, and – as in Bran's destination – the island of women. Here, Mael Duin sleeps with the queen, and his men with other maidens, and they are offered eternal youth, immortality and constant sex. Despite Mael Duin's understandable reluctance to leave, the crew's homesickness leads to their eventual departure. On the final island, an Irish falcon guides them home. Mael Duin forgives his father's killer and narrates his adventure.

The story of Mael Duin directly influenced the story of St Brendan's voyage, which was enormously popular throughout Europe in the Middle Ages, although some scholars suggest that the influence was the other way around, or at least that there was mutual borrowing as both stories developed orally. Written down in the tenth century, this recounts the mythical voyage of the Irish abbot Brendan (c. 486-578 CE, but estimates of his dates vary widely), who was known to have travelled at least as far as Iceland. The course of Brendan's legendary journey is almost identical to that of Mael Duin's, and many incidents are Christian reworkings of events in the Celtic story. Brendan sets out with 17 monks in a curragh in search of the Land of Promise of the Saints (a reference to chapter 20 of the Book of Revelation, where Christ will reign with the saints and martyrs for a thousand years before the establishment of the New Jerusalem; in the apocalypse of Paul, the Land of Promise is located in the second heaven). In Brendan's story, this land is an earthly paradise, teeming with ripe fruit,

where night never falls and day never ends.[23]

During their seven-year voyage across the Atlantic, they diligently observe the Christian feasts, masses, and the pattern of daily prayers at fixed times. As in Mael Duin, they find wonders on a series of islands, but there is a Christian slant to all their encounters: in the paradise of birds (similar to several islands in Mael Duin), the birds sing praises to God, and they celebrate one mass on the back of a whale. They sail by the outskirts of hell, a flaming island with wailing inhabitants and a noxious smell, and meet Judas, who, because it is a Sunday, has a brief respite in the crashing waves from his fiery torments. In the Land of Promise of the Saints they reach a river, which an angelic youth tells them they cannot cross as they are still alive.

There has been considerable discussion as to whether the story was based on an actual voyage. In 1976-77, Tim Severin re-enacted Brendan's voyage in a curragh from Ireland, around Britain, and across the Atlantic, landing in Newfoundland, to demonstrate that such a journey was achievable in practice and that the wonders Brendan described could be accounted for by natural phenomena.[24]

The Irish vision literature also grew out of the Celtic Otherworld voyage stories, taking familiar motifs from the Jewish and Christian apocalypses and adapting them to Irish saints. One of the most popular of these visions was that of Tundale, written in Latin in 1149 by an Irish monk, which was translated into at least 13 languages in the Middle Ages.

Tundale is an Irish knight, a sinner, who is struck supposedly dead. During the three days and three nights of what can be described as a near-death experience, his guardian angel leads his soul on a tour of hell and heaven. Most of the focus is on the imaginative tortures of hell, and Tundale's soul is purged through various punishments, so that he eventually returns to life repentant and changed – which was of course the moral purpose of the story. Leaving hell, they follow a rising path, encountering ever more righteous souls arranged hierarchically according to degree of virtue, through the not very evil, to the not very good, to the truly virtuous and pure. The description of heaven is familiar from the earlier apocalypses: it is a temple/ palace with walls of silver, gold and precious stones, gates, thrones, the Elysian/Celtic motif of a beautiful flowery field where there is no night, and plenty of singing of praises to God.

Sexual purity and asceticism are particularly rewarded in this vision of heaven (just as sex outside marriage or by the clergy is most heavily punished in Tundale's hell). Tundale sees sexually active people who have been subsequently purified through leading ascetic lives or by martyrdom. He is forbidden from entering deepest heaven, which is reserved for pure monks and the virtuous who deserve to be among the angels, because, the angel tells him, he is not a virgin.

This and other medieval visions of heaven and hell[25] were heavily influenced by the views on sex and purity of the early Church fathers, and the contemporary monastic zeal for asceticism and virginity. These views built on the interpretation of Paul's 'transformed' resurrected body that we saw in Chapter 1, and the quote from Jesus in the gospel of Mark 12:25:

For when they rise from the dead, they neither marry nor are given in marriage, but are like angels in heaven.

Clement of Alexandria (c. 150-215 CE) had written that sexual differentiation would disappear in heaven, and that men and women, though human, would cease to be sexual beings. His contemporary Tertullian argued that the resurrected body would contain all the same organs, but would have no need to use the organs of sex or digestion. For Augustine, a complete person who lives for eternity in heaven is composed of a soul joined to a sexless body free from all desires; heaven is therefore a community of perfected beings, like angels, singing eternal praises to God.

This is the heaven of Tundale's vision. As Alan Segal has pointed out, the Zoroastrian, Muslim (and Celtic) heaven is sexual; the Jewish heaven is equivocal; but the pre-Renaissance Christian heaven is sexless, pure and virginal.[26]

Dante's *Paradiso*

Dante's *Paradiso* ('paradise' or 'heaven') is the culmination of this tradition of Christian ascents to heaven, which had originated in the Jewish and Christian apocalypses more than a thousand years earlier. Durante degli Alighieri (c. 1265-1321), called Dante, was born in Florence and became Italy's foremost poet as well as a political activist, spending the latter part of his life in exile. His epic poem *The Divine Comedy* (although he titled the original simply *Commedia*), completed soon before his death, is generally considered the greatest work of literature ever composed in Italian.

Dante intended it as an allegory about free will, reward, punishment and justice, and a warning to the corrupt society he saw around him. The poem describes Dante's own journey through the afterworld realms in three parts: hell (*Inferno*), purgatory (*Purgatorio*) and heaven (*Paradiso*). Through the first two he is guided by the Roman poet Virgil, and through heaven by Beatrice (Bice di Folco Portinari, 1266-1290), the dead, unrequited and idealised love of his youth. The structure of each of the three realms follows a pattern of several levels with an additional one: hell has nine circles, with Lucifer/Satan's level at the bottom; purgatory has seven terraces, based on the seven deadly sins, with the Garden of Eden at the summit; and heaven has nine levels, followed by the highest, where God resides, called the empyrean (from the Latin *empyreus*, 'fiery', but probably understood to symbolise pure light).

There are many echoes of the earlier Jewish and Christian apocalypses in *Paradiso*: multiple levels of heaven, the traditional guide, the hierarchies, well known people met in the different levels, music and praises sung to God, and this whole section of the poem begins in the earthly paradise on top of Mount Purgatory. The use of the word 'purgatory' within the Catholic Church to refer to a particular place for the cleansing of sins probably dates to the late twelfth century. The need for a process of purification for the moderately wicked, through temporary rather than permanent punishments, in order to qualify for heaven, though, was a much older idea, and had certainly been much discussed by Christian and Jewish thinkers since at least Clement of Alexandria in the late second/early third centuries CE (and purgation of the soul by fire was also incorporated into the mystical strand of Judaism known as Kabbalah, at about the same time as purgatory became formalised in Christianity). As we have seen, punishment took place in the lower levels of multiple heavens in the earlier apocalypses, and Tundale was purged of his sins during his journey through hell, just before the concept of purgatory became spatialised. By the time of Dante, the purification process had moved to a specific place called purgatory, through which he enters heaven.

Dante's nine levels of heaven are based on the then established cosmology of the spheres, recalling Cicero's 'Dream of Scipio': counting upwards, the moon, Mercury, Venus, the sun, Mars, Jupiter, Saturn, and the fixed stars to the outermost sphere, the *primum mobile* ('first moved'), which is the shell or skin of the cosmos and the sphere that moves all the others. Beyond that is the empyrean, described by Dante as the heaven of pure light. As in the earlier medieval visions, including Tundale's, there are grades of reward in heaven. Angels reside in the *primum mobile*. Just below are the most blessed humans, as in Tundale the monastic contemplatives, emphasising again the importance of sexual purity and asceticism. The highest of these is Bernard of Clairvaux (1090-1153), the influential Cistercian abbot, who saw contemplation as the key to Christian spirituality. Many of the medieval visions had a deliberate Cistercian bias, demonstrating their superior rank in heaven.[27] It is not surprising, therefore, that Beatrice is succeeded by Bernard as the guide to the empyrean, where he invites Dante to look directly upon God – the Beatific Vision, the ultimate aim of medieval Christian conceptions of heaven.

Modern visions of heaven

With his *Divine Comedy*, Dante effectively brought to an end the long tradition of visionary Christian journeys to heaven (and hell). Yet, despite its enormous popularity, Renaissance paintings mostly depict heaven as a city or building – rather than Dante's nine levels – and very explicitly incorporate the classical motifs of Elysium as well as a degree of sensuality missing in earlier Christian visions.[28] For example, in the paintings of Fra Angelico (c. 1395-1455), we get both city and garden paradise, with trees, birds, flowers, meadows, fountains, tents and boats. This was still the common depiction of heaven at the time of John Milton's *Paradise Lost*, published in 1667.

A very different heaven appears in the visions of Emanuel Swedenborg (1688-1772), an eminent Swedish scientist in a variety of fields. After a personal religious crisis in the mid-1740s, he wrote a vast number of religious and spiritual works, sharing his visions of the other world. These essentially record his journeys to heaven. Swedenborg claimed that only a narrow sea separated the living from the dead, and that he frequently travelled back and forth between the afterworld and this world.

Swedenborg's heaven was a continuation of life on earth. Based on love, it was bodily and sensual, just like our earthly lives, with friends and family, marriage, weddings and sex – but no pregnancies or babies. He claimed that no great change took place in the personality or lifestyle of the individual, and that the afterlife was so similar that sometimes the dead did not know they were dead.

His heaven was a fully built environment, just like on earth.

There are some echoes of older visions of heaven. He records seeing magnificent palaces, as if of gold and precious stones, which he explicitly relates to the biblical Book of Revelation's New Jerusalem. There were shining parks, with leaves glistening as if of silver, fruit as if of gold, and flowers forming rainbows of colours. He even included his own drawings of what these heavenly cities looked like, and they still included churches.

Swedenborg records that he frequently talked with angels, who were actually former humans. These angels lived in houses – the male angels grew long beards – and they had jobs in heaven, for example in church, civil or domestic affairs. But this heaven still had grades: a natural heaven, a spiritual heaven, and a celestial heaven, depending on one's degree of spiritual development. Everything in heaven was constantly changing. This was not a picture of heaven as an eternity of praising God. Those living forever in heaven carried out lots of charitable activities for each other. It was an active eternal life, with individual and social progress and development.

Although Swedenborg never had a huge popular following – and the philosopher Immanuel Kant famously dismissed his visions as 'nonsense' – he did influence other writers, poets, artists and philosophers, such as William Blake, William Butler Yeats, August Strindberg and Johann Wolfgang von Goethe. In the United States, Swedenborg had a major indirect influence through the book *The Gates Ajar*, written by the then 22-year-old Elizabeth Stuart Phelps (1844-1911), though not published until 1868, which became the second best-selling novel of the nineteenth century (after *Uncle Tom's Cabin*) and was translated into French, German, Dutch and Italian. Phelps was familiar with Swedenborg's writings, which clearly influence her vision of heaven, and she cites him in her book. In this fictional diary set at the time of the American Civil War, a grieving young woman's aunt provides comforting visions of a social heaven of family, friends, houses with flowers in the windows, pets, pianos, gingersnaps and happiness. It is also a creative heaven, with sculptors, painters, poets, musicians, writers and orators:

'Yes, I believe we shall talk and laugh and joke and play... I expect that you will hear some of Roy's very old jokes...'[29]

The dread of loss of personal identity, memory and connections haunts the book, which is also filled with voluminous footnotes which are essentially biblical interpretation in support of this view of heaven. Some of these footnotes contradict her earthy vision of heaven – and undermine the presence of gingersnaps, strawberries and pianos – by discussing, at great length, Paul's idea of the spiritual resurrected body (see Chapter 1):

... after death it will be raised a spiritual body... needing no more food, rest, sleep, or recreation; no longer capable of relishing animal pleasures...[30]

Despite the enormous popularity of the book, which, according to her autobiography, spawned a diverse range of linked products, including cigars, songs, patent medicines and floral funeral arrangements, Phelps' rather wholesome depiction of heaven was not universally admired. The last story ever published by her contemporary Mark Twain (1835-1910), *Extract from Captain Stormfield's Visit to Heaven*, was a deliberately satirical response to Phelps, in which the dead captain has a series of bizarre adventures and conversations in heaven. Having problems flying with his new angel's wings, he knocks down a bishop, then sends the wings to a laundry before storing them in a cupboard, saving them for a special occasion to wear with his halo, harp and palm branch. Taking particular aim at the popular picture of a human-centred heaven and its celebrities such as Adam, Twain includes people in heaven from other planets and systems who look down on humans and their achievements.

Many scholars have credited Swedenborg with at least indirect responsibility, through his influence on others, for the modern popular notion of heaven as a perfect continuation of earthly life, with its focus on reunions with friends and family, sex, and the opportunity to be creative and active. There had always been a tension within Christianity around sex (and its absence) in heaven and around the prospect of worshiping God for eternity, which for many seemed rather dull. Of course, the idea of meeting friends and relatives in heaven had a very long precedent in visions of the afterlife. Already in the *Odyssey* and the *Aeneid*, Odysseus meets his mother and Virgil his father. Augustine, in his *Confessions*, believes his parents are in heaven. Dante's father is actually consigned to hell, but the poet meets other friends and relatives in heaven.

The difference with Swedenborg and many other modern visions of heaven is that friends and family have become the prime focus of heaven. Augustine had insisted that he and his parents would not be focused on one another but on God, and the Beatific Vision is also the focus of Dante's heaven. But the modern heaven, from the eighteenth century onwards, is more social and centred on human relationships, and God becomes slightly peripheral or sometimes disappears altogether. Towards the end of *The Gates Ajar*, Phelps insists that God comes first, but the only way in which she is able to articulate this is to reimagine God in social form and talking to Jesus as a friend. This picture of a social heaven was also the basis for the popularity of the spiritualist movement from the mid-nineteenth century on, with mediums relaying messages from dead family and friends, and of electronic voice phenomena, tape recordings of the voices supposedly of the dead especially by Friedrich Jürgenson and Konstantin Raudive from the late 1950s on.[31]

This social picture continues in the modern visions of heaven recorded in many near-death experiences (NDEs). An NDE can occur when the body is under severe stress, close to or even after clinical death – and since death is a process, the dividing line between 'life' and 'death' is not clear-cut and clinical pronouncements of death are not infallible. A variety of common sensations are typically experienced, including feelings of peace, a dark tunnel, an out of body experience, a strong light, a life review, meeting others, glimpses of heaven, and the return to life. In recent years, there has been an explosion of interest in NDEs, with a vast amount of books and other media – a random search on Amazon recorded nearly three thousand books dealing with NDEs. For many people, NDEs are proof of life after death. Most scientists are sceptical and believe that there are physiological, or even psychological, explanations; they note that the experiences are not actually of final, permanent death, and at the most they tell us something about the experience of the process of death, but not how long the experiences continue or anything about life after death. That some sort of consciousness, experience or memory is present after normal brain functions have shut down raises questions about the relationship between the mind and the brain, to which we will return in Chapter 8.

Carol Zaleski, in her *Otherworld Journeys*, concludes that NDEs are best treated as works of religious imagination which convey meaning through symbolic forms rather than describe verifiable facts, and which do not necessarily say anything certain about immortality or what happens after death. She explores similarities and differences between modern NDEs and the ancient and medieval journeys to heaven and hell (such as the early apocalypses and Tundale – some of which, but by no means all, might be accounts of early NDEs). Essentially, NDEs are accounts of journeys to the afterlife – whether real, as many of those who have experienced them believe, or imagined, as most scientists argue – and they round out our picture of how heaven can be understood in the present day.

The heaven that often appears in NDEs consists of flowery meadows, colours, lakes, splendid buildings or heavenly cities, and it is filled with light. It is peopled mostly by deceased relatives and friends. We can see that most of these elements have parallels to earlier journeys to heaven, with the mix of a heavenly city and a paradise garden, the standard body of water, and meeting people. But there are also significant differences. These modern heavens are not multiple, or graded, there are no ordeals, pain or suffering, no agonising about asceticism and sex, and there is no link to virtue or lack of it – the typical life review is just a review, it is not judgmental. Although the content has similarities to earlier journeys, the cultural form or interpretation of the journey has changed, in line with modern expectations, hopes, beliefs and fears. Whatever their ultimate cause, these do not seem to be disinterested and objective accounts – they are culturally conditioned. If they were not, then we would expect to see accounts of modern NDEs similar to those of medieval examples, like Tundale, with its horrific tortures and obsession with sexual purity.[32] But the heaven of modern NDEs is more Swedenborg and *The Gates Ajar* than it is Enoch, Baruch, Tundale or Dante. It is mostly a glimpse of a heaven of human relationships, peace and happiness – surely the golden triangle of modern human hopes – with hell, sin and punishment conspicuously absent, unlike earlier visions (although a small proportion of modern NDEs do report dark and unpleasant experiences). And it is to visions of the underworld and hell that we now turn.

Ancient journeys to the underworld

Depictions of hell as a place of fiery torment and punishment for the wicked are very similar across cultures. They first appear in Jewish apocalypses in the Hellenistic period, but many of the details of our modern notion of hell derive from the tradition of journeys to the underworld. The most famous and influential of these is Dante's *Inferno*, but this itself borrowed from and built on a very long tradition going back to the ancient Near East, where the genre was popular.

The fullest ancient Near Eastern account of a journey to the underworld concerns the Sumerian goddess Inanna (known in the Akkadian language as Ishtar). This is recorded on 13 clay tablets from the Mesopotamian city of Nippur, dating to the first half of the second millennium BCE, although it was composed earlier. This Sumerian version is a longer and more detailed account than the later Akkadian version of Ishtar's descent to the underworld.[33]

Inanna/Ishtar was the goddess of sex and war and the most important female deity in ancient Mesopotamia. It is likely that the story was re-enacted in a ritual, with the goddess' cult statue making a journey from her home town of Uruk to Kutha, seat of the underworld deities. This was a seasonal ritual connected with the myth of the dying and rising god Dumuzi, her lover, and the fertility of the earth.

For an unknown reason, Inanna/Ishtar leaves heaven and visits the underworld, threatening to crush its gates and raise up the dead, who will outnumber and eat the living. As she passes through each of the seven gates of Kurnugi, the land of no return (a Sumerian term for the underworld), her garments and jewels are removed piece by piece. Finally, she arrives naked before Ereshkigal, her older sister and queen of the underworld. She is turned into a corpse and hung from a stake for three days and three nights. Drought and infertility descend upon the earth. Eventually, she is revived and leaves the underworld, but is accompanied by the dead and demons to seek a substitute – her lover Dumuzi, who will have to spend half the year in the underworld.

This theme of journeys to the underworld became popular later in Greece and Rome, both for gods and heroes, including the myth of the dying and rising Persephone and Orpheus' rescue of Eurydice. Odysseus' visit in Book 11 of the *Odyssey*, in order to find his way home, lacks a detailed description of the underworld, apart from his conversations with the dead and mention of the punishments meted out to particular people: Tityos picked at by vultures; Tantalus standing in water but unable to drink; and Sisyphus condemned forever to push a boulder uphill. The first really detailed underworld journey, that in fact describes a recognisably modern hell – a combination of fire with punishment for the wicked – is found in Book 6 of Virgil's *Aeneid*.

Above, we saw how Aeneas, once over the River Acheron, turned right on a divided path towards Elysium and his dead father. On the left, though, the path leads to Tartarus, well known in classical mythology as a place of punishment for the wicked, and, according to Plato, as the place where souls were judged after death.

Virgil describes Tartarus as having wide battlements, a triple wall and a huge gate, encircled by a river of red-hot flames, the Phlegethon ('the flaming'):

Groans resound from the depths, the savage crack of the lash, the grating creak of iron, the clank of dragging chains.[34]

Inside is a monstrous Hydra, with fifty black gaping jaws. The Sibyl explains the sorts of wickedness that are punished here: striking one's parents, fraud, adultery, miserliness, causing civil war, treachery and incest. There are varied punishments:

Some trundle enormous boulders, others dangle, racked to the breaking point on the spokes of rolling wheels.[35]

Tours of hell

Jewish apocalypticism also had a tradition of tours of hell, and Jan Bremmer has suggested that apocalyptic writings, and in particular 1 Enoch, may have been a significant source for Virgil for images of a fiery underworld, and also for the idea of a guide to the underworld – Enoch is led by an angel, Aeneas by the Sibyl – neither of which had clear classical prototypes.[36]

The earliest apocalyptic journeys are in the form of cosmic tours in which the mysteries of heaven, earth and hell are revealed to the seer by angelic guides; they are ascribed to ancient seers like Enoch, Elijah and Moses. The oldest is 1 Enoch chapters 17 to 36, dating to the third or early second century BCE, in which Enoch is taken to a mountain on the western edge of the world. There he sees the four chambers in which the four categories of the dead are kept until the day of judgment. Here, for the first time in Jewish literature, and in marked contrast to the earlier bleak, undifferentiated Sheol (see Chapter 1), we have the theme of reward and punishment after death: the righteous souls are in a chamber with light and a fountain, while the other chambers are dark.

Chapter 54, the latest strand of 1 Enoch, probably dating between the first centuries BCE and CE, introduces a fiery abyss, as part of Enoch's journey to the heavenly throne room and through the cosmos:

> Then I looked and turned to another face of the earth and saw there a valley, deep and burning with fire. And they were bringing kings and potentates and were throwing them into the deep valley. And my eyes saw there their chains while they were making them into iron fetters of immense weight.[37]

The valley mentioned here is referred to elsewhere by Enoch and other apocalyptic writings as 'the accursed valley', 'the abyss', or specifically Gehenna (or Gehinom), a name which means the Valley of Hinnom. Gehenna became the name for the Jewish hell.

In the Hebrew Bible, the Valley of Hinnom, near Jerusalem, was condemned by the prophet Jeremiah as the location of the idolatrous worship of the Canaanite gods Molech and Baal. This consisted of sacrificing young children by passing them through a fire and into the hands of the gods. It has been suggested that the altars and cultic places there were considered an entrance to the realm of the gods, and that as a result the Valley of Hinnom – Gehenna – may naturally have been adopted as the name of the underworld. As the notion of an afterlife and resurrection developed among Jewish apocalyptic sects, Gehenna came to represent the place of judgment and punishment of wicked Jews, eventually expanded to include all wicked everywhere.

Punishment by fire in Gehenna became an increasingly popular motif in Jewish and Christian texts – probably because fire was linked to the original Molech cult – usually in a fiery lake or abyss, as in 1 Enoch (perhaps the source for Virgil) and in the Christian gospels. In the gospels, Gehenna, often described as 'the hell of fire' (where the word 'hell' is an English translation of Gehenna), is used by Jesus metaphorically as the place of eternal fiery judgment, where 'men will weep and gnash their teeth'.

In the tours of hell in the later apocalypses, from the first century CE onwards, the travellers are normally accompanied by a guide, and the descriptions mainly focus on the punishments for different types of wickedness. Sexual sins are often mentioned, in all sorts of variations, particularly in Christian apocalypses which were concerned with purity. Common are 'hanging punishments', in which the dead are hanged by the parts of their bodies used to commit the sin: sex offenders by their genitals, breasts, eyebrows or hair; speech offenders by their tongues or ears. Punishments by fire are also dominant, especially immersion in a fiery river or a burning furnace, or impalement on wheels of fire. In the second-century CE apocalypse of Peter, liars have their lips cut off and fire burns their mouths and entrails, murderers are tortured in the sight of the souls of their victims, and slanderers have their eyes burned by red-hot irons. The fourth- or fifth-century CE apocalypse of Paul, which continued to be popular in Christian Europe late into the Middle

Ages, with 12 different versions translated into many languages, singled out underperforming and sinful church officials for specific punishment. One of the versions shows the continuing influence of classical journeys to the underworld, by directly paraphrasing words from the *Aeneid*. Compare the *Aeneid*:

> No, not if I had a hundred tongues and a hundred mouths
> and a voice of iron too – I could never capture
> all the crimes or run through all the torments,
> doom by doom[38]

with the apocalypse of Paul:

> there are 144,000 pains in hell, and if there were 100 men speaking from the beginning of the world, each one of whom had 104 tongues, they could not number the pains of hell.[39]

By the time of Augustine (354-430 CE), hell as a literal lake of fire was the orthodox Christian church view. Some of these motifs were incorporated into Zoroastrian ideas and tours of hell in Persia. Judgment, torture of sinners, and different punishments for different sins are encountered in the explicitly drug-induced journey through hell of Arda Viraz, dated to the ninth century CE or later, mentioned above. The bulk of this text is a horrific list of sins and punishments, especially focused on adultery and other sexual sins, including the familiar hanging punishments, bodies constantly gnawed by various creatures, and eternally eating excrement, blood and refuse.

The Zoroastrian journey of the high priest Kirdir, recorded on two inscriptions dating to the third century CE, included what was to become a very popular motif, also included in the later journey of Arda Viraz: a perilously narrow bridge – the Chinvat Bridge – over the bottomless pit of hell, full of reptiles, which the dead had to cross to reach heaven. This bridge is described in the Avesta, the collection of sacred Zoroastrian texts, which is notoriously difficult to date. When the wicked cross, the bridge narrows and they fall into hell; for the righteous, it widens and they cross successfully and ascend into heaven. The Zoroastrian hell was not eternal, however, but was destined to be destroyed, together with all evil, at the end of time.

The idea of Gehenna was adopted by Islam, in its Arabic form Jahannam, and the word appears frequently in the Quran as the name of hell, alongside *al-nar*, 'the fire'. In some Quranic verses, hell seems to be depicted as an animal, ready to hurl itself at the damned. Mostly, though, it is a place of blazing fire, and the gruesome details are familiar from earlier apocalyptic traditions, which were still current in the region.

Architecturally, the Quranic hell comprises seven concentric circles or levels in the form of a crater or abyss, with seven gates (echoing the seven gates of the underworld in Inanna/Ishtar's descent). Some later interpreters regarded Jahannam as specifically the upper level of hell, a temporary place of punishment for Muslim sinners. A later inclusion, possibly borrowed from Zoroastrian tradition, is a perilously narrow bridge – Al-Sirat – over the fiery chasm of hell, which has to be crossed by the dead in order to enter paradise. Bridges to heaven became a popular motif in other cultures: narrow bridges over the fiery lakes or rivers of hell occur in medieval visions such as Tundale's; and, in later Norse mythology, the burning rainbow bridge Bifröst connects earth with Asgard, the realm of the gods.[40]

Most of the punishments meted out to the wicked in the Quran are connected with fire and heat. Later Islamic texts – handbooks or tours of hell which expanded the tradition of Muhammad's ascent to heaven, the *mi'raj*, with an increased focus on hell – embellished them and added more extreme punishments, such as decapitation, gibbeting, stoning, throwing down from heights, drowning, and trampling by animals, as well as the 'hanging punishments' known from apocalyptic texts. In one later tradition, the fire of hell is so intense that the upper lip of the sinner

is rolled up until it reaches the middle of his head, and his lower lip will hang down until it beats on his navel.[41]

In none of these early traditions about hell is the devil or Satan reported as being its ruler. In the Hebrew Bible, the term used for God's opponent is Satan, which means 'adversary' in Hebrew. The English word 'devil' comes from the Greek *diabolos*, which means 'slanderer'. In apocalyptic and early Christian texts, the devil is an angel who falls from grace and is banished from heaven.

The Quran expands on these traditions. There, the proper name of the devil is Iblis, possibly a corruption of the Greek *diabolos*. Iblis refused to bow down to Adam and is condemned to be thrown into hell at the last judgment, but he is not described as its ruler. According to the Quran, the angel Malik (a name probably derived from the Semitic word for 'king') is the lord of hell, whose role is to inform those condemned to hell that they must remain there for eternity. In later tradition, Satan is most prominently portrayed as the ruler of hell, with the rebellious angels as his followers, in *Paradise Lost* by John Milton (1608-1674).

The tours of hell, derived from the Hebrew tradition of Gehenna, continued to be popular for over a thousand years, alongside parallel descriptions of heaven, well into the medieval period. Martha Himmelfarb, in her *Tours of Hell*, has shown that they formed a distinct literary genre with common elements. Hell is portrayed as a fiery place; it is divided into levels or compartments, each relating to a distinct sin; the traveller is led by a guide; they stop to view each level or compartment; at each stop, the guide explains the nature of the sin and describes the (usually extreme) punishments meted out; they often include criticism of contemporary religious and political authorities. The most detailed description of particularly vivid and horrendous tortures is in the twelfth-century vision of Tundale, whose journey to heaven through the horrors and punishments of hell we encountered above. Typically for this genre, the most savage and imaginative tortures are reserved for sexual sins such as adultery, fornication, promiscuity and sodomy, and especially those committed by the clergy, since they are judged worthy of the greatest pain; for example, monks and nuns tortured in their genitals which gush with worms, and both sexes made pregnant by a beast that swallows then vomits them up into a frozen swamp, after which they beget serpents that sting their entrails, with men giving birth through all parts of their bodies.

As we have seen, these stories were not parochial, but were incorporated into Jewish, Christian, Zoroastrian and Islamic traditions and shared by those communities in Asia, Africa and Europe. The tradition found its culmination in Dante's *Inferno*, which continues to be the best known and most influential description of a Christian hell.

Dante's *Inferno*

In the *Inferno*, Virgil guides Dante through hell, and they stop on the way to speak with various dead people. Among these are contemporaries of Dante, including several popes, who in Dante's estimation are clearly not destined for heaven, as well as historical and legendary figures. Each circle of hell is reserved for those who have committed particular sins, the lower the circle the greater the sin, and, for each, Dante describes increasingly horrific punishments. At the bottom, in the ninth circle, those guilty of treachery are buried in an icy lake; and, at the centre of hell, encased in ice, Satan's three faces eternally chew the heads of the arch-traitors Brutus, Cassius and Judas.

Of course, *The Divine Comedy* has such a great reputation

because of the beauty of its language, the richness of its images, and its ambitious scope: no wonder Dante chose his ancient countryman Virgil as his guide, as this was the most epic treatment of the afterlife since the *Aeneid*, and Dante deliberately adapted its framework and motifs. However, if we are interested in the *Inferno* mainly as a medieval description of hell, and seek to understand where it sits alongside earlier descriptions, then we need to acknowledge what Dante borrowed from those earlier traditions, and what was new. It did, after all, become the most influential vision of hell until the present day.

Dante adapted the following elements from the long tradition of earlier journeys to the underworld and tours of hell, including the *Odyssey* and the *Aeneid*: hell as a series of concentric circles; sins divided into compartments or levels; specific punishments for specific sins; frequent fiery punishments, such as burning rivers, sand and rain; the idea of a guide through hell; and conversations with the dead, many of whom include religious or political figures.

What is new about Dante's hell? Firstly, it is explicitly autobiographical: it is Dante himself who undertakes the journey (although 1 Enoch was attributed to Enoch, in fact this was a compilation of five independent works of different dates; similarly, although some of the medieval journeys are written in the first person, they are clearly at least compiled by someone else, and there is no indication that they are truly autobiographical). This allows him to incorporate many of his friends and contemporaries into the story and to comment on current political matters.

Secondly, we might have expected the lowest circle to portray the classic fiery hell and the harshest of burning punishments, but instead the sinners there are frozen in an icy lake. The usual explanation is that this lowest circle is the furthest away from the warmth of God's love, and cold and ice do occasionally feature in descriptions of hell in the apocalypse of Paul and early medieval visions, such as Tundale's. However, we cannot discount that Dante was also encouraged in this idea of an icy hell from early transmission across Europe of the *Gylfaginning*, the first part of the *Prose Edda*, the renowned narrative of Norse mythology written by the Icelandic historian and politician Snorri Sturluson (1179-1241) about a hundred years before *The Divine Comedy*. In that work, all those who die of sickness and old age (as opposed to slain warriors, who go to Valhalla and Fólkvangr) end up in Niflheim, a realm of primordial ice and frozen rivers, and abode of the goddess Hel. Around the time of Dante or a little later, too, the Beijing Temple of Eighteen Hells includes the hell of cold ice. Here, each hell graphically depicts in clay figures a different form of torture fitting the crime, many of them similar to those in the medieval Christian visions. Whatever Dante's source, it is clear that cold and ice were common components of hell across cultures, alongside fire.[42]

Thirdly, the nine circles with their graded sins and punishments are also new. Helpfully, Dante tells us where this idea came from. In Canto 11, Dante's guide Virgil outlines the structure of the nine circles of hell and explains its reasoning. In response to a question from Dante on why certain sins are not punished in the same way, Virgil explicitly refers to Aristotle's *Nicomachean Ethics* as the explanation of hell's framework.[43] Clive James' accessible modern translation clearly explains this reasoning:

> Don't you recall how Aristotle shows,
> In the *Ethics*, that three different kinds of state
> In humans breed all crimes that can oppose
> Themselves to heaven's will? Incontinence,
> Malice and brutishness? And of those three,
> Incontinence is held the least offence
> By God, and so is punished less? You see,
> Or ought to, how this basic teaching yields

The reason that all those we left outside
And higher up in their respective fields
Are separate from the wicked who reside
Down here. These were more guilty. Hence, divine
Justice assails those less than it does these.

The word 'incontinence' here is from the Greek *akrasia*, which Aristotle used in his *Ethics* to refer to a voluntary action based on weakness of will or lack of moderation, which is not as severe or as culpable as sins of violence ('brutishness') or fraud ('malice'). It is this appeal to Aristotle's ethical system that creates the innovative graded structure of the nine circles of Dante's hell. All sins are divided into three main groups, the deeper the circle, the greater the sin and the harsher the punishment: sins of incontinence in Circles 2 to 5 (lust, gluttony, avarice, anger); sins of violence in Circle 7 (divided into three: violence against one's neighbour, against oneself, and against God); and sins of fraud in Circles 8 and 9 (including flattery, hypocrisy and, in Circle 9, betrayal and treachery).

Limbo (Circle 1, for unbaptised infants and virtuous non-Christians) and the sin of heresy (Circle 6) are omitted in this canto, because they are specifically Christian themes that were not covered by Aristotle. The idea of limbo as a specific place was brand new in Dante's time, although the post-mortem fate of dead, unbaptised children had been discussed by Christian thinkers since the fourth century. In fact, there were generally thought to be two limbos, one for unbaptised infants and one for the pre-Christian Old Testament patriarchs. Unusually, though, Dante also placed virtuous non-Christians, including Aristotle, in limbo, rather than placing them in heaven or hell, which was the orthodox practice of his time.

Many commentators have pointed out that no previous or subsequent Christian vision of the afterlife invokes a classical philosopher as its source or authority. *The Divine Comedy* quickly became a classic, and already Dante's first biographer, Giovanni Boccaccio (1313-1375), referred to him as the heir to Homer and Virgil. The *Inferno* in particular has been a huge inspiration for poets, writers and artists, who have been drawn to it more or less constantly up to the present. Its detailed imagery of the savage punishments in hell, together with the descriptions in the earlier apocalypses and medieval visions, such as Tundale, influenced medieval sculpture and painters such as Hieronymus Bosch (c. 1450-1516), whose nightmarish depictions of hell belong to the same Christian moral universe. Among the great artists who have illustrated the *Inferno* are Sandro Botticelli (1445-1510), William Blake (1757-1827), Paul Gustave Doré (1832-1883), probably the most successful illustrator of the nineteenth century, who for many brought hell and heaven to life through his evocative illustrations, Auguste Rodin (1840-1917), and Salvador Dalì (1904-1989). For T.S. Eliot (1888-1965), Dante represented the most 'universal' poet ever, and he often made references to the *Inferno* throughout his own work.

It is probably true that the structure of hell – or at least a Christian hell – that is mostly understood today is one based on Dante's description. Even Swedenborg – who was admittedly less interested in hell than in heaven, and whose picture of heaven arguably conditioned modern understandings of a happy social afterlife – came up with what reads like a poor man's version of Dante's hell: the place farthest from God, dark and mostly cold apart from the fires of malice, with a horrible stench, where people torture each other. *The Divine Comedy* remains immensely popular: when Clive James' verse translation was published in 2013, it became a bestseller. The *Inferno* continues to have a high profile in popular culture: Botticelli's map of hell, based on Dante, is a central motif in the thriller *Inferno* (2013) by the American author Dan Brown and in the film of the same name (2016).

Summing up: which heaven and hell?

Religions and cultures, especially those with a belief in resurrection, have imagined different types of heaven and hell. In the ancient Near East and the classical world, heaven was the abode solely of the gods. Deceased humans ended up in a bleak underworld – although the winterless paradise gardens of classical Elysium and the Isles of the Blessed were set aside originally for heroes and later the righteous. Judaism and Christianity developed the idea of single or multiple heavens for the virtuous, with heaven imagined as a temple or palace, and angels singing eternal praises to God on his throne. Heaven could also be, or could include, a paradise or pleasure garden, as in Islam, with God (Allah) less evident. Some of the early conceptions of heaven included places for punishment, or this could be located in a separate hell, commonly depicted as a place of fiery torments. In some traditions, there is a narrow bridge over the pit of hell leading to heaven, which the righteous cross easily (originally a Zoroastrian concept). The Celtic heaven consisted of the fantastic islands of the Otherworld. Or, heaven can simply be a perfect continuation of earthly life, focused on friends and family, with no prospect of pain, suffering or punishment.

What were these beliefs based on, and why did they change or adapt? There seem to be three main factors which contribute to a choice or development of one idea of heaven or hell over another: religious, cosmological, and cultural.

Religious factors include the original stimulus for a heaven and hell, the need for a system of afterlife rewards and punishments. This was developed by persecuted Jewish groups and linked with the new idea of resurrection. It developed especially as a system of rewards for a chosen group, or for what were considered particularly righteous behaviour or beliefs. From those beginnings, the idea of heaven as a temple or palace was influenced by the understanding of its being a heavenly counterpart of the temple in Jerusalem. The idea of a fiery hell –

a popular motif across many cultures – developed from the cults of the Canaanite gods Molech and Baal in the Valley of Hinnom (Gehenna).

The way different cultures understand their universe – their cosmology – has a huge impact on how the afterlife is understood. The simple tripartite cosmos of the ancient Near East and the early classical world – heaven, earth, underworld – meant that humans had no place in heaven. But improved astronomical observations and a new understanding of the movements of the celestial bodies led to heaven being located beyond the known planetary bodies rather than in an underworld, which then led to the idea of multiple heavens arranged according to the planetary bodies. The Celtic heaven was similarly influenced by cosmology: a series of fantastic islands at the end of the world to the west across the vast, mysterious Atlantic.

Cultural factors include explicit borrowings from other cultures, but also tensions and expectations developing within societies, which have an impact on their understanding of the afterlife. The paradise or pleasure garden motif, as we have seen, was often explicitly borrowed from classical Elysium, which itself may possibly have been influenced by the ancient Egyptian Field of Reeds. Sex or its total absence is a common feature of different conceptions of heaven. The tension within Christianity about sex led to the ideals of sexual purity and asceticism in early and medieval Christianity, with particularly horrific punishments in hell for sexual sins and the higher levels of heaven reserved for the sexually pure, virgins and ascetics. On the other hand, sex is a key focus of Islamic, Zoroastrian and Celtic heavens. The Christian attitude to sex was initially based on interpretation of Jesus' sayings recorded in the gospels concerning the lack of marriage in heaven, and the later zeal for monasticism, although it also goes back to the Platonic idea of the pure, intellectual soul being contaminated by bodily desires; whereas Islam's encouragement of sex in heaven may have more to do with its origins as a religion of conquest and conversion, with a need to offer attractive rewards for potential converts. Cultural factors are also at play in the most influential picture of a Christian hell, with the nine circles of Dante's *Inferno* based on the ethical system of a classical philosopher, Aristotle. More modern cultural factors include the change of focus of heaven from God to human relationships and a particularly earthly type of human happiness, as society has increasingly developed the importance of the individual and his/her fulfilment as persons. Is God even present in those heavens? For similar reasons, there is a peculiarly modern expectation for activity and progress in the afterlife – an eternity of praising God just does not cut it any more for many people – and much less expectation of judgment and punishment.

Taking a very broad overview of how these ideas have developed across human cultures, one pattern stands out. The idea of what heaven is, and who it is for, has been completely flipped around. In our earliest records, from the ancient Near East, heaven was reserved for the gods. In modern times, it seems it is mostly for humans, and the fulfilment of individual human desires, with the gods (or God) much less apparent. Of course, this is an exaggeration, but it is noteworthy that Jeffrey Burton Russell's defence of a Christian heaven as the Beatific Vision, in his misleadingly titled *A History of Heaven*, culminates in Dante's *Paradiso*. He calls it the ultimate Christian view of heaven, lauding it for its adherence to Christian theology.[44] Russell does not even mention Swedenborg or any developments of heaven after Dante, presumably because God is no longer at their centre.

Part 2

Transmigration and Transformation

Chapter 4

Reincarnation and the eternal spirit

As a caterpillar, having come to the end of one blade of grass, draws itself together and reaches out for the next, so the Self, having come to the end of one life and shed all ignorance, gathers in its faculties and reaches out from the old body to a new.
– *Brihadaranyaka Upanishad*

The word 'reincarnation' comes from Latin, and means 'entering the flesh again'. It is the belief that an aspect of a living being goes through a cycle of rebirth each time it dies biologically. Each rebirth begins a new life in a different physical body or form.

This chapter and Chapter 5 use the word 'reincarnation', but other terms commonly found are more or less interchangeable. 'Transmigration' means to pass or migrate into a different body. 'Metempsychosis' comes from the Greek *meta empsychos*, meaning literally 'after' or 'beyond (in) the soul', and was the term used for reincarnation in ancient Greek philosophy. More rarely we find the word 'palingenesis', from the Greek *palin*, 'again', and *genesis*, 'birth', meaning 'rebirth' or 're-creation', used for example by the Greek writer Plutarch to refer to reincarnation.

Belief in reincarnation is central to all major Eastern religions, including Hinduism, Jainism, Buddhism, and Sikhism, in which each successive incarnation is determined by karma (the law or principle that one's actions determine one's fate in the next incarnation, explained more fully below). These religions all had a common ancestor in Hinduism, and have shared features, but also significantly different understandings and interpretations of what becomes immortal through the process of reincarnation, even within the individual religions. Their shared presupposition is that the present existence is merely one part of a longer process of spiritual development towards release from the chains of bodily desires and absorption in self.

Reincarnation was a popular belief in classical Greece and Rome, and it was the Greek philosophers, particularly Plato, who first speculated about the idea and attempted to validate it intellectually. There have also been certain sects within Christianity, Islam and Judaism which have believed in reincarnation. It has been a popular belief in the Western world since the theosophical movement of the late nineteenth century.

Reincarnation, or something like it, is part of the beliefs of indigenous societies particularly in Australasia, North America and parts of Africa. Generally, these are animist cultures in which everything is sentient and has spirit: not only humans and other animals, but plants, trees, rocks, mountains, water and wind. While there are undeniable similarities with some aspects of Eastern religions, especially Buddhism, in most indigenous animist cultures what happens after death is more to do with transformation than reincarnation as such – transformation into other humans, animals or plants. Crucially, this transformation is intimately connected with the continuing role of ancestors in the life of the community, which has profound implications for how they regard and treat their dead. It does more justice to those beliefs to treat them separately, and not purely as other examples of reincarnation, and they are covered in Chapter 5.

One of the key aspects the current chapter attempts to bring out is what, exactly, is believed to be immortal in the process of reincarnation. This apparently simple question is made complex because there are many different traditions. One of the misunderstood aspects of reincarnation is that, in most (but certainly not all) traditions, the individual 'personality' or 'self', with all its memories and foibles, does not survive into the next life: in fact, in most Eastern religions the ultimate aim is to break out of the cycle of births and deaths and relinquish the idea of 'self'. This makes it very different from the immortal soul of later Christianity which is the locus of personal identity.

In order to understand the main differences in understandings of reincarnation, this chapter follows its developments chronologically, starting with the Eastern religions and the earliest evidence for belief in reincarnation within Hinduism.

The earliest evidence for belief in reincarnation

What is the earliest evidence for belief in reincarnation? In fact, this is a controversial issue. Some scholars claim that there are hints concerning reincarnation in the Rigveda, the oldest text of Indian literature, but others disagree. The reasons for the uncertainty and the controversy lie in the very nature of the text.

The Rigveda is the oldest and most extensive of the four Vedas, the earliest sacred texts of Hinduism, the other three being the Samaveda, Yajurveda and Atharvaveda. It was probably composed between 1400 and 1000 BCE, but transmitted orally for possibly more than two thousand years, before being first written down in around 1000 CE, although the oldest extant manuscripts date to the fourteenth and fifteenth centuries CE. The various manuscripts exhibit differences, so there is no single canonical version.

The term 'Rigveda' comes from the Sanskrit *veda*, 'knowledge', and *rig*, 'poem' or 'hymn'. The text is a collection of 1028 hymns arranged in ten cycles or mandalas. Most of these are hymns that were recited by a priest during ritual performance, including animal sacrifices.

The problem of interpretation largely arises because the texts were written in an archaic form of Sanskrit which is difficult to interpret and so has led to numerous different – sometimes radically different – translations, commentaries and understandings. For example, one translation of a line from the famous riddle hymn reads:

The immortal self will be reborn in a new body due to its meritorious deeds.[1]

This appears to be a very clear hint at reincarnation and at least a rudimentary understanding of karma as merit, although the idea is not developed and it does not use those later terms. However, an alternative translation of exactly the same line reads:

The living one keeps moving by the will of the dead one; the immortal one shares the same womb with the mortal one.[2]

Despite the reference to immortality, something to do with birth, and the dead somehow motivating the living, this version no longer hints at reincarnation quite so unambiguously. The radically variant readings are due to both the difficulty of the archaic language, and the fact that this particular 'riddle' hymn is deliberately ambiguous and evasive and has hidden meanings, leaving it open to very different interpretations. It is not surprising, therefore, that there is confusion and disagreement about whether or not reincarnation is mentioned in the Rigveda. If you hope to find it in this most ancient of Indian texts, then there will be a translation to support your assumption, and vice versa. A dispassionate observer looking for a clear answer has little choice but to either accept that we do not know for certain, or choose one or other version by assessing the linguistic details of Sanskrit offered by different translators in support of their interpretation.

Some scholars have proposed that the idea of karma has its origins in the Vedas, although the term itself is not mentioned. The suggestion is based on the development of the concept of transfer. The ritual of *shrāddha*, which first appears in the Vedas, consists of offering food and drink to deceased relatives in order to help them into the afterlife. The hypothesis is that, eventually, food was combined with merit: living relatives gave part of their own food and merit to help the dead, giving rise to the idea that merit could be transferred in order to produce rebirth.[3]

The earliest unambiguous explanations of the concepts of reincarnation and karma are found in the Upanishads, which form the root of all Indian philosophy and religions. The Sanskrit word 'Upanishad' is composed of three elements: *upa*, 'near', *ni*, 'down', and *sad*, 'sit', meaning 'to sit down near to' – literally, to sit at the feet of a teacher. As the word implies, essentially these were records of sessions of spiritual instruction by unnamed sages. Technically, they were commentaries on the Vedas: where the Vedas deal with ritual, the Upanishads deal with wisdom, insight, and understanding of the true nature of reality. Each Upanishad was embedded at the end of one of the four Vedas, although they were composed later. The oldest were composed between 800 and 400 BCE in northern India, and some as late as the fifteenth century CE, though repeating older ideas. Altogether, there are about 200 Upanishads, but traditionally ten are considered the 'principal Upanishads', according to the mystic, philosopher and poet Shankara (788-820 CE). They are of different lengths, and some are very short indeed, comprising only a few verses. Some are in prose, others in verse, and many are in dialogue form.

The central purpose of all the Upanishads is to show that the individual soul or self (*atman* in Sanskrit) is really part of Brahman, the eternal, imperishable, single ultimate reality. The Upanishads explain that life is about learning how to leave separate individuality behind and achieve union with the infinite spirit of Brahman. This is not about intellectual knowledge, but transcendent, transformative experience. Once we understand that central vision of the Upanishads, it is relatively easy to see that the notions of karma and reincarnation follow on logically from it. Since the soul or self is eternal, being part of Brahman, it cannot die, but it cannot achieve true union with Brahman until it sheds its individuality and feeling of separateness. To shed all individuality and achieve union with Brahman is extremely difficult and cannot be achieved within one lifetime. And so the self or soul is constantly reborn in a new temporary body until it reaches that state of realisation of unity. Each rebirth is based on one's conduct in the previous life, and gives new opportunities to learn until, finally, identification with Brahman breaks this cycle of birth, death and rebirth.

The Shvetashvatara Upanishad sums this up:

On this ever-revolving wheel of being
The individual self goes round and round
Through life after life, believing itself
To be a separate creature, until
It sees its identity with the Lord of Love
And attains immortality in the indivisible whole.[4]

Reincarnation itself is not immortality, but the path to immortality, leading to liberation from the cycle of birth, death and rebirth (this cycle is called *samsara* in Sanskrit). Moreover, immortality here is not 'everlasting life', but union with the infinite beyond death and life.

This scheme is already fully worked out in the earliest (and longest) of the Upanishads, the Brihadaranyaka. Here we find the identification of the soul or self with Brahman; a description of humans as being made of and driven by desires; that one's actions in one life determine the nature of the next life and the opportunity to continue learning; and that by freeing ourselves from all desires we break out of the cycle of *samsara* and become one with Brahman:

We live in accordance with our deep driving desire. It is this desire at the time of death that determines what our next life will be. We will come back to earth to work out the satisfaction of that desire.

But not those who are free from desire; they are free because all their desires have found fulfilment in the Self. They do not die like the others; but realising Brahman, they merge in Brahman. So it is said:

When all the desires that surge in the heart
Are renounced, the mortal becomes immortal.[5]

The soul or self in the Upanishads, though immortal, is very different from the Christian, Jewish or Muslim soul we encountered in Chapter 2. Although it appears to us to be separate, in fact it is part of Brahman. Everything is ultimately one – all reality is consciousness, there are no separate minds, and the oneness only appears to be multiplied into many separate entities:

There is only one Self in all creatures.
The One appears many, just as the moon
Appears many, reflected in water.[6]

The feeling of separateness is an illusion, as is the whole world of senses and phenomena. The Sanskrit word for phenomenal reality and the illusion of a world of separate entities is *maya*, literally 'deception', 'illusion' or 'appearance'. It essentially means that the world is not as it seems to the senses. That separateness is deceiving, and *maya* masks the reality that everything is one:

We see not the Self, concealed by maya;
When the veil falls, we see we are the Self.[7]

By continuing to live in the phenomenal world of fleeting pleasures and senses, and believing in a world of separate entities, we remain in the cycle of death and rebirth:

Who sees multiplicity
But not the one indivisible Self
Must wander on and on from death to death.[8]

But the nature of the next rebirth – the next incarnation – is not chance. It is determined by our actions, thoughts and desires in the previous life, and is led by our needs for spiritual development. The purpose of the next incarnation is to give opportunities for spiritual growth on the continuing journey to relinquish self and realise unity with Brahman. This is *karma*, a Sanskrit word that means 'action'. In the Upanishads, and within Hinduism and other Eastern religions, it is a natural law of cause and effect – that every one of a person's actions has a consequence that may not be immediately apparent. It is about both judgment and education, as many passages in the Upanishads and in the later Bhagavad Gita, the best known of the Hindu scriptures, make clear:

The Self takes on a body with desires,
Attachments, and delusions, and is
Born again and again in new bodies
To work out the karma of former lives.
The embodied self assumes many forms,
Heavy or light, according to its needs
For growth and the deeds of previous lives.[9]

The cycle of reincarnations is not necessarily constant progression. The passage above refers to rebirth in 'heavy' or 'light' forms, while the Katha Upanishad refers to rebirth in 'embodied creatures', probably meaning animals, or as 'a lower state of evolution', probably meaning plants,[10] but both Upanishads underline that it is determined by the need for spiritual growth. In this sense, we have control of our own destiny, and the Upanishads stress constantly that the way to relinquish self and achieve unity with Brahman is through meditation. It is not enough to understand it intellectually: you can only achieve unity through deep spiritual experience.

Meditation in the Upanishads is a way to forget the self, leave the transient behind, control one's actions and thoughts, and renounce all desires, in the search for the joy of unity: as the Katha Upanishad urges, to rise above 'I' and 'me' and 'mine'.[11] Of course, the consequence is a loss of personal identity, or rather the blending of personal identity and individuality into a unified greater consciousness – a very different type of immortality from all the versions of the Christian, Jewish and Muslim heaven. The Prashna Upanishad uses a memorable metaphor of individual rivers running into the sea to make this point. It refers to sixteen forms of the self or soul, which include the senses and mind and the whole phenomenal world of time and space, and stresses the loss of personal individuality – which, according to the teaching of the Upanishads, is in any case an illusion:

As rivers lose their private name and form
When they reach the sea, so that people speak
Of the sea alone, so all these sixteen
Forms disappear when the Self is realized.
Then there is no more name and form for us,
And we attain immortality.[12]

Reincarnation in Jainism, Buddhism and Sikhism

The major Eastern religions of Jainism, Buddhism and Sikhism all developed from the roots of Hinduism, in different ways and at different times. The early texts of all three share the concepts and terminology relating to karma and reincarnation, but they differ in what aspect they believe to be immortal. This section attempts to explain those key differences succinctly.

The founder of Jainism was Mahavira (c. 497-425 BCE, but his dates are disputed and estimates vary widely), who was probably born in India. He taught that the way to spiritual liberation was through non-violence towards every living creature and extreme asceticism. His teachings were transmitted orally for centuries and only written down in the late first millennium BCE, and many Jain documents date to the first millennium CE.

Jainism believes in an independent, individual, eternal soul (*jiva*). When linked with matter, including the body, the soul is in bondage. The individual soul can be liberated from matter and thus from the cycle of death and rebirth by achieving perfection, especially through practising asceticism. In this sense, this view is the opposite of Hinduism and does not subscribe to the oneness espoused in the Upanishads. Individual souls still caught in the cycle of *samsara* can be reborn an infinite number of times in one of four *gati* or forms of existence, depending on their karma: as heavenly beings, humans, animals or plants, or hell-beings (in places of torture, torment and retribution, not dissimilar to Christian and Muslim depictions of hell, but temporary). The Bhagavati-sutra, a Jain document which allegedly records Mahavira's answers to a range of questions, links specific *gati* to specific karmas: for example, murder and violence lead to rebirth as a hell-being, while falsehoods lead to rebirth as an animal or plant. But, once liberated from the cycle, each soul becomes a *siddha*, an individual, perfected, immortal soul. The Jain universe is not based on unity with the infinite: it is pluralistic. Its goal is the liberation of individual souls from the bondage of matter.

There is a different understanding of the self or soul in Buddhism, too. Buddhism was founded by Siddhartha Gautama, now usually known as the historical Buddha. Born in Nepal into a Hindu culture, his usual dates are c. 563-483 BCE, but more recent suggestions are c. 480-400 BCE. He preached for over forty years, and his teachings were preserved orally and not written down until the late first millennium BCE, about 400 years after his death. The oldest surviving Buddhist manuscripts are the Gandharan Buddhist texts found in Afghanistan, written on 27 birch bark manuscripts dating between the first century BCE and the third century CE. These include the Dhammapada, a collection of sayings of the Buddha, one of the most widely read and best known of Buddhist scriptures. However, there is no scholarly consensus on whether this records the actual words of the historical Buddha and, indeed, on most of the historical facts of his life.

As Buddhism spread from India to China, Tibet, Japan and the countries of south-east Asia, different traditions arose with varied understandings of key concepts around reincarnation and the afterlife, making it impossible to define a single set of Buddhist beliefs. Alongside the myriad names of the different schools and sub-schools of Buddhism, such as Mahayana and Hinayana, the two great schools, and Theravada, Vajrayana or Zen (many of which also have alternative names), to name just a few, this makes it very confusing for newcomers to the topic.

In most Buddhist traditions, there is no permanent soul or self. Although, when directly asked whether a self existed or not, the Buddha reportedly refused to respond,[13] one of his sayings from the Dhammapada is less unambiguous:

'All things are not-self' – when one sees this with wisdom, one turns away from suffering. This is the path to purification.[14]

This belief in a lack of soul is called *anatman* in Sanskrit (or *anatta* in the Pali dialect) – literally, the opposite of *atman* – 'no-self' or 'no-soul', meaning that the self or ego is not permanent but transitory, changeable and prone to suffering. Unlike Hinduism, there is no permanent soul or self that moves from one incarnation to another and ties the lives together. Instead, all living beings are believed to be aggregates that dissolve at death and are reincarnated as a new being. Five aggregates make up the personality of an individual, all of which are subject to change.

So what, then, reincarnates, if there is no soul or self and therefore no apparent sense of personal identity that continues? One of the five aggregates is consciousness, and most Buddhist traditions believe that this, though itself changeable and evolving, is the link between incarnations – that consciousness transmigrates to a new body after death – but it is categorically not the basis of a personality or self. So it is not a 'soul' that migrates from one body to another; instead, something like a new temporary state of existence is generated – a new birth – conditioned by the karma of the previous state. Certainly within Theravada Buddhism, widespread throughout south-east Asia and based on the direct teachings of the Buddha, the new incarnation is effectively a new individual being, who is also temporary. But the issue of precisely what aspect of a person reincarnates, and if there is, in any sense, continuity with the 'self' of the previous life, is much debated within the different Buddhist traditions. Indeed, some regard the denial of the soul and the affirmation of karma and reincarnation as a contradiction, because the concept of karma seems not to make much sense if not attached to a self which performs the actions, experiences their consequences, and takes responsibility. There is a current trend of 'secular' Buddhists who attempt to reinterpret reincarnation scientifically, proposing that rebirth occurs constantly as cells in our bodies die and are replaced, so that we are reborn every moment and with every action. After death, the molecules from which the body is composed mix with other molecules to create a new birth and a new individual.[15] The unorthodox Vatsiputriya school of Buddhism, which originated in c. 240 BCE, took a completely different tack by affirming the concept of an individual self which continues through incarnations, accumulating karma, and even continues to exist in nirvana (for which see below).

As in Jainism, there are *gati* or modes of existence into which a Buddhist is reincarnated depending on their actions, but there are six of these. Three are good or higher – gods, humans and 'lower gods' (*asuras* – the Sanskrit word literally means 'demon' or 'evil spirit') – and three are bad or lower – animals, ghosts and hell-beings. Reincarnation is into one of three worlds or spheres of the universe: the world of desire, mostly of humans and animals, where sex and other desires predominate; the world of form, populated by gods, in which desire for sex and food is less, but enjoyment continues; and the formless world, a realm of pure consciousness.

Buddhist traditions vary in their understanding of the mechanisms of rebirth. For example, in Theravada Buddhism, rebirth is immediate; Tibetan Buddhism believes in *bardo*, an intermediate state of up to 49 days between death and rebirth, through which the *Bardo thödol*, popularly known as the Tibetan Book of the Dead, is a guide; while within Japanese Zen Buddhism reincarnation itself is accepted by some but rejected by others who regard it as no more than a superstition lingering on from Buddhism's early development from Hinduism.

The goal of spiritual practice and the purpose of the successive reincarnations in Buddhism is to achieve liberation and enlightenment by doing away with the ego and the passions and desires that drive it. The ultimate aim is to achieve *nirvana*, a Sanskrit word that means 'extinguished'.

There are different interpretations of nirvana within Buddhism, and some of them appear contradictory. Tellingly, the Buddha refused to make a clear statement concerning the nature of nirvana. In early texts, it is a liberation from the cycle of karma and *samsara*; in Mahayana Buddhism, which arose in the first century CE in India and spread widely, it is conceived as oneness with the absolute and freedom from the illusions of *maya*, not dissimilar to Hinduism; in some sutras – summaries of ideas in short and practical statements – it is merely an end to suffering. Overall, nirvana is regarded as another mode of existence, and many texts use the metaphor of an extinguished flame that, although it has gone out, has not passed away but has become invisible by passing into the space from which it originally came. In this sense, nirvana is immortality outside time and space. But, in many ways, it is impossible to state categorically what nirvana is and what becomes immortal, if anything – whether it is some sort of positive state or mere annihilation, as the Sanskrit word perhaps implies. The important aspect within Buddhism, which regards all existence as suffering, is that nirvana is an end to suffering, which is a sufficient goal for spiritual effort, and whatever nirvana might be beyond that is irrelevant. In the Pali version of a collection of sutras, written centuries after his death, the Buddha emphasises that considerations of immortality are unimportant in the face of suffering:

> Malunkyaputta, bear always in mind what it is that I have not elucidated and what it is that I have elucidated... I have not elucidated that the saint exists after death, I have not elucidated that the saint does not exist after death. I have not elucidated that the saint both exists and does not exist after death... And what, Malunkyaputta, have I elucidated? Misery... the origin of misery... the cessation of misery... the path leading to the cessation of misery.[16]

In Mahayana Buddhism, entry into nirvana can be postponed by someone who has achieved enlightenment, but chooses to actively help others by taking on their suffering and transferring his own karmic merit. This is a *bodhisattva*, an 'enlightened being'. Nirvana is postponed until all beings are liberated from suffering. Because a *bodhisattva* has achieved enlightenment and the sense of unity with the absolute, they alone are aware of their previous lives. In Japanese Zen Buddhism, too, which developed in the sixth and seventh centuries CE and seeks to apply Buddhism to everyday life, nirvana is not separated from this world, but is a realisation of the true nature of the mind through wisdom.

Sikhism also focuses more on the current world. One of the world's younger religions, it was founded by Guru Nanak (1469-1538 CE), born into a Hindu family in what is now Pakistan. It is often portrayed as an attempt at a synthesis or bridge between Hinduism and Islam, which by the fifteenth century had been present in India for centuries. The aim of Sikhism is union with God, called Ik Onkar, which means 'one all-pervading spirit' in the Punjabi language, effectively an alternative name for Allah or the Hindu creator god Brahma. The focus of Sikh practice is on social justice and selfless service for the benefit of all humanity.

Afterlife beliefs, though not a primary concern, are very similar to those in Hinduism: Sikhs believe in karma, reincarnation, *maya*, and in the existence of the soul. Liberation from the cycle of *samsara* is achieved by union with God, through living an ethical life and devotion to God. This liberation is effectively immersion in the divine soul, and a loss of personal identity, as in the concept of unity with Brahman within Hinduism, and Sikh hymns often use a similar metaphor to the Upanishads of drops of water immersed in an ocean or stream to describe this unity. A key difference from Hinduism and Buddhism is that liberation cannot be achieved just through meditation and ethical living, but through the grace, intercession and will of God. Like a Buddhist *bodhisattva*, one can be liberated from the cycle while still alive.

Reincarnation in the classical world

There has always been speculation whether the Eastern religions influenced early Greek ideas about reincarnation, mainly because the earliest Upanishads pre-date the earliest Greek writing on the topic by many centuries, but there is absolutely no evidence either way: so it has to remain speculation. Most scholars, though, conclude that the concept of reincarnation is a common enough belief within humanity for it to have been independently introduced in Greece. Who first introduced it, and when, however, is debatable. Claims for introducing reincarnation into Greece are variously made for Pherecydes of Syros, Pythagoras, and Orphism. Some sort of case can be made for each one, but the evidence for the primacy of any one of them is extremely weak.

Little is known about Pherecydes, who lived in the sixth century BCE. Reputedly the first writer of Greek prose, the fragments of his writings that survive concern the birth of the gods and the creation of the cosmos. It is much later sources – including both Cicero and Augustine – that claim he was the first to teach reincarnation and was the teacher of Pythagoras, but there is no real evidence for either of these claims.

Pythagoras (c. 570-495 BCE) was born on the island of Samos and migrated to Croton in Italy in c. 530 BCE. Much of his later fame was related to mathematics and musical theory. By all accounts he was a mix of philosopher, priest and showman, and in later centuries he was regarded as an omniscient figure who originated much of Greek philosophy and mathematics. Since he wrote nothing himself, and there are no detailed accounts of his philosophy by his contemporaries, it is impossible to know exactly what he believed and discovered as opposed to what was attributed to him by later tradition.

The earliest and best evidence for his belief in reincarnation is Fragment 7 by Xenophanes, a poet and contemporary of Pythagoras:

Once he [i.e. Pythagoras] was present when a puppy was being beaten,
they say, and he took pity and spoke this word:
Stop! Do not strike it, for it is the soul of a man who is dear.
I recognised it when I heard it screaming.[17]

This suggests belief in a form of reincarnation in which human souls are reborn into animal bodies, and perhaps implies that personal identity is preserved through incarnations, as Pythagoras recognised something distinctive about the soul. Pythagoras' reputation as believing that humans can reincarnate as animals became widespread in the classical world, and even found its way into the plays of William Shakespeare and his contemporary Christopher Marlowe:

> I was never so be-rhymed since Pythagoras' time, that I was an Irish rat, which I can hardly remember.[18]

The reference to memory may be based on Diogenes Laertius' report, in his third century CE biography, that Pythagoras remembered his own previous human incarnations.[19] Not much else can be said about Pythagoras' own concept of reincarnation. Later Pythagorean tradition, as reported by Alexander Polyhistorius in the first century BCE, believed that the souls of the dead filled the atmosphere and provoked dreams and premonitions, but also emphasised purity, asceticism and vegetarianism, which provided a standard gag for comedy. By then, reincarnation was regarded as a myth, useful mainly to encourage people to avoid leading wicked lives.

Orphism is also often said to be the origin of belief in reincarnation in early Greece. However, it is difficult to get a handle on exactly what Orphism was, and the picture of it as a religious movement or a sort of mystery cult in Greece from the fifth century BCE or earlier is largely a modern scholarly construct. What we have is a collection of pseudepigraphical literature ascribed to Orpheus, the mythical singer, whose failed attempt to bring his lover Eurydice back from Hades made him the figurehead for afterlife beliefs. Orphic literature consists of theogonies (accounts of the origins and relationships of the gods), hymns and ritual texts, including some which attest belief in reincarnation. However, the authors of some of these texts are known to have been Pythagoreans, and even Pythagoras himself is suspected of composing or editing poems under the name of Orpheus. There are certainly parallels to elements of Pythagorean belief in reincarnation, but insufficient evidence to conclude influences or primacy of invention. All we can conclude is that belief in reincarnation was present in Greece by the sixth century BCE, but we cannot be certain when and where it originated and who influenced whom.

There are elements of Pythagoreanism and Orphism in the philosophy of Empedocles (c. 495-435 BCE), a poet, philosopher, scientist and politician who is best known for his theory of physics in which everything in nature is composed of the four elements of fire, water, earth and air, which are moved in a cyclical pattern by two opposing and balanced forces, Love and Strife. Details of his life and work are uncertain, and most of our information comes from the biography written centuries later by Diogenes Laertius. It is clear that Empedocles was inspired by Pythagoreanism and accepted some form of reincarnation. His own vegetarianism was informed by the belief that the eating of flesh was a sin which impacted on the divinity of the soul, and he argued against animal sacrifice on the basis that it involved the killing of creatures with a human soul. A passage from Empedocles' poem *Purifications* suggests that he believed that human souls are reincarnated as plants as well as humans and animals:

> I was once a boy and a maid,
> A bush and a bird, and a dumb fish leaping out of the sea.[20]

It was, inevitably, the great Plato who brought all these strands together most coherently, and for the first time ever offered an intellectual argument for reincarnation. Plato believed that human souls reincarnated in both human and animal bodies, and he often referred obliquely to the ideas of Pythagoreanism and Orphism. His argument for reincarnation, presented in the *Phaedo* (see Chapter 2), is based on the principle of opposites. Everything that has an opposite is generated from that opposite: for example, weaker from stronger, sleeping from waking, and therefore living from dying, and vice versa:

> ... the living have come from the dead no less than the dead from the living. But I think we decided that if this was so, it was a sufficient proof that the souls of the dead must exist in some place from which they are reborn.[21]

He further argued that, if the living did not come from the dead, eventually everything would be dead and nothing alive. In terms of the mechanics of reincarnation, in the *Phaedo* Plato states that the newly dead are judged: those who lived a neutral life are sent to the underworld's River Acheron, where they undergo purification from bad and reward for good deeds; the incurably wicked are hurled forever into Tartarus; while the curably wicked also go to Tartarus, but only for a year, and can only leave once their victims allow them to join the other souls awaiting reincarnation by the banks of the Acheron. Despite this period of punishment, the wicked are reincarnated according to the characters they developed in life, for example as donkeys, wolves or hawks. But those who practised self-control and integrity reincarnate as more useful creatures, such as bees, wasps, ants or even humans. Those who attained purity and intellectual wisdom in life break the cycle of reincarnation and become pure, immortal souls and exist in a sort of beautiful, immaterial heaven.

In Book 10 of *The Republic*, Plato tells the myth of Er, which gives a slightly more detailed – and subtly different – account of this process. Er, a warrior killed in battle, is chosen to come back to life to tell others of his journey to the afterlife (reminiscent of the otherworld journeys we saw in Chapter 3). After death, he and other souls come to a place with two openings through the earth and two through the sky. Between the openings sit judges who order the souls which openings to go through: good souls go through the sky, and bad ones down through the earth. Er learns from those returning from below that they had to stay a thousand years to suffer for their wicked deeds, although murderers and tyrants remained in Tartarus forever. Those returning pure and clean from the skies tell of the delights and beauty of heaven.

The souls then travel to the spindle of Necessity, attended by the Fates, the daughters of Necessity, which is an allegory of the workings of the universe. Influenced by the discoveries of Greek astronomy, like many of the journeys to heaven in Chapter 3, the eight rims of the whorl represent the orbits of the moon, sun, Venus, Mercury, Mars, Jupiter, Saturn and the fixed stars. There, the souls have to draw lots to choose their next life, whether animal or human: for example, the soul of Orpheus chooses a swan, while Agamemnon, who hates humanity because of the sufferings it caused him, chooses an eagle; Odysseus, cured of all ambition, chooses the life of an ordinary man. Sometimes, those returning from heaven choose unwisely, as they do not have experience of suffering. Having chosen their new lives, the souls drink from Lethe, the river of Oblivion, to forget their previous life, go to sleep, and with earthquake and thunder they are all swept away to be re-born.

Much of this imagery was portrayed faithfully later by Virgil in the *Aeneid*:

"And who are they
who crowd the banks [of the Acheron] in such a growing throng?"
His father Anchises answers: "They are the spirits
owed a second body by the Fates."[22]

Virgil follows Plato closely by referring to a lengthy period of punishment of the wicked:

> ... once they have turned the wheel of time
> for a thousand years: God calls them forth to the Lethe,
> great armies of souls, their memories blank so that
> they may revisit the overarching world once more
> and begin to long to return to bodies yet again.[23]

Plato's theory of reincarnation was developed by Plotinus (c. 205-270 CE), who was educated in Alexandria and then taught in Rome. He is regarded as essentially the founder of Neo-Platonic philosophy (his Alexandrian teacher, Ammonius Saccas, is often so credited, but since he did not publish anything the extent of his influence is uncertain). Neo-Platonism is a modern name for Plotinus' renewal and development of Plato's philosophy, which became the dominant philosophy in the ancient word until the sixth century CE, and strongly influenced Christian, Islamic and Renaissance thought, including such thinkers as Augustine. Plotinus wrote 54 treatises, which his student Porphyry collected and edited into six groups of nine, hence the name *Enneads* (an ennead being a group of nine).

Several passages in the *Enneads* show that Plotinus believed in reincarnation and retained some of Plato's ideas, for example reincarnation into human or animal bodies, and having a choice of new lives. Plotinus especially emphasised the importance of intellectual purity. He argued that all modes of being – mind, soul, and nature – come from the 'One', an ultimate immaterial reality, which he claimed Plato referred to in his *Parmenides* and as 'the Good' in *The Republic*. But Plotinus developed this much further. The aim was to become oblivious to self and to the world. By achieving this, the soul would see the One alone and experience joy. This is not dissimilar to the Upanishads and their key concept of unity with Brahman, and indeed some passages in the Upanishads and the *Enneads* express similar sentiments regarding knowledge of the absolute, separation and unity. Compare:

> How can the knower ever be known?[24]

with:

> For it will know by the knowing, which it itself is, and it will know the intelligible, which it itself is.[25]

Or:

> In truth who knows God becomes God.[26]

with:

> But if anyone admits that intellect knows God, he will be compelled to agree that it knows itself also.[27]

These similarities have been explained by suggesting that Plotinus had contact with Indian travellers during his time in Alexandria. Of course, Plotinus emphasises the intellect above the soul, while the Upanishads do the opposite, but he too refers to breaking out of the cycle of bodily reincarnations by achieving consciousness of the One:

> But there will be a time when the vision will be continuous, no longer troubled by any bodily trouble.[28]

Reincarnation in Christianity

In Chapter 2, we followed the tensions within the early Christian Church between physical resurrection and the immortal soul, and saw that many of the early Church fathers were well versed in Plato's philosophy. It is not, therefore, all that surprising that Plato's ideas about reincarnation occasionally came to the fore, flirted with by some and rejected by the orthodox majority. Some of the early Christian believers in reincarnation were pejoratively labelled Gnostics, as they did not accept orthodox teaching. Both Tertullian and, later, Augustine felt the need to explicitly refute reincarnation in their writings, the former singling out Pythagoras and Plato for critique and the latter adding Plotinus to the list.

Justin Martyr (c. 100-165 CE), on the other hand, who was martyred in Rome for his Christianity, tried to find links between Christianity, Platonism and Judaism, and his writings include a dialogue between himself and Tryphon, a Jew, in which he defends the Platonic doctrine of reincarnation into human and animal lives and lack of memory of previous lives.

Origen, as we saw in Chapter 2, believed in the pre-existence of souls, but it is unclear if he believed in reincarnation as such, despite being a Platonist. Even belief in pre-existence was deemed heretical enough, though, and nearly 300 years after his death the Fifth Ecumenical Council of 553 CE in Constantinople, under the aegis of the emperor Justinian, issued the 'Anathemas against Origen', in which the very first sentence curses anyone asserting the pre-existence of souls.[29]

Belief in reincarnation was one of the tenets of the Cathars (also known as the Albigensians), a heretical Christian movement in southern Europe, especially northern Italy and southern France, between the eleventh and fourteenth centuries. Essentially, they were anti-orthodox Catholics, consisting of diverse groups with varying beliefs, not really properly or centrally organised, but jointly opposed to what they regarded as the corruption of the established Church. Many of them were ascetics and vegetarians with a respect for all living things, who believed that human souls were originally the souls of angels and needed to renounce the material world to regain the state of angelic perfection.

Cycles of reincarnation were a form both of punishment and improvement, and the cycle could only be broken by denying the material world completely and through a special ceremony to achieve perfection – a ceremony which itself was specifically denounced by the Church. It was largely in response to such beliefs about reincarnation that Aquinas and others at that time emphasised in their writings that resurrection entailed the soul returning to the same body, and that the dead would rise in their own bodies, the bodies they had now (see Chapter 2). The Cathars were consistently persecuted by the Church – the Inquisition was founded in the twelfth century to deal with their heresy – and the Albigensian Crusade between 1209 and 1229 attempted to eradicate them totally, although this was not fully accomplished until the fourteenth century.

Later in the fourteenth century, the beginnings of the Renaissance in Florence were essentially prompted by the rediscovery of classical art and philosophy, and it brought renewed interest in thinkers such as Pythagoras, Plato and Plotinus. The two foremost philosophers of the Renaissance, Marsilio Ficino (1433-1499) and Giovanni Pico della Mirandola (1463-1494), were both influenced by Plato and the Neo-Platonists and discussed reincarnation at length in their writings. Both had to be careful how they phrased their thoughts on reincarnation, though, as it was regarded as heretical by the Church, and was condemned by the Inquisition in 1490. While both wanted to speculate about Christian theology in the light of classical philosophy, they also needed to be seen as orthodox Christians, and Ficino was in fact ordained as a priest in 1473.

Ficino, who was supported by the Medicis in Florence and became the young Lorenzo de Medici's tutor, translated the works of Plato and Plotinus and was the first head of the Platonic Academy in Florence, an attempt to revive the spirit of Plato's ancient academy. In his *Platonic Theology*, Ficino discussed Plato's arguments for reincarnation and the pre-existence of the soul. In his care to avoid the charge of heresy, he tried to show that Plato used ideas of reincarnation allegorically and symbolically: for example, referring to reincarnation from humans to animals, that what Plato really meant was that human souls had bestial capacities within them. He constantly described Plato's references to reincarnation as 'poetic', and claimed that he was repeating a Pythagorean story he did not himself believe – in effect, blaming Pythagoras for any un-Christian ideas that would put Plato in a bad light. In his commentary on Plotinus, however, Ficino boldly stated that Plato was reincarnated as Plotinus.[30] While this could be understood metaphorically, it is possible that Ficino's ideas about reincarnation were complex and perhaps inconsistent.

Pico based himself more on Plotinus, but was a little less circumspect. In his *Oration on the Dignity of Man*, he wrote openly that

the soul passes out of one body and enters another.[31]

This oration, written in 1486, was actually a speech he was prevented from giving by the Pope, as it was full of dangerous, unorthodox ideas, including the importance of magic and kabbalah, which influenced much of his thinking. In other writings, influenced by Plotinus, he states that the soul of a sinner

lives the life of a beast after death.[32]

While this could be understood literally as reincarnation into an animal body, some scholars regard such statements as allegorical, in the same way as Ficino interpreted Plato.

That Ficino and Pico were correct to be careful how they wrote about reincarnation was demonstrated later by the fate of the very unorthodox Italian Dominican friar, Giordano Bruno

(1548-1600). Interested in the occult and astral magic, he is best known for his cosmological theories, initially based on the then still heretical Copernican theory, that neither the earth nor the sun are the centre of the universe, which is infinite. But he further identified the universe with God, and argued that all souls were one (an idea he almost certainly adapted from Plotinus). Influenced by Pythagoras, Plato and the Neo-Platonists, he believed in reincarnation, the lack of memory of previous lives, and also in a form of karma (which he called High Justice), stating that each act brings an appropriate reward or punishment in another life. The Inquisition accused him of heresy for denying several core Catholic doctrines, including the divinity of Christ, and for believing in reincarnation, especially into animal bodies. In his defence, he asserted that he was a Catholic and believed that souls are immortal and go to paradise, purgatory or hell; but, speaking as a philosopher, and based on the views of Pythagoras, the idea of reincarnation seemed to him likely, even if not proved. He was found guilty of heresy and burned at the stake in Rome. A commemorative statue now stands on the spot of his execution.

Reincarnation continues to be a strand within Christianity, even though it is not mentioned in the Bible (unless one indulges in some very creative reading between the lines). According to a survey by the Pew Research Center in 2009, 22 per cent of US Christians believe in reincarnation,[33] and reincarnation within Christianity is becoming an increasingly popular topic of debate on online forums. In a series of books, the philosopher and priest Geddes MacGregor has proposed a case for a Christian form of reincarnation. He argues that the Church has never formally condemned the idea of reincarnation (although, as we have seen, over the centuries prominent Christian thinkers have, and it was condemned as a heresy by the Inquisition). MacGregor sees reincarnation and resurrection as different but not incompatible forms of embodiment. He interprets reincarnation in the light of the Christian notion of purgatory (see Chapter 3) as an opportunity for an ongoing process of development and growth across multiple lives, the cycle eventually being broken by a final resurrection.

Reincarnation in Jewish kabbalah

Chapter 2 referred briefly to kabbalah, the mystical strand of Judaism that developed in the twelfth and thirteenth centuries in southern France and Spain. From the very beginning, a core part of kabbalah was belief in reincarnation, called *gilgul*. The concept of *gilgul* first appeared, clouded in metaphor and parable, in the *Sefer ha-Bahir*, a work of Jewish mystical literature, sometime between 1150 and 1200. By the late thirteenth century it was enshrined in the Zohar, the principal book of kabbalah, and became normal in kabbalistic circles. The Zohar includes explicit discussions about reincarnation and the lack of memory of previous lives:

> ... all souls must undergo transmigration; but men do not perceive the ways of the Holy One... they do not perceive the many transmigrations... which the Holy One accomplishes.[34]

Over the ensuing centuries, as different Jewish rabbis expounded on *gilgul*, it came to encompass many different models of reincarnation: human to human, animal, plant or angel; more than one soul in a body; a maximum of three or four reincarnations, or up to a thousand, or sometimes with no limit. But the kabbalists also believed that, at the final judgment, there would be a physical resurrection, in a body that would be transformed and perfected, although over time the idea of physical resurrection was downplayed in favour of a more spiritual resurrection. The purpose of reincarnation also varied, although overall its aim was to purify the soul. It gave opportunities for self-improvement, to fulfil unrealised potential, to make amends for sins committed, or it could function as punishment or reward.

Jewish kabbalists were an influence on the Renaissance philosophers Ficino and Pico, who refer to their writings alongside those of Plato and Plotinus, and the influence may well have gone both ways. Much of this Jewish mysticism and belief in reincarnation was eventually incorporated into Jewish Hasidism from the eighteenth century on, and became part of the East European Jewish folk tradition.

Reincarnation in Islam

Since the seventh century CE, Islam has been divided into two main branches, the Shiites and the Sunnis. The split was caused by violent disagreement over the succession to the office of caliph – leader of the Muslim community – soon after Muhammad's death. Shiites believe that Muhammad's cousin and son-in-law, Ali ibn Abi Talib, was his designated successor, while Sunnis claim that Muhammad did not appoint a successor and that Abu Bakr was the rightful caliph. While Sunni Islam has based itself on the words and actions of Muhammad as an authoritative guide to righteous conduct, within Shia Islam authority resides in individual imams or religious leaders who are the sole legitimate guides for their communities on religious, moral and, often, political matters. As a result, Shiism is actually a large group of very different sects, with varying practices and beliefs. While reincarnation is not part of orthodox Islam, and is not found in the Quran, it is not that surprising that when it does appear, it is in radically unorthodox Shiite sects, who are consequently regarded as deviant or even heretical by other Muslims.

The Arabic word for transmigration, *tanasukh*, actually has two meanings. One meaning refers to the divine spirit passing into certain humans, a belief held by the Druze and certain Shiite and Sufi sects (Sufism is the mystical wing of Islam, originating in the ninth century CE, based largely on personal spiritual experience of Allah).[35] The more usual meaning of the soul reincarnating into different bodies is held by some unorthodox Shiite sects, especially the Alawites (also known as the Nusayris), who emerged in Syria in the late first millennium CE and in recent decades have been the ruling sect there under the Assad family. The Alawites believe that a Muslim sinner reincarnates as a Jew, Sunni Muslim or Christian, while non-believers return as animals, especially donkeys and dogs. There are seven degrees of reincarnation, and the virtuous soul which has passed through them rises to the stars from which it originally came (reminiscent of the seven heavens we saw in Chapter 3, which are an accepted part of Muslim cosmology).

The Druze, the present-day neighbours of the Alawites in Syria, Lebanon and also in Israel, share a belief in reincarnation. Although the Druze are not Muslims, and indeed were persecuted by Muslim caliphs, their religion grew out of Ismailism, a Shiite sect, in Egypt around 1000 CE, and was also influenced by Greek and Neo-Platonic philosophy. The Druze faith is exclusive: one can only be born a Druze, not converted. It is also extremely secretive: the tenets of the faith have been kept secret since the eleventh century. The community is divided into those who share this secret knowledge, and the uninitiated, who are given a strict moral code to live by. According to the Druze, the number of souls is fixed, so when a Druze dies, another Druze is born, the soul of the deceased entering a new body of the same sex instantly. Some accounts claim that the wicked return in the bodies of dogs, monkeys and pigs, but not all accounts confirm this belief. Once the soul is fully developed – a process described as a long journey of successive incarnations – the cycle is broken, and the soul achieves a beatific vision of God.

While the Yazidis, a Kurdish tribal group in northern Iraq, Syria and Iran, are also not Muslims, their religion combines elements of many different religions, including Islam. Among the Yazidis, the aim of successive reincarnations is spiritual purification, and souls reincarnate into bodies of men and animals, with successive existences separated by 72-year intervals. Marriage outside the community leads to automatic expulsion, and is regarded as terminating the soul's spiritual growth.

The theosophical movement and the popularisation of reincarnation

In much of the Western world, after the suppression of the Catharists in the fourteenth century and the interest shown by Renaissance philosophers, reincarnation was largely forgotten but remained of academic interest. It was particularly popular among German philosophers and writers in the eighteenth century. Among them was Gotthold Ephraim Lessing (1729-81), who saw reincarnation as integral to his view that the history of mankind was an educational progress towards perfection:

> Why should I not return as often as I am capable of acquiring fresh knowledge and further power? Do I achieve so much in one sojourning as to make it not worth my while to return? Never![36]

These so-called German transcendentalists influenced others in England and America, including writers such as Edgar Allan Poe (1809-49), whose stories 'Morella' and 'Ligeia', both written in the 1830s, have reincarnation at their core. Indeed, in 'Morella', Poe specifically mentions two of the German philosophers, Johann Gottlieb Fichte (1762-1814) and Friedrich Schelling (1775-1854), alongside the 'palingenesis of the Pythagoreans'.[37]

Wider public knowledge of reincarnation and interest in Eastern religions in general was only sparked once translations of Eastern religious texts began to appear in the nineteenth century. The very first translation of a Hindu text into a European language was by Abraham Hyacinthe Anquetil-Duperron (1731-

1805). His Latin translation of a Persian version of 50 of the Upanishads was published in 1801-1802. This was the translation that had a huge impact on the philosopher Arthur Schopenhauer (1788-1860), and was his favourite book which he read every night before going to sleep. Although there are many parallels between Schopenhauer's philosophy and the Upanishads, it is clear that he had already developed his key philosophical ideas before he encountered the Upanishads.[38]

German and English translations started to appear in the mid-nineteenth century, particularly led by Max Müller (1823-1900), who also inaugurated and edited the monumental 50-volume series Sacred Books of the East, which appeared between 1879 and 1910. It was the availability of translations, introducing new and radically different ideas to a mostly Christian world, that lay behind the success of the theosophical movement, which for the first time popularised in the West the reincarnation ideas of the Eastern religions.

The Theosophical Society was founded in New York City in 1875 by Helena Petrovna Blavatsky (1831-1891), a controversial and much ridiculed figure born in the Ukraine, who studied in India and Tibet, had an interest in the occult and paranormal, and claimed psychic powers. Theosophy is an eclectic mixture of ideas derived from Hinduism, Buddhism, Gnosticism and Neo-Platonism – indeed, the word 'theosophy' means 'divine wisdom' in Greek, and was first used by the Neo-Platonists.

Absolutely central for the theosophists were karma and reincarnation, which in their view laid the foundations for ethical conduct. Karma and reincarnation were regarded as a universal law of evolutionary progress, providing infinite possibilities for growth and development:

Intimately, or rather indissolubly, connected with Karma, then, is the law of re-birth, or of the re-incarnation of the same spiritual individuality in a long, almost interminable, series of personalities. The latter are like the various costumes and characters played by the same actor, with each of which that actor identifies himself and is identified by the public, for the space of a few hours.[39]

In their view, only reincarnation could explain the problem of good, evil and injustice, which were the results of actions in present and past lives. They also attempted to tackle the problem of lack of memory of previous lives:

> 'Why do I not remember my past lives?' is really based on a misconception of the theory of reincarnation. 'I,' the true 'I,' does remember; but the animal-man, not yet in full responsive union with his true Self, cannot remember a past in which he, personally, had no share. Brain-memory can contain only a record of the events in which the brain has been concerned...[40]

Most theosophists did not believe in reincarnation in animal bodies, however, and much theosophical writing regards humans as a higher order of being, as 'nature's crowning masterpiece',[41] too superior to be reincarnated as animals. In theosophical thinking, too, the cycle of reincarnation was not something to be escaped from, unlike the Eastern religions. The focus was very much on this (human) world and its infinite possibilities for development. In this way, it paralleled the absolutely contemporary focus on the social heaven within Christianity that we saw in Chapter 3, which was a re-creation, in heaven, of the network of family and social relationships with opportunity for progress. The Christian social heaven and the theosophical focus on constant development through reincarnation addressed the same contemporary concerns about the afterlife and were two sides of the same coin.

The theosophical movement opened the floodgates for publication of accounts of past lives, spawning a huge literature that shows no sign of slowing down even today, and which has undoubtedly influenced the interest in reincarnation generally and also within Christianity that we saw earlier in this chapter.[42] Annie Besant (1847-1933), a leading early theosophist and social campaigner, apparently remembered more than 50 reincarnations, from mineral to vegetable to animal to human, both male and female, including becoming the unfortunate Giordano Bruno, who was burned at the stake in 1600.[43]

In the wake of this surge in popularity of reincarnation, scientists began to investigate the claims of memories of past lives, whether spontaneous or under hypnosis, to see if there was evidence to back them up. The leading figure in this was Ian Stevenson (1918-2007), a professor of psychiatry, interested in the paranormal, and himself from a theosophical background. Stevenson was the first to undertake a series of systematic experiments, with full analysis and publication, investigating the memories of past lives, especially focusing on the spontaneous memories of young children. Stevenson reported many cases, especially in India, Sri Lanka, Brazil, Alaska and Lebanon, and some in Europe and the USA, of children who spontaneously remembered their past lives, often in astounding and accurate detail, long before they could have had any first-hand knowledge of the people and places they referred to, and which were also unknown to their parents and family friends. He came to the conclusion that many of these accounts were true and were evidence of reincarnation. Largely ignored or treated with scepticism by his scientific peers, but hugely influential among believers in reincarnation, we will consider his findings, and the critique of other scientists, in Chapter 8.

Chapter 5

Immortal ancestors: death as transformation

Our dead never forget this beautiful world that gave them their being. They still love its winding rivers, its great mountains and its sequestered vales, and they ever yearn in tenderest affection over the lonely-hearted living, and often return to visit, guide and comfort them.
– Chief Seattle's speech

In many human societies across the world, ancient and modern, reincarnation is only one of several different types of transformation. Humans – dead or sometimes alive – are believed to transform into other humans, animals, plants or spirits. These transformations are intimately connected with the continuing involvement of ancestors in the daily life of the communities: ancestors keep watch over the traditions of the society – though their actions are not always benevolent – and they can be reborn back in their community. In this way reincarnation, other transformations, and the continuing role of ancestors are a way of preserving the social structure of such societies, which are found in North and South America, Africa, Australasia, the Pacific, and also existed in medieval Europe.

Animism, ancestors, and transformation

What links the understandings that these societies have of the way the world works is that they are – albeit in different and culturally distinctive ways – animist, a word that requires some explanation. 'Animism' derives from *anima*, the Latin word for 'breath', 'soul' or 'spirit'. The word 'animism' was introduced into the study of religion and anthropology by the anthropologist

Edward Tylor (1832-1917) in his book *Primitive Culture*, first published in 1871. Tylor referred to animism as the earliest stage of the evolution of religion, which he believed to be common among primitive peoples, that is, a belief in souls and spirits: that everything in the world has its own soul or spirit, not only humans, but animals, plants and even, sometimes, supposedly inanimate entities such as rocks, rivers, clouds and thunder, and that there are mechanisms through which the human and spirit worlds interact and influence each other. This old understanding of animism attempted to fit other, exotic cultures into pre-existing schemes of cultural progress and, since the term was coined in the Victorian period, animism was compared unfavourably with the highest level of civilisation and intellect of Victorian England. As a result, the word 'animism' soon came to be used pejoratively and dismissively, referring to beliefs that were somehow backward, simplistic, local rather than universal, and that lacked sacred texts, religious institutions and a systematic theology.

In recent years, animism has been reappraised and redefined in light of current understanding of what it means to the peoples who believe and practise it. The 'new' animism is a recognition

that the world is full of persons, only some of whom are human, and that life is always lived in relationship with others.[1]

A 'person' is defined as a being capable of valuing its own existence, with its attributes of consciousness, intentionality, language, reasoning and moral awareness. In animism, personhood extends to other species, and includes the living and the dead. For Linda Hogan, a Native American poet and scholar, animism means that

every particle in the universe is alive.[2]

This 'new animism' does not dismiss belief in 'spirits', but it questions what 'spirits' means:

> 'Spirits' might just be a way in which some people try to convey an idea about their personal relationship with trees, animals, rivers or ancestors that others consider inanimate or inert... Do people possess a soul or spirit? If they do, are there other beings that are similarly animated by souls or spirits?[3]

Contemporary animism also questions the terms 'life' and 'death'. In animist societies, they are not so distinctly separate: 'death' is not a fixed state opposed to 'life', but another type of transformation. In most if not all animist cultures, the death of a person merely transforms the nature of the relationship with the living. The deceased is still a person, and still part of the community. The fact that they are 'dead' is the least important aspect: mourning, contact and connection continue through different mechanisms such as myth, ritual, shamanistic mediation, and transformation into other or reborn forms of 'life'. Contemporary understanding of animism, then, is about relationships between persons, human and non-human, 'alive' and 'dead'.

Animist societies, in general, have an abiding concern for ancestors, whose souls or spirits continue to influence the living community in different ways. The term 'ancestor' usually refers to specific, named individuals, and not a vague grouping of all who have died. In animist societies, social distinctions continue after death, and not all those who die become ancestors. These ancestors are not supernatural beings, unreachable and out of touch with the living world. In some senses, these 'dead' ancestors are actually 'alive'. They are known, named, talked to and listened to, are involved in the daily life of the community, and they have the power to act and intervene. Among the Maori of New Zealand, for example, ancestors are important members of the human community, participating in ceremonies, and their presence is recognised in various forms, visible and invisible.

Similarly, among the Trobriand Islanders of the Pacific, the spirits of the dead appear during particular ceremonies, especially after the harvest, and sometimes the spirits send messages and keep watch over the maintenance of traditional customs. The spirits of the dead are believed to go to a place called Tuma, a sort of spiritual paradise which nevertheless includes a sexual life, but eventually they become human again and are reincarnated into the same tribe, though sometimes after a gap of many generations. The islanders believe in a fixed pool of ancestors from which souls cycle between earth and Tuma and back again.[4] In other parts of the Pacific, woven into the warp and weft of ancestors and transformations into animals and insects, there are varying afterlife beliefs, not dissimilar to the range we saw in Chapter 3: descent to a gated underworld, a heaven and hell, idyllic islands for the deceased elite, and hazardous voyages to otherworld islands.[5]

Often, in animist societies, shamans are responsible for contact with ancestors and the non-human world, usually through dreams or trance states. Shamans are healers and priests, but above all they are mediators who have the power, skill and authority to mediate the relationships between the living community and the ancestral and non-human world that others cannot or do not want to manage. Among the Wari' in the Amazon rainforest in South America, dead humans become animal spirits and then animals. They are identified by shamans and offer themselves as self-sacrificing animals to be hunted and to feed their family as peccaries, a type of wild pig. Subsequently they return as spirits again and again and continue the cycle of incarnations to feed their descendants, in a system that is about sustaining the subsistence of the tribe indefinitely.

In some societies, shamans have the power to transform themselves while still alive in order to interact with non-human

persons. Among Native Americans, there are lots of stories of
shamans who change into animals and back again, sometimes
after an initial human death, but who retain their human
consciousness. Transformations can also happen the other way
around. In Chewong mythology, in the Malaysian rainforest,
each species has its own body or cloak, but these can be changed
by those with shamanic abilities, who are able to put on the body
or cloak of another species. There are many stories, for example,
about frogs which appear in human shape and behave in a
human manner, unseen except by other shamans.

There is evidence that medieval societies in Europe were
essentially animist and had similar traditions of transformations
and the importance of ancestors. The best evidence survives
in the Norse sagas, which were less influenced by Christian
traditions than other European countries. The Norse sagas are
full of human transformations into animals, and the ability
to change shape was part of the essence of being human. The
dead were believed to transform into dwarves, elves and spirits
connected to a specific place, and could return as revenants,
flesh and blood beings who looked, spoke and acted like living
humans and interfered in human society, often maliciously,
usually back in their own community. Revenants sometimes
transformed into animals such as seals, horses, bulls, birds or
dragons. They appeared especially in winter, in connection with
festivals commemorating the ancestral dead. There is occasional
mention of reincarnation in the Norse sagas, and newborns were
given the names of ancestors in order that they might possess
the ancestor's qualities.

Turning to reincarnation as a form of transformation, a
general, though not exclusive, pattern across animist societies is
the expectation that reincarnation occurs in relatives, particularly
grandchildren. Grandparents are expected to be reincarnated
in grandchildren. Often, a newborn can be identified as a
specific ancestor (though not among the Trobrianders). In

contrast to Eastern traditions of reincarnation, the goal of rebirth is not spiritual development in order to escape from the cycle of reincarnation, but continuity of the family and wider community, a maintenance of the connection with ancestors and social traditions.

The best documentation we have for reincarnation in animist societies is for Native American groups,[6] and they are the subject of the first case study below. The evidence from other geographical areas has not been collated systematically, and it must be admitted that it is patchy. It is also not entirely reliable, for various reasons: uncorroborated accounts of early travellers; misunderstandings of indigenous worldviews and mistaken assumptions in reports by colonial administrators, missionaries, explorers and early anthropologists, who often did not recognise the significance of reincarnation or other types of transformation because they were alien to their own experience; subjects not being entirely forthcoming about their beliefs to missionaries who wanted to convert them; and disagreements in interpretation between experts, who sometimes, frankly, simply ignore what does not interest them. For many – or even most – of these areas, it is probably too late to record systematically the traditional afterlife beliefs of the societies, as they have already been irrevocably changed or heavily overlaid by Christian or Muslim concepts, especially in Africa, South America and Oceania.[7] As a result, the origins of these traditional beliefs remain unclear. Some claim that the rebirth beliefs of Native Americans are older than the reincarnation beliefs of the Eastern religions, but the lack of hard evidence means that really we have no way of knowing for certain.

Reincarnation and transformation among Native Americans

The earliest mention of Native American reincarnation beliefs was by European settlers and missionaries in the early seventeenth century, especially observations by Jesuit missionaries among the Huron. Despite the influence of Christianity, those beliefs continue to exist today, though often much diluted and altered. Reincarnation concepts vary widely between culture areas and groups, and certainly not all Native Americans believe in reincarnation.

One reincarnation belief that is reportedly shared by all Native American groups is that hunted animals reincarnate, depending on how they are treated by the hunter. There are special rites which ensure that the killed animal will return to be hunted again, and so will continue to provide food for the hunter's family. For example, the hunter has to pray for pardon and, if he does not, he will be punished in some way; often, there are ceremonies to return certain animal body parts to the water or to the land in order to ensure the animal's reincarnation. The Cherokee believe that an animal has a predefined lifespan that cannot be ended by violent means. If it is killed before its allotted time, the death is only temporary, and the body is resurrected from the blood drops. At the end of its full lifespan, the animal's spirit joins others in the spirit world.

Among Native American groups, it is not generally an expectation that all humans will be reincarnated. For many groups, reincarnation is only one of a number of possibilities of what happens to the human spirit or soul after death; some believe that the soul goes to the spirit world, though it retains some involvement with the human world. The soul is regarded as pre-existing in an underworld, the rising sun, the clouds or the Milky Way. Many Native American groups believe in a dual soul – the Huron believe they have five or more souls – one of which retains a sense of personal identity and can be reborn.

A belief in human reincarnation is reportedly strongest in the northern and north-western part of the continent, among the Inuit,[8] the Northwest Coast groups and the Native peoples of the Western Subarctic. Not surprisingly, this distribution corresponds to the areas least affected by the proselytising of Christian missionaries, who tended to argue that belief in reincarnation was the Devil's work and tried to stamp it out. As a result, these groups have managed to maintain their cultural beliefs and subsistence base far more than those of other areas.

Where belief in human reincarnation is found, the most widely shared belief is in the reincarnation of children and warriors, that is, those who died prematurely. Children who died stillborn or at an early age are believed to be reborn into the same families; while warriors killed in battle may be reborn and are identified from birthmarks corresponding to their wounds.

A common theme in Native American myth are human-animal transformations, and vice versa, not all necessarily related to reincarnation. Sometimes, it is not clear if a deceased human transforms into an animal temporarily and then again into a human, and if it is spirit or tangible. There are stories of an Inuit shaman, Avôvang, who was murdered and transformed himself into a series of animals to avenge his own death. Eventually, he went on to live the life of every creature on earth, before becoming a human once more.

References to humans reincarnating as animals after death are most frequent among the California groups, where a bad person might return as a grizzly bear or a rattlesnake. The Mojave believe in multiple reincarnations: at death, first the deceased becomes a spirit; then an owl; then a different kind of owl; then another kind; then a water beetle; and finally turns into air. Among the Kwakiutl, a human soul can inhabit an animal body while retaining the consciousness of a human. At death, sea hunters become killer whales, land hunters become wolves, and ordinary people become owls. When, eventually, the animal dies, its soul is reincarnated into a human baby. There is, therefore, a strong belief among these groups that the souls of their ancestors are among them as animals. Both human and animal bones have to be treated with proper respect to ensure the regeneration of the bodies; bones are believed to have the capacity to remember, and can bring those memories to a new incarnation.

Some of the Northwest Coast groups believe that twins are the reincarnation of salmon. One informant remembered his life as a salmon, and being caught, cooked, canned and shipped. As a result, twins are regarded as only half human and as dangerous beings.

As regards reincarnation into a human body, among Native American groups there is an expectation that rebirth occurs in the same family, and that ancestors return to live among them. Occasionally, though rarely, rebirth happens outside the community, or even among non-Native Americans. In this way, in general, the belief system incorporates the living and the dead seamlessly. The reincarnated person remains essentially the same social individual and tends to marry the same category of person as in the previous incarnation.

Reincarnated ancestors are identified in numerous ways: through similar birthmarks, dreams announcing their birth, usually to relatives, and special knowledge or particular skills that the reincarnated person shares with the ancestor. In most cases, memories of the previous life fade as the person grows older.

In Northwest Coast groups, it is not unusual for an elder to predict their own reincarnation. For example, among the Tlingit of Alaska, it is common for the dead person to decide the details of their future reincarnation, such as the place of rebirth and who the mother will be. Either they inform a relative that they will be returning, and instruct them to name the child after them, or their return is announced through a dream. A potential mother might also seek the reincarnation of a particular relative by placing the hand of the dead person against her breast.

The mechanisms of reincarnation are described by various informants. A Winnebago shaman, Thunder Cloud, described his two previous lives and the time between them. After his first life, his spirit was taken to the west where he lived with an old couple in a village of the dead, organised as a human society, with a chief. He received permission from the chief to be reborn, in order to exact revenge for the death of his relatives in his previous life. When he died a second time, he watched his own burial, then went to the west once more. There he remained in the village of the dead for four years before being reborn again. Similarly, among the Siberian Yukaghirs, the dead waiting to be reincarnated live in log cabins and tents, and eat and drink, although day and night, winter and summer are reversed.

There are, nevertheless, huge variations between Native American groups concerning the mechanisms of reincarnation, including whether humans can be reincarnated as animals. One variation is whether humans can reincarnate into the opposite sex, which is most common among the Inuit and in the Western Subarctic. Among the Inuit, in cases of cross-gender reincarnation, cross-dressing is not uncommon until puberty; in any case, in this culture gender is malleable, and aspects of transvestitism are quite normal. Multiple simultaneous reincarnation – where a soul reincarnates into different people simultaneously – is most widely reported for the Inuit and some Northwest Coast peoples. Normally, all the simultaneous incarnations occur within the bodies of their own descendants, although among the Inuit sometimes a person is said to be reborn in a different Inuit community.

Australian Aboriginal societies: the Dreaming, ancestors, totems and reincarnation

The spirituality of Australian Aborigines is based on ancestors and the land. Ideas of reincarnation play some sort of part, but they have not been systematically studied and collated in the same way as for Native Americans, and for various reasons the picture remains unclear.

Defining 'traditional' Aboriginal beliefs unaffected by any sort of external contact is tricky. Even before the English fleet carrying convicts landed at Botany Bay in 1788, to found the penal colony that became the first European settlement in Australia, Aboriginal beliefs had been influenced by contact with Melanesians and Indonesians. The first accounts of Aboriginal beliefs and customs were not published until later in the nineteenth century by missionaries, explorers and colonial administrators, so it is virtually impossible to reconstruct pre-contact beliefs and practices. The impact of Christian missions in Australia was huge, and as a result 70 per cent of Aborigines now describe themselves as Christians.[9] In some ways, traditional beliefs and Christianity are not seen as separate, but have become integrated. Furthermore, many contemporary urban Aborigines have lost touch with their ancestral lands and traditions. In the past, much of the information about 'typical' Aboriginal culture came from the areas remote from European settlement, such as parts of Central, Northern or Western Australia, where a traditional culture is still practised today, which of course gives rise to questions about how representative those areas might be. Aborigines are divided into more than 500 tribal groups, and there are significant regional differences in customs and beliefs.

Nevertheless, more recently there has been a revival of Aboriginal spirituality and of links to ancestral lands, and a growth of Aboriginal self-determination. Aboriginal authors now publish their own accounts of their traditions, which often differ quite significantly from those of professional anthropologists. As with Native Americans, there are areas of knowledge and practice which are restricted and often not fully accessible or revealed to 'outsider' experts, while the native accounts can provide far more insight. This explains why descriptions of Aboriginal beliefs, especially related to the afterlife and contact with the non-human world, can be inconsistent: what is found in one account is not necessarily echoed in another, and it may even be substantially different.

The core of Aboriginal spirituality is the Dreaming, a mythical time when the world was created by ancestral beings who took on numerous changeable forms, for example, the Rainbow Snake, whose image is seen on cave walls throughout Australia and which features prominently in myth, story and song. Tribal land and the Dreaming are inseparable, and each part of the landscape is explained through myth and story. The topography of the land – its hills, rivers, valleys and stones – is believed to have been formed by the explicit actions of ancestral beings in the Dreaming. The landscape of a tribal land is regarded as the transformed substance of these ancestral beings, and is full of the signs of the ancestors as they travelled, fought, copulated, menstruated, gave birth and defecated. So the landscape is itself sacred and symbolic, and in this way the Dreaming is ever present and part of the rhythm of daily life.

The creation, life, death and transformation of humans are also woven into the narrative of the Dreaming and the land. Every individual in an Aboriginal tribe is born into a totem, all of which bear the name of a natural entity – an animal, plant, water, sun, cloud or wind – and, together with the other people in that totemic group, shares the characteristics of that totem. There are a number of different totems within each tribe, and the need for balance between totems and their essential characteristics also determines who one can marry, in order to maintain harmony. The totem is, of course, linked to the creation myths of the Dreaming. It is the embodiment of each individual in their primeval, rudimentary state before they were transformed into humans by the ancestral beings. The totem represents an Aborigine's pre-existent condition, his constant contact with the Dreaming, and forever links them to their origins. They not only identify with the totem in an intellectual sense, but are regarded as actually identical with it; for example, if you are identified with the kangaroo, you really are the kangaroo, you share its flesh and therefore you cannot eat its meat, otherwise you are eating yourself. An Aborigine also adopts a father's totem after his death, and takes on its attributes.

Each Aboriginal individual is believed to be a reincarnation of a primordial totemic being in the Dreaming. No one is a unique individual, but a reincarnation of an ancestor. This rebirth of a totemic being means that the Dreaming is a living actuality, not a distant myth. Death is regarded as the spirit departing to the realm of the dead – sometimes described as a river of the dead, an interpretation of the Milky Way – but it is also seen as a transformation into an ancestor and becoming part of the ever-present Dreaming. Some Aboriginal groups have ceremonies to get the dead to their destination and explicitly transform them into ancestors.

As a result of the lack of systematic research on Aboriginal reincarnation beliefs, the mechanisms of reincarnation are not well understood and, as with Native Americans, they appear to vary across tribes and regions. In some tribes, the deceased is believed to merge with their totem, and so lives on in that totem; but in others, the reincarnated spirit changes totem and gender. It has been reported that most Aborigines do not recognise sex as the prime mover in conception, and that a human spirit is carried into a mother's womb, usually by herself at the behest of a totem; but in some Central Australian tribes, the spirit deliberately chooses its own mother. Certainly for the Aborigines of Central Australia, the souls of all the dead are believed to be reborn as infants, and every living person is believed to be the reincarnation of a dead person who lived a longer or shorter time ago. Features of the landscape are populated by the souls of the dead waiting to be reborn. Sir James Frazer also reported in 1913 that some Aborigines believed that the spirits of the dead were sometimes reincarnated in 'white people'.[10] Not enough research has been carried out – especially given the constraints described above – to determine if such reincarnation beliefs were or still are widespread, and if they fit into the typical patterns recorded for other animist societies.

While the mechanisms of reincarnation across Aboriginal societies are not entirely understood, may vary, and in many cases have been reshaped by Christian concepts, most of them believe that in death the spirit returns to the ancestral lands to await being reborn, and, importantly, continues to be regarded as part of the living community. The physical remains of the deceased are reintegrated into the land, ready for the process of reincarnation. The land binds together the living, the dead, the human and the non-human as a community. It is for this reason that Australian Aborigines, as well as other indigenous groups such as New Zealand Maori and Native Americans, feel deeply the need to repatriate and rebury the human remains of their ancestors that were taken to museums, often in other countries, as specimens for research and exhibition. For Aborigines, the ancestral dead are part of the living community, which includes the ancestral lands formed as part of the Dreaming. Taking the remains of ancestors away from the land unbalances everything and is a wound felt by the whole community for generations. Repatriation and reburial of the human remains of ancestors is a healing process, and returning the ancestors to the tribal lands, the life source from which they were created, among their own community, is seen as a wrong put right.

Reincarnation and transformation in Africa: some examples

Systematic documentation of reincarnation in Africa is meagre. It was cursorily recorded by early ethnographers, but the beliefs are now so deeply influenced by Christianity and Islam that the opportunity for more detailed study may have been lost. Many of those early reports were synthesised by the psychic researcher Theodore Besterman (1904-1976), who concluded that over a hundred tribes across Africa believe in some form of human reincarnation, whether as humans, animals or both.[11] A few examples, based on more recent ethnographic fieldwork, give an indication of the variety of traditional beliefs.

Among the Igbo of Nigeria, following the general pattern in animist societies, reincarnated ancestors return to relatives, though not necessarily into the same nuclear family. In a society in which social position is important, reincarnation is seen as an opportunity to achieve previously unattained objectives and a higher status in the new life. The wicked – the incestuous, murderers, witches and sorcerers – are not reincarnated, which is regarded as a terrible punishment.

Also in Nigeria, the Benin believe that everyone is reincarnated 14 times. The Benin explicitly examine a newborn for characteristics shared with a deceased relative, and choose an appropriate name to create strong ties with an ancestor.

Elsewhere, we find different kinds of transformations after death, and evidence that the attitudes of ancestors are not always positive. Among the Ju/'hoansi San in the Kalahari in southern Africa, dead humans are transformed into spiteful spirits which spread dissent, disease and death among humans by spying on them and shooting tiny, invisible arrows into their bodies. Until changes were forced on their culture, this necessitated regular healing ceremonies to deal with the actions of these malicious ancestors.

The Shona of the Zimbabwe plateau (also found in Botswana, Mozambique and South Africa) believe that places are owned by the ancestors whose spirits reside there: even if the group moves, the previous place, though abandoned, remains the ancestral home and has spiritual value for them. There are regular ceremonies to welcome back home the spirits of the deceased as ancestors. Those ancestors protect the living, but they can also punish them through witchcraft or illness. The spirits of dead chiefs can come out of a burial and transform themselves into lions to protect their group.

The zombies of Haiti

Probably the best known post-mortem transformation of a human being in popular Western culture is the zombie, although this is admittedly more about reanimation than a form of immortality. The word 'zombie' was known earlier, but it was American journalist William Buehler Seabrook (1884-1945) who introduced zombies as 'walking dead men' to English-language readers in 1929, in the rather sensationalised account of his travels in Haiti, *The Magic Island*:

> ... they were corpses walking in the sunlight, and they themselves and all the people knew that they were corpses... and as they approached the graveyard, they began to shuffle faster and rushed among the graves, and each before his own empty grave began clawing at the stones and earth to enter it again...[12]

In fiction, especially film and television, a zombie is a soulless, undead being created through the reanimation of a human corpse. The development of this idea of the zombie is usually credited to the influential, low-budget 1968 film *Night of the Living Dead*, directed by George A. Romero, in which the reanimated dead who eat human flesh are called 'ghouls'. This popular notion of the zombie was adapted from Haitian folklore, though it may have had an African origin, brought to Haiti, or developed there, by enslaved Africans.

In Haiti, zombification is believed to be, essentially, a rare, extreme and carefully considered form of social punishment. Such punishment is imposed by the Bizango guild, a society normally active by night that maintains order and ethical behaviour in rural communities and protects community resources, especially land. Traditionally, the punishments at its disposal involve sorcery and poison. The ultimate sanction, zombification, is carried out on individuals who have become pariahs in their community, as a result of stealing other people's land, jobs or wives. The process of zombification results in the victim being – at least apparently – put to death, but then revived as a slave, with loss of individual freedom and will, and subject to the will of a sorcerer (a *bokor*) who controls the zombie's soul. In this way, zombies can be made to work, to atone for their misdeeds and to be useful to the community.

The most holistic and influential explanation of the zombification process has been that of Wade Davis, a Harvard-trained ethnobotanist, who went to Haiti to study the toxic plants and animals used in zombie preparations. He concluded that the key ingredient was tetrodotoxin, a highly lethal neurotoxin found in certain marine fish and other organisms. Its ingestion causes malaise, dizziness, respiratory paralysis and death. According to Davis, tetrodotoxin induces a state of paralysis and lowers the metabolic state of the victim to such a level that they are considered dead. While the initial dose induces this deathlike stupor, it is also capable of inducing a prolonged psychotic state which renders the victim liable to loss of self-will.

The process is accompanied by a magical rite to capture the essence of a person's soul – their personality, character and willpower – which is the explanation for why a zombie appears cataleptic, a characteristic already recorded by Seabrook:

> The eyes were the worst. It was not my imagination. They were in truth like the eyes of a dead man, not blind, but staring, unfocused, unseeing.[13]

Their body basically becomes an empty vessel subject to the command of the *bokor*. Davis relates the story of a man returning to his community many years after his death (or disappearance), and claiming that he had been a zombie during the intervening period.

Davis' interpretation has been challenged by others, who

think that he has been too gullible in believing folk accounts of the zombie state. Many scientists dismiss tetrodotoxin as the cause, citing experimental evidence that it does not have the effects that Davis reports. He has also been criticised for believing that *bokors* can keep zombies in a pharmacologically induced trance for years.

Others have suggested an entirely different explanation for the zombie phenomenon, for example, mental illness such as schizophrenia, which can manifest itself as a catatonic state and is not uncommon in rural Haiti. However, such limited explanations do not account for the elaborate folklore around the whole process of zombification as a social punishment. To be convincing, any interpretation needs to take into account wider aspects of the culture. Like the other societies described in this chapter, where the boundary between life and death is experienced as permeable and malleable, it is a transformation intimately connected with the preservation of the traditional social structure.

Part 3

Longevity and Legacy

Chapter 6

From Gilgamesh to cryonics: the search for the everlasting body

I do not want to die – no; I neither want to die nor do I want to want to die; I want to live for ever and ever and ever.
– Miguel de Unamuno, *The Tragic Sense of Life in Men and in Peoples*

This chapter focuses on the search for everlasting life on this earth, rather than in a post-mortem afterlife. It is about staving off death and the longing for immortality within our human bodies. The quest for earthly immortality has been central to ancient legends and epics, through classic fiction, to modern popular cinema and television. Immortality continues to be an extremely popular subject for the media: it's still a story people want to hear. Newspapers regularly report on scientific and medical advances with headlines such as 'Scientists bring dead back to life' or 'We're gonna live forever', feeding a public appetite for that sort of immortality, making it appear tantalisingly achievable and not just the stuff of legends. Some of this is simply about slowing the ageing process and extending life by a few years, but there is also the (still) fantasy possibility of bringing the dead back to life and extending human lifespans through cryonic technologies, which are based on the hope that future medicine and technology will someday be able to revive and restore them to youth and health.

The search for earthly immortality has been a staple theme of stories ever since humans started telling them: from what is often labelled as the oldest story in the world, Gilgamesh, first written down in the late third millennium BCE; through classical myths and legends; stories about the First Emperor of China's quest for the elixir of everlasting life in the third century BCE;[1] medieval legends of the Holy Grail; Henry Rider Haggard's 1886 bestselling romantic adventure, *She*; all the way through to modern cinema (including the *Indiana Jones* and *Monty Python* films, which take up the Arthurian legend of the Holy Grail; or the British science fiction television series *Misfits*, which used the memorable marketing slogan 'If being immortal doesn't help me pull, nothing will'). A typical recurrent theme of the ancient stories and myths is the hero or heroine seeking some elixir, plant, sacred fire or vessel that would make them immortal, the punch line usually being that they lose it at the last minute, don't realise they will become old, or that their loved one cannot join them in that immortality.

It is not the purpose of the first part of this chapter to provide some sort of brief anthology of stories about the search for immortality from all over the world. Instead, it focuses on a select group of stories, myths and legends, originating from three different cultures and time periods: Gilgamesh from the ancient Near East, tales about Achilles from classical Greece and Rome, and the Holy Grail legends from medieval Europe. These stories became so popular that they have been constantly adapted, rewritten, edited and transformed over hundreds or even thousands of years. They were popular not only within the cultures that created them, but these same stories have survived into our own times, where they are still being retold and re-imagined in different media, on occasion deliberately throwing a different perspective on particular modern issues. It is notable that the immortality theme was not part of the original stories of Achilles and the Holy Grail, but that thread has become dominant in modern interpretations. The aim is, therefore, to demonstrate the ongoing power and popularity of these stories, which seem to speak to a longstanding human concern about immortality and the heroic battle to defeat death. They often conclude, though, with an acceptance that death cannot be defeated. Arguably it is the failure to achieve immortality in these ancient tales that explains their popularity through the centuries: the failure of the heroes perhaps makes it easier for the rest of us to accept the inevitability of death. Their shared message seems to be: life is short, accept your lot.

Gilgamesh through the ages

Stories about Gilgamesh and his search for fame and immortality were popular for over two thousand years in the ancient Near East, influenced episodes in the *Odyssey* and the *Arabian Nights*, and, since their rediscovery in the nineteenth century, have been retold and reinvented in myriad ways. They feature the adventures of Gilgamesh, considered in Babylonian tradition to be a real king of the city of Uruk. Although there is no contemporary proof of his reign, Gilgamesh is named as the second king of Uruk after the Flood in a later list of kings who ruled Sumer, the southern part of Babylonia (roughly corresponding to the southern part of modern Iraq), and credited with a reign of 127 years. That would place him around 2600 BCE, if he really existed. None of the rare documents from that time mentions him, but both he and his father have divine status in cuneiform tablets written a century or two later.

The first stories about Gilgamesh are five fragmentary poems in Sumerian, the language of southern Babylonia until the late third millennium BCE. These stories were probably first written down in the cuneiform script on clay tablets in about 2150 BCE, but were most likely based on an older, oral tradition of storytelling. The longer integrated version that today we call the Epic of Gilgamesh is known from tablets dating to the first millennium BCE, about 1500 years later. This is known as the standard version, and is in Akkadian, the Semitic language of Babylonia and Assyria from the mid-third millennium BCE until the first century CE. The standard version is the fullest account of Gilgamesh's adventures, and almost certainly incorporates episodes which originally appeared in early Sumerian poems of the late third millennium BCE that are now missing or completely lost. For that reason, it is easier to understand the whole story using the standard version as a starting point, and then work back to the first Sumerian poems to explore how Gilgamesh's quest for fame and immortality evolved over many centuries.

The standard version is known from 73 cuneiform tablets, 35 of them from the library of King Ashurbanipal (668-c. 627 BCE) at Nineveh, the rest from other cities in Assyria and Babylonia. Ashurbanipal was interested in collecting copies of all known cuneiform literature, and instigated a deliberate programme of acquiring cuneiform tablets from other cities and libraries, ordering his scribes to copy them out. The tablets in Ashurbanipal's library are the oldest of this version, while the latest one from Babylon dates to c. 130 BCE, a full 2000 years after the story of Gilgamesh was first written down.

The standard version is divided into 11 sections, each on a separate tablet, so it is common to refer to the sections as tablets I-XI (a twelfth tablet contains a translation of part of one of the Sumerian poems). But there are still considerable gaps: only four of the tablets are more or less complete, and about one-fifth of the epic is totally missing, while other parts are badly damaged and difficult to read.

The epic is set in Uruk, the greatest city of its day. In antiquity the story was known as 'He who saw the Deep', after its opening words, which was the usual way to refer to works of literature, just as today we have an index of first lines in poetry collections. In fact, the first eight tablets do not even allude to immortality, but concern Gilgamesh's quest for fame and his adventures with Enkidu, the wild man. Briefly, those eight tablets introduce Gilgamesh as two-thirds god, one-third man, who tyrannises the people of Uruk; the gods create Enkidu to rival him; Gilgamesh defeats Enkidu in a fight and they become friends; they go to the Cedar Forest and kill its ferocious guardian, Humbaba (an older variant of this name is Huwawa); Gilgamesh spurns the advances of the goddess Ishtar, who asks her father Anu to send the bull of heaven to kill Gilgamesh, but instead Gilgamesh and Enkidu kill the bull; the gods decree Enkidu's death, he dies, and is given an elaborate funeral.

The last three tablets deal with the quest for immortality. In tablet IX Gilgamesh considers his own mortality, in response to his grief at the death of Enkidu. He sets out to find the only immortal man, Utnapishtim, the sole survivor of the Flood, to learn the secret of eternal life:

I am afraid of death, so I wander the wild,
to find Uta-napishti...
who attended the gods' assembly, and found life eternal:
of death and life he shall tell me the secret.[2]

In tablet X, a wise tavern keeper, Siduri, guides him to the ferryman, who takes Gilgamesh across the waters of death to Utnapishtim. In tablet XI, the old man explains how he gained immortality after surviving the Flood, but not eternal youth. He suggests Gilgamesh might succeed if he goes without sleep for a week. Gilgamesh fails – in fact he sleeps for the full seven days – and realises he has no hope of conquering death. Utnapishtim offers Gilgamesh a final opportunity: he can pick a plant from the seabed that has rejuvenating powers:

But if you can possess this plant,
you'll be again as you were in your youth.[3]

Gilgamesh dives and plucks the plant, but a snake eats it while he is bathing in a pool, and he acknowledges his failure. Returning to Uruk, he shows the ferryman the city walls that will be his legacy, the only form of immortality he can hope to achieve.

This standard version of the epic of Gilgamesh is the longest known composition written in Akkadian. It is likely that it was read out or sung as entertainment in many different contexts: in royal courts, homes, tents and around campfires, on trading caravans crossing the deserts and on long sea voyages. Although the standard version is known from first-millennium BCE copies, its composition is credited to an earlier Babylonian scribe and priest, Sin-leqe-unninni, who lived between the thirteenth and eleventh centuries BCE. His name appears in later colophons, which were a bit like title pages at the ends of tablets. It is uncertain how much his version was an original composition and how much just collating and editing existing versions. At that time, the late second millennium BCE, it is clear that the story was popular over a wide area, and there were many versions of the Gilgamesh story in different languages: tablets with parts of the story have been found outside Assyria and Babylonia in the Hittite capital of Hattusa in Anatolia, at Emar and Ugarit in Syria, and at Megiddo in Palestine.

Indeed, Sin-leqe-unninni most likely made use of an earlier integrated version from the Old Babylonian period in the eighteenth century BCE, which included episodes from the early Sumerian poems but added new compositions to form, for the first time, a connected story around kingship, fame and the fear of death. This was called 'Surpassing all other kings' in antiquity, and it is simpler and sparser than the later standard version, though only parts of it survive. Most of the extant tablets concern Gilgamesh and Enkidu and the Cedar Forest expedition. Only one tablet, reportedly from Sippar, a city on the River Euphrates in southern Iraq, deals with Gilgamesh wandering the wild, seeking eternal life. However, there are passages here which are missing from the later standard version (these older passages are often used to fill in gaps in the standard version). These include Gilgamesh being warned of the futility of his quest by the sun god Shamash and Siduri, the tavern keeper (although her name does not survive on this tablet). Siduri expands on this theme, explaining that only the gods are immortal, and that the task of a man is to enjoy life while he can, and nurture his family to produce descendants:

> O Gilgamesh, where are you wandering?
> The life that you seek you never will find:
> when the gods created mankind,
> death they dispensed to mankind,
> life they kept for themselves.
> But you, Gilgamesh, let your belly be full,
> enjoy yourself always by day and by night![4]

The precursor to this first Old Babylonian integrated version were the earliest Sumerian poems about Gilgamesh, to which we now return. In these, his name is Bilgames. They are known almost entirely from versions copied out by eighteenth-century BCE trainee scribes in schools, although the oldest existing version dates a few hundred years earlier. The poems are short, individual tales, without the common themes that were added later in the integrated versions.

Only one of the five poems concerns Bilgames' search for immortality, known today as 'The Death of Bilgames', and in antiquity as 'The great wild bull is lying down'. The story here is different to that later expanded and retold in the integrated versions. Bilgames is on his death-bed, and in a vision the gods review his heroic career, including a brief allusion to his journey to meet the immortal survivor of the Flood, called Ziusudra (the Sumerian equivalent of the Babylonian Utnapishtim). The gods consider whether Bilgames should be mortal or immortal. The god Enki decides that Ziusudra alone achieved immortality, in special circumstances, and that Bilgames, despite his divine birth, must die and descend to the underworld (for a description of the ancient Near Eastern underworld, see Chapter 1):

From that time we swore by the life of heaven and the life of
earth,
from that time we swore that mankind should not have life
eternal.
And now we look on Bilgames:
Despite his mother we cannot show him mercy![5]

Bilgames will nevertheless have an honoured position in the
underworld, where he will be reunited with his family and
Enkidu, and will be commemorated by the living in an annual
festival. The god Enlil explains that Bilgames cannot escape the
fate of mortal men:

O Bilgames, I made your destiny a destiny of kingship, but I
did not make it a destiny of eternal life.[6]

Bilgames awakes and recounts his vision, but his listeners reply
that death is inevitable. He builds his tomb, lies down, and the
doorway is sealed.

No Sumerian poem is known that describes Bilgames'
journey to reach Ziusudra or the detail of his failure to achieve
immortality. Yet, the single passing reference to the Ziusudra
episode in the poem 'The Death of Bilgames' ('you reached
Ziusudra in his abode!')[7] implies that the details of Bilgames'
quest and failure were well known to the audience. This
indicates that there must have been other Sumerian poems
about Bilgames – now lost completely or lying unrecognised and
undeciphered in museum stores – including one about his search
for immortality, as later described, probably in an expanded
form, in the standard Babylonian version; or that additional
details were expected to be improvised by inventive storytellers
familiar with other stories about Bilgames.

Despite the lack of detail in the fragmentary Sumerian poems,
the theme of a failed search for immortality and acceptance of

death as the inevitable fate of humans is already a key part of the tale of Bilgames/Gilgamesh in these earliest stories from the late third millennium BCE, one that would be expanded and adapted over the following two millennia to form a central theme of the integrated Babylonian epic. There is evidence, however, that the story of Gilgamesh may have influenced the literature of other ancient cultures. The episode of Calypso and Odysseus in Book 5 of the *Odyssey* is acknowledged to have several close parallels with that of Siduri, the tavern keeper, who appears in the Old Babylonian and standard versions of the Gilgamesh story, though not in the extant Sumerian poems. In the *Odyssey*, Calypso is an immortal nymph who rescues the shipwrecked Odysseus and keeps him as a lover on her island of Ogygia for seven years, enticing him to stay with promises of immortality and eternal youth, until the gods persuade her to let him go.

Despite differences of detail, there are numerous parallels between these episodes. Both Siduri and Calypso are lone females; they both serve alcohol to a wandering hero, who in both cases is inconsolable, though for different reasons. Compare the description of Gilgamesh in the standard version, fearing death, with that of Odysseus, desperately homesick:

... why are your cheeks so hollow, your face so sunken,
your mood so wretched, your visage so wasted?
Why in your heart does sorrow reside,
and your face resemble one come from afar?
Why are your features burnt by frost and by sunshine...[8]

By day he sat
out on the rocky beach, in tears and grief,
staring in heartbreak at the fruitless sea.[9]

To prepare for the forthcoming voyage, Gilgamesh and Odysseus each takes an axe to cut and trim trees, the first to make punting-poles, the second to build a boat. In both episodes, the women send the hero off on an ocean voyage described as perilous. And of course the theme of immortality comes up in both: Gilgamesh seeks it, Odysseus rejects it, but neither achieves it.

It is unlikely that we are dealing here with deliberate borrowing, and it is not all that surprising to find such parallels. The *Odyssey*, though written much later (in fact, at about the same time as the standard version of Gilgamesh was being copied by Ashurbanipal's scribes), is supposedly set in a fictionalised, heroic Mycenaean age at the end of the second millennium BCE. At that time, the Gilgamesh story was known in Syria and Palestine,[10] which had close trading contacts with Mycenaean Greece, so there was plenty of opportunity for traders and itinerant storytellers to swap stories. We know that the *Odyssey* developed from a long oral poetic tradition which started at that time and culminated in the written version hundreds of years later, so it is entirely possible for such stories to have been exchanged, adapted and integrated into other works with different settings.

A similar process of oral transmission, re-use and adaptation of traditional stories explains the extremely close resemblances between elements of the story of Gilgamesh and the tale of Buluqiya in the *Arabian Nights* (properly called *One Thousand and One Nights*).[11] This is a compilation of folk stories from the Middle East and India collected over many centuries from diverse sources. A number of these stories were translated into Arabic in the eighth century CE and formed the core of what was later expanded into the *One Thousand and One Nights*, with further additions over the centuries.

The story recounts how Buluqiya, a young king of Israel, sets out with a companion to obtain Solomon's ring, which bestows power over all things and which will enable them to travel to the fountain of life and drink the water of immortality. There are many direct parallels to the story of Gilgamesh. It has even been suggested that the name Buluqiya may ultimately be derived from Bilgames. The protagonist is a young king who seeks immortality, and journeys into the desert with his companion, here called 'Affan. They are offered a plant which gives eternal youth to those who eat it, like the plant offered to Gilgamesh by Utnapishtim. Just as they are about to get hold of the ring, 'Affan is reduced to a handful of dust. Buluqiya, alone and despairing like Gilgamesh after the death of Enkidu, continues his journey. He travels through a subterranean passage to a kingdom where the trees have leaves and fruit of precious stones, echoing a passage in Gilgamesh where he travels beneath the mountains and finds similar trees. Eventually, Buluqiya meets a king, Sakhr, who has achieved immortality by drinking from the fountain of life. The fountain is guarded by Al-Khidr, a sage known in many Islamic and other traditions, whose name some suggest is an abbreviation of Atrahasis (in Arabic, Hasisatra), an alternative name for Utnapishtim/Ziusudra, the immortal survivor of the Flood found by Gilgamesh. Sakhr tells Buluqiya the early history of the world, which echoes the passage in which Utnapishtim reveals to Gilgamesh the mystery of the gods. Then Buluqiya is spirited back to his kingdom.

These similarities running through the whole story of Buluqiya cannot be dismissed as coincidence, but are clearly a further adaptation of the story of Gilgamesh. There are other similar examples of the adaptation of older stories, notably the close resemblance of the episodes of the Cyclops and Circe in the *Odyssey* to two of the stories of Sinbad, which were added to *One Thousand and One Nights* much later.

Meanwhile, the original form of the story of Gilgamesh was forgotten. The last known copy of any part of it in cuneiform dates to the late second century BCE, and by the first century CE writing in cuneiform on tablets and the use of the Akkadian language died out completely. At that time Mesopotamia had become part of the Parthian empire, with a mix of Persian and

Greek culture and, eventually, the introduction of Christianity. This was a different world, and the old gods, traditions, myths and epics were forgotten.

Fast forward to the 1850s, when Sir Austen Henry Layard (1817-1894) and his assistant Hormuzd Rassam (1826-1910) discovered the ruins of Ashurbanipal's library in Nineveh, and excavated thousands of cuneiform tablets and fragments. The tablets came to the British Museum in London, where scholars began the painstaking process of identifying and deciphering them. One of these scholars was the self-taught George Smith (1840-1876), an engraver by trade, who in 1872 identified the fragments on his desk as the story of the Flood: what today we call tablet XI of the Gilgamesh epic. Apparently, when he realised what he was reading, Smith

> jumped up and rushed about the room in a great state of excitement, and, to the astonishment of those present, began to undress himself![12]

Smith's lecture on his discovery to the Society of Biblical Archaeology that year, in the presence of the Prime Minister, William Gladstone, caused a sensation. Before his early death from dysentery just four years later in Aleppo, Smith deciphered much of the Gilgamesh epic and his pioneering translations of 1875 and 1876 were the first to reveal Gilgamesh once more to the world.

The revival of the ancient epic immediately inspired novelists and poets, who produced inventive rewritings which often strayed very far from the original story. Like Gilgamesh, Henry Rider Haggard's *She*, published just ten years after Smith's first translations appeared, describes a perilous journey in search of the one person who has the secret of immortality. In both cases the journey is triggered by love and grief, although in different ways. *She* tells the tragic love story of Ayesha, 'She-who-must-be-obeyed', who lived for two thousand years (66 generations) after finding the secret of immortality and eternal youth through the Fire of Life, only to wither away by trying to renew its effects. Translated into 44 languages, and filmed 11 times since 1899, it has never been out of print. Haggard had a deep interest in ancient civilisations, amassing a collection of antiquities from the ancient Near East, Egypt and the Classical world,[13] and was clearly influenced by ancient tales of lost immortality and eternal youth such as Gilgamesh and the classical myths, mixed in with his experiences as a colonial administrator in South Africa where he was exposed to traditional Zulu tales.

Fuller and more reliable translations of Gilgamesh started appearing after the First World War, and Nancy Sandars' 1960 prose translation for Penguin in particular became very popular and reached a wide readership. For nearly 150 years, the story has been treated in fiction, poetry, theatre, classical music (operas, oratorios, cantatas, songs), pop music, film, television, painting, children's books, comic books, *anime* and video games. Ironically, in some of the more recent offerings Gilgamesh is in fact immortal. Theodore Ziolkowski, who has gathered together and commented on the modern reception of Gilgamesh, writes that

> Gilgamesh constitutes a finely turned seismograph whose reception registers to a significant degree many of the major upheavals of the past century.[14]

The most fascinating modern approaches are those in which the story of Gilgamesh has been re-worked in order to reveal new (or, in this case, very old) perspectives on contemporary political or social issues. In the 1950s, concerns about the Cold War were reflected in a BBC radio play by Douglas Bridson, *The Quest of Gilgamesh*, broadcast in 1954, in which the Flood is a tidal wave caused by an atomic explosion. Later geopolitical worries were addressed in the introduction to his 2004 adaptation by Stephen Mitchell, who compared Gilgamesh's raid on the Cedar Forest and the killing of Humbaba to the recent 2003 invasion of Iraq and the toppling of Saddam Hussein. Mitchell felt that the much critiqued morality of the pre-emptive strike on Iraq had ancient echoes in one of the early Sumerian poems, 'Bilgames and Huwawa', in which the god Enlil criticises Gilgamesh and Enkidu for their actions in words strikingly reminiscent of the language used by modern critics of the Iraq war:

> Why have you done this thing?
> Was it commanded that his name be wiped from the earth?[15]

More recently, Gilgamesh has been called into action in support of gay rights, feminism and environmental consciousness. Ziolkowski claims that no other masterpiece of world literature – including Homer, Virgil and the Bible – has had such a varied and pervasive cultural impact. It has often been said that, like any great work, Gilgamesh still has much to tell us about ourselves, our values, what we strive for, and what we long for. It is not only its continued popularity, but the ways in which the themes of Gilgamesh have been reinterpreted for the modern age that demonstrate the continued relevance of the story after more than four thousand years.

Achilles and the late heel

Although nothing can match the antiquity of the Gilgamesh story and the diverse ways it has been adapted by different cultures into the present day, it is not alone in retelling the theme of the failed search for immortality and eternal youth over hundreds of years. Another ancient character familiar in modern times is Achilles, greatest of the Greek heroes in the Trojan War. The phrase 'Achilles' heel' in the English language has come to embody the fatal flaw, the one point of vulnerability that undermined Achilles' immortality and caused his death.

Achilles is best known from Homer's *Iliad*, probably composed between 750 and 650 BCE (see Chapter 2), in which he is the central character. Indeed, despite its title, derived from Ilion, an older name for Troy, the *Iliad* is not really about the Trojan War as such, but about the wrath of Achilles. This sets in motion all of the key action of the epic, as the famous opening words make clear:

> Sing, goddess, the anger of Peleus' son Achilleus
> and its devastation...[16]

The *Iliad* does not begin until the tenth year of the siege of Troy, and finishes 41 days later with the burial of Hector and the city still under siege. In fact, two of the most famous episodes in the Trojan War are not even mentioned in the *Iliad*: the wooden horse (alluded to several times in Homer's *Odyssey*, particularly in Book 8, but most fully described centuries later in Book 2 of Virgil's *Aeneid*); and the death of Achilles. The *Iliad* ends with Achilles still alive, although his forthcoming early death is predicted. Later accounts of his death differ widely, although the god Apollo usually plays a role, either as the killer himself or directing the weapon of Paris; Achilles' heel is not mentioned until hundreds of years later. The *Iliad* makes no mention of his heel or of any immortality or invulnerability: on the contrary, the god Hephaestus has to make him a new 'immortal' armour to protect him in battle, and despite that he is still wounded. The Achilles of the *Iliad* is very mortal and vulnerable.

After Homer, other poets, dramatists and legends filled gaps and made additions to the story of Achilles, mostly regarding details about his youth and death. Over the centuries, many of these incidents and legends were inconsistent with each other. Achilles was a popular character: there was a cult of Achilles, and Alexander the Great identified with him and reputedly always carried a copy of the *Iliad*.

The earliest reference to the attempted immortality of Achilles is later than Alexander, and is found in the *Argonautica* of Apollonius Rhodius, a Greek author who lived in Alexandria in the first half of the third century BCE. The *Argonautica* is an epic poem about Jason and the Argonauts, which reworked events in Homer and later poets and was a major influence on Virgil's *Aeneid*. It includes an episode in which Achilles' mother, the goddess Thetis, kills her children by thrusting them into a fire and covering them with ambrosia (the elixir of life and food of the gods, from the Greek word *ambrotos*, 'immortal'), in a failed attempt to purge them of the mortal elements inherited from their father and make them immortal and eternally young:

> For she ever encompassed the child's mortal flesh in the night with the flame of fire; and day by day she anointed with ambrosia his tender frame, so that he might become immortal and that she might keep off from his body loathsome old age.[17]

His father, Peleus, manages to save the seventh child, the young Achilles, before he is incinerated.

The first extant reference to the legend of Achilles' heel is not in ancient Greek literature at all, but in the *Achilleid*, a fragment of an unfinished epic about Achilles written in the late first century CE by Publius Papinius Statius (c. 45-96 CE), a Roman poet. Here we find a brief allusion to the now well-known story of Thetis dipping the baby Achilles in the River Styx to make him immortal and invulnerable:

> ... at thy birth I fortified thee with the stern waters of Styx.[18]

That is all we get here: there is no specific mention of Thetis holding Achilles by the heel and his subsequent vulnerability in that spot. The next brief allusion to the heel of Achilles is in the *Genealogiae*, a handbook of mythology probably dating to the second century CE, attributed, perhaps falsely, to the Latin author Gaius Julius Hyginus (c. 64 BCE-17 CE):

Apollo in anger, taking the form of Alexander Paris, struck him with an arrow on the heel which was said to be vulnerable, and killed him.[19]

This work was only published for the first time in 1535 by the printer Jacob Micyllus, who renamed it *Fabulae* (Fables), but in the process destroyed most of the original manuscript, so that the printed version is now the sole authority for the text, apart from a few surviving fragments.

The first fuller account of the Achilles' heel story does not appear until the late fifth century CE, in the *Mythologiae* of the Christian writer Fabius Planciades Fulgentius, a collection of allegorical interpretations of pagan myths:[20]

Then after Achilles was born his mother dipped him in the waters of the Styx to make him a perfect man, that is, she protected him securely against all trials, but his heel alone she did not dip... Then he dies of love for Polynexa and is killed as it were because of his heel.[21]

Fulgentius' *Mythologiae* was widely read in the Middle Ages, which probably explains the enduring popularity of the Achilles' heel story; in addition, quite a few of the mythological collections from classical antiquity were first published in the sixteenth or early seventeenth centuries. Despite the fact that the Achilles' heel motif is a late addition, 700 to 800 years after Homer, in modern times it has become the best known fact about Achilles. Certainly by the late seventeenth century it was already common to refer to the human calcaneal tendon as the Achilles cord or tendon.[22] The seventeenth century was a good time for Achilles, with the first of many operas about him composed by Francesco Cavalli, Jean-Baptiste Lully and Alessandro Scarlatti, as well as the now famous painting by Peter Paul Rubens, *Thetis dipping the infant Achilles into the river Styx*, painted between 1630 and 1635.

The first mention in English of Achilles' heel as a metaphor for vulnerability is by the poet Samuel Taylor Coleridge (1772-1834). In 1809 he had started a weekly paper, *The Friend*, devoted to literary, moral and political essays, in which he himself wrote regularly. Like most poets – and their audiences – of the time, he was steeped in classical mythology, and in an 1810 edition of the paper he used the phrase

... the alarming state of Ireland, that vulnerable heel of the British Achilles.[23]

This was the period of the Napoleonic Wars, and Coleridge was defending his earlier support of the Royal Navy's seizure of the Danish fleet at Copenhagen in 1807, citing his concern that Ireland was vulnerable to an attack by the Danes on behalf of Napoleon, as the first step in an invasion of Britain. Following his lead, by the mid-nineteenth century, according to etymologies in many dictionaries, 'Achilles' heel' had come into regular use to refer more generally to an area of weakness or a vulnerable spot.

Achilles has continued to be a popular subject in poetry, books, drama, visual art and music more or less non-stop since the seventeenth century. In 2012, Madeline Miller won the Orange Prize for Fiction for her *Song of Achilles*, which portrays the relationship between Achilles and his friend Patroclus as a romance, an approach with precedents in antiquity. The 2004 film *Troy*, with Brad Pitt as Achilles, on the other hand, departs from the ancient sources by keeping Achilles alive in order to take part in the wooden horse episode. Although there is brief allusion to the legend that Achilles cannot die, the stress throughout is on fame and heroic deeds keeping his name alive forever. Inevitably, the heel motif is called upon right at the end, when Paris kills Achilles by shooting him initially through the heel, which makes him vulnerable. Despite being non-Homeric, and a very late addition, this powerful story was too good, and had become too popular, to omit.

> Now he was reduced to ashes, and of the great Achilles there remained only a little handful, scarcely enough to fill an urn: but his glory lived on, and filled the whole world. The extent of his fame is in keeping with the man himself, and by that fame the son of Peleus is as great as he ever was, and is not conscious of Tartarus' empty void.[24]

The Holy Grail and immortality

At the end of the 1989 film *Indiana Jones and the Last Crusade*, loosely based on the supposed Nazi search for the Holy Grail, the villain Donovan hopes to achieve immortality by drinking from the Grail cup. Yet, when the Grail first appeared in literature in the late twelfth century, it had nothing to do with immortality. So how did this meaning become embedded in late twentieth-century popular culture?

The Grail first appears in *The Story of the Grail* (*Le Conte du Graal*) by Chrétien de Troyes, an unfinished poem set in the times of King Arthur, probably written in France between 1180 and 1190. It tells the story of Perceval and his development from boy to knight. Perceval comes to the Fisher King's fortified house, where a girl enters the dining hall holding a grail (in Old French, *graal*, a word for a large serving dish). Although its shape is not described, it is made of gold and precious stones, and its appearance is accompanied by a brilliant light. Later in the poem, a single host or Mass wafer served from the grail suffices to sustain the life of the king's father. That is all we learn specifically about the Grail on its first mention.

The unfinished story was taken up by many other writers in the next 50 or so years, some creating original compositions, others attempting to continue Chrétien's tale. In most of these, the Grail – first called the 'Holy Grail' in one of the continuations – is described as the chalice, platter or bowl used by Jesus at the Last Supper, and/or as the vessel into which Joseph of Arimathea collected the blood that flowed from Jesus' wounds at the Crucifixion. It has miraculous sustaining and healing properties, is accompanied by a great brightness, only the pure can approach it, often it moves of its own accord, and sometimes vanishes – hence the Arthurian quests to find it. It was these descriptions of the Grail and its properties that predominated later on.

But one of the stories took a rather different tack, providing the first hint of the immortality theme. *Parzival*, written by Wolfram von Eschenbach (c. 1160/80-c. 1220) in Germany between 1200 and 1220, is generally acknowledged to be the greatest of the medieval Grail romances. As with Chrétien's earlier poem, to which it refers, it tells the story of Parzival's growth from youth to knight at King Arthur's court and his quest for the Holy Grail. In this story, though, the Grail is a stone, also called *lapsit exillis*, an obscure, much discussed term which sounds like Latin but is not. Once again the Grail is associated with the host, but in addition it has miraculous properties that renew life and bestow eternal youth:

> Moreover, never was a man in such pain but from that day he beholds the stone, he cannot die in the week that follows immediately after. Nor will his complexion ever decline. He will be averred to have such colour as he possessed when he saw the stone – whether it be maid or man – as when his best season commenced… Such power does the stone bestow upon man that his flesh and bone immediately acquire youth. That stone is also called the Grail.[25]

Of the later medieval writers, only Albrecht von Scharfenberg hinted at this theme. In his work known as *The Younger Titurel*, a continuation of another of Wolfram von Eschenbach's poems, probably written in the 1270s, the Grail is again a stone, but this time fashioned into a dish. Albrecht was mostly interested in the Grail's spiritual impact, but there is some indication that it had life-renewing as well as sustaining properties: he uses the same metaphor as in Wolfram's *Parzival* of a phoenix rising from the ashes.

But in the greatest English version of the Arthurian tales, *Le Morte Darthur* by Sir Thomas Malory (c. 1415-1471), a collection and reworking of Arthurian stories from various sources first published in 1485, the Grail is a vessel which still contains some of the blood of Jesus, strongly associated with the host, and it is its properties of healing that are highlighted again and again. Lancelot, Perceval and Ector are all healed by the Grail (usually called the Sangreal by Malory):

O Jesu, said Sir Percivale, what may this mean, that we be thus healed, and right now we were at the point of dying? I wot full well, said Sir Ector, what it is; it is an Holy vessel that is borne by a maiden, and therein is part of the holy blood of our Lord Jesu Christ...[26]

The only tentative hint at the Grail's power to bestow eternal youth is when it appears at Camelot and the knights seem transfigured:

Then began every knight to behold other, and either saw other, by their seeming, fairer than ever they saw afore.[27]

This is not as direct and obvious as Wolfram von Eschenbach's earlier description in *Parzival*: for Malory, it may be more of a spiritual transfiguration, and any rejuvenating effect is not mentioned the numerous times that knights are healed by the Grail. There is certainly no immortality in Malory's Grail.[28]

When stories about the Grail reappear in the nineteenth century, they mostly endow the Grail with its traditional sustaining and healing properties.[29] The first explicit linking of immortality with the Grail was by the French writer Edgar Quinet (1803-1875) in his *Merlin l'Enchanteur* (*Merlin the Enchanter*), published in 1860. In this reworking of the Merlin legends, an eternal wanderer, unable to die, asks if drinking from the Grail will bring on death – to which the response is that drinking from the Grail will make one immortal.

It is these tenuous threads linking the Grail with immortality that surface in the film. However, it is impossible to track a direct line back to any of the medieval sources, even *Parzival* in the thirteenth century (in which the Grail was of course a stone): although the film does portray water from the Grail as healing the hero's father, there is no indication of eternal youth; on the contrary, the knight who has guarded the Grail for 700 years is aged and weak, though immortal.[30] One is tempted to conclude that the hotchpotch of powers in the Indiana Jones Grail is due to pure invention and the popularity of the idea of immortality in modern times, rather than being based on any historical tradition. It is yet another example of the continuous reinvention of powerful stories – like Gilgamesh and Achilles – in which faithfulness to the original sources does not get in the way of a good immortality story, especially one that ends badly. The Holy Grail legend in particular has always been susceptible to imagined new meanings, occult and secret wisdom and conspiracy theories. It would be remiss, though, not to point out a wonderful irony within the film. To achieve immortality, Donovan has to drink from the Holy Grail, but must first choose the right cup – according to the film, only the true Grail will bring you life, whereas the false Grail will take it from you (another pure invention). Unfortunately for him, he drinks from the wrong cup, and is reduced to a pile of dust. The irony is that the 'wrong' cup he drinks from, which kills him, is gold inlaid with precious stones, exactly like the very first description of the Grail by Chrétien de Troyes. In that sense, it should have been the right cup, and had Donovan and the filmmakers known their Grail history, he would indeed have chosen wisely.

From halting ageing to cryonics: resurrection and immortality?

Until recently, the wish for immortality was the realm of myths and stories and reports of magical elixirs, as in Gilgamesh, Achilles and the Holy Grail legends. Of course, humans have always tried to prolong life for as long as possible.[31] With the coming of the Scientific Revolution, some of these attempts were put on a more rigorous footing. Francis Bacon (1561-1626), a key figure in the development of the modern scientific worldview, included observations and experiments on ageing and the degeneration of the body, with possible remedies to prolong life, in his *The History, Natural and Experimental, of Life and Death*, first published in Latin in 1623.

But these attempts, before and after Bacon, were about prolonging life by a few years, not, realistically, about immortality; just as today's advice to eat healthily, exercise regularly and not smoke will not make you immortal. The sociologist Zygmunt Bauman has argued that these are all feasible tasks that redefine death as a series of manageable problems which we can do something about, which might prolong life, and which stop us thinking about their ultimate futility:

There are so many causes of death... If I defeat, escape or cheat twenty among them, twenty less will be left to defeat me. One does not just die; one dies of a *disease* or *murder*. I can do nothing to defy mortality. But I can do quite a lot to avoid a blood clot or a lung cancer.[32]

The computer scientist Aubrey de Grey is notorious for claiming in 2008 that the first person to live to a thousand years had already been born and may be well into middle age, and that living indefinitely in a youthful state is possible in the future through medical technology.[33] Recent more sober scientific assessments conclude that, theoretically, the maximum human lifespan is at around 125 years, although of course these figures are disputed.[34] However, scientists now also suggest that attempts to stop ageing are futile, as it is mathematically impossible to halt ageing in multicellular organisms like humans. Why humans age is not completely understood, but the result is that cells degenerate and die. The only way to stop ageing is to get rid of poorly functioning cells – cells that are getting older and slower – but that then allows cancer cells to proliferate. So while you have fixed one problem, you are still faced with another: either all your cells will become sluggish (that is, you age), or you will get cancer. Ageing can be slowed down, they conclude, but it cannot be stopped.[35]

A 125-year lifespan is therefore perhaps the maximum we can hope for. That might seem like quite a lot to many of us, but it is still a far cry from immortality. In 1964, a physics and maths teacher named Robert Ettinger (1918-2011) suggested a bold new approach:

> Most of us now living have a chance for personal, physical immortality.[36]

Inspired by a science fiction story he read as a boy, in which a body is preserved for millions of years by freezing and the brain is revived and repaired by aliens, Ettinger's essential idea was that it was possible to preserve dead people indefinitely at very low temperatures, followed by the assumption that, eventually, medical science should be able to repair almost any damage to the human body. Initially he explored the idea in his own science fiction story, published in 1948, but his book, *The Prospect of Immortality*, first privately printed in 1962 and then as a hardback in 1964, translated into many languages, was the foundation of modern cryonics (derived from the Greek word meaning 'cold'):

> It is simply proposed that, after one dies a natural death, his body be frozen and preserved at a very low temperature – perhaps near absolute zero, the lowest possible temperature – which will prevent further deterioration for an indefinite period. The body will be damaged by disease or old age which is the cause of death, and will be further damaged (although in some cases probably not much, as we shall see) by our current freezing methods. But it will not decay or suffer any more changes, and one assumes that at some date scientists will be able to restore life, health, and vigor – and these, in fact, in greater measure than was ever enjoyed in the first life.[37]

Ettinger had grand ideas about how future medical science might improve human bodies and minds:

> After awakening, he may already be again young and virile, having been rejuvenated while unconscious; or he may be gradually renovated through treatment after awakening. In any case, he will have the physique of a Charles Atlas if he wants it, and his weary and faded wife, if she chooses, may rival Miss Universe. Much more important, they will be gradually improved in mentality and personality.[38]
>
> You and I, as resuscitees, may awaken still old, but before long we will gambol with the spring lambs – not to mention the young chicks, our wives.[39]

He was honest, though, about the lack of guarantees of success:

Clearly, the freezer is more attractive than the grave, even if one has doubts about the future capabilities of science. With bad luck, the frozen people will simply remain dead, as they would have in the grave.[40]

The publication of his book stimulated the foundation of various cryonics institutes. The first person to be cryonically suspended was Dr James Bedford, a 73-year-old retired psychology professor. Frozen a few hours after his death on 12th January 1967 in California, he remains preserved to this day. Quite a few other early attempts were not so successful, with frozen bodies thawing out and decomposing.

Cryonics is still regarded as a speculative practice at the outer edge of science, and its take-up has not been resounding. According to the latest available figures,[41] since Bedford in 1967, around 250 people have been cryopreserved in the United States, and about 1500 have made legal and financial arrangements to be cryopreserved after death. Modern cryonics has essentially followed Ettinger's basic principles: it involves cooling a recently deceased person to liquid nitrogen temperatures (-196° C.) in order to keep the body preserved indefinitely. It continues to express the hope that, in the future, the cryopreserved person can be revived and their lifespan radically extended. An option is neurocryopreservation, the practice of removing and cryopreserving only the head of a dead person. This is based on the assumption that only the information contained in the brain is of any importance, and that techniques for cloning or regenerating a new body will be developed in the future.[42]

In one sense, cryonics is based on the hope that, in the future, scientific advances will enable a dead person to be brought back to life. However, this is not a blanket resurrection of the dead, only of the recently dead who have been properly treated and preserved immediately after legal death. While societies require definitions of legal death in order to function, death is usually a process and not a sudden event. At clinical death, however it is defined, a majority of the body's tissues remain intact at a cellular level. The goal of cryonics is to halt the process of physical decay as quickly as possible after legal death, giving future doctors the best possible chance of reviving the patient.

It is a process which comes at a cost. While cryonics institutes insist that the costs of cryopreservation are often funded through life insurance, the costs vary greatly: current prices (2018, in US dollars) vary from $28,000 to $200,000, which are not insignificant sums. One cannot help drawing a parallel with the ancient Egyptian evidence concerning the costs of achieving the afterlife (ironically, the individual pods in which cryopreserved subjects are placed into liquid nitrogen strongly resemble Egyptian sarcophagi). Chapter 1 made the point that in ancient Egypt it was only the elite who could afford the expensive preparations to ensure the transition to the afterlife. Cryonics is not much different: it is the hope of immortality for those who can afford it.

Cryonics rests on assumptions and hopes about what might be achievable in the future. Rather surprisingly, there has been little discussion about what sort of life a revived person might lead. John Harris makes the point that cryopreserved people wish *their lives* to continue, and those lives are not just biological lives but are inextricably linked into a particular social world, with homes, friends, relatives, skills, jobs and hobbies that they are familiar with, and which most likely will no longer be there when they are revived. Harris admits that continued existence in such circumstances may be preferable to no existence at all, but that adjustment to a new world would be hard.[43]

The bad news is that there is a strong possibility that cryopreservation will irreparably damage human organs and cells:

Their optimism may well be ill-founded by present standards

of knowledge, since if they were 'dead' by our present criteria before being frozen too much damage is likely to have been done to the brain to make it worthwhile to attempt resuscitation in the future.[44]

As of now, not a single human or mammal has been cryopreserved and revived, and cryonicists continue to acknowledge – as did Robert Ettinger – that it remains unknown whether future science will be able to revive cryonically frozen subjects. As things stand, cryonics must take its place alongside the long list of magic elixirs, plants, sacred fires and holy vessels in the history of the human imagination as the hope of those reaching for immortality on this earth.

Chapter 7

'I will establish for ever a name eternal!'

*If there be any truth in poets' prophecies, I shall live to all eternity,
immortalised by fame.*
– Ovid, *Metamorphoses*

The simplest – and some might say the only – way to achieve
any sort of immortality is to be remembered forever: to leave
some memory, legacy or heroic deed that will be remembered
down the ages, memorialised in epics and on public monuments.
Another legacy is to have children: the individual may not
survive, but the family line, and ideally the family name, will,
and your children will remember you and tend your grave – at
least for a time. Already in the earliest versions of the world's
oldest epic, the hero Gilgamesh, having failed in his search for
real immortality, had come to this conclusion: fame and progeny
are the only route to immortality.

This chapter traces the pursuit of immortality through fame by
mythical and real heroes, by the rulers who 'make history', and
by ordinary people, who have always had their own strategies
for commemorating and immortalising their dead.

The legacy of Bilgames/Gilgamesh

We saw in the previous chapter that the earliest stories about
Gilgamesh are five Sumerian poems, dating to the late third
millennium BCE but known from eighteenth-century BCE copies.
Already in these, the hero – Bilgames in Sumerian – expresses
his fear of death, craves deeds of glory to establish his name, and
is taught the importance of descendants. In one poem, Bilgames
regards the killing of the monster Huwawa as the road to fame:

... since no man can escape life's end
I will enter the mountain and set up my name.[1]

Another of the Sumerian poems ends with Bilgames' funeral and reflects that men live on after death in the memories of those still living. It refers to the practice of placing votive statues in temples as a way of ensuring the remembrance of the name of the dead person. It also explains that the gods have given men families to continue their line:

Men, as many as are given names,
their (funerary) statues have been fashioned since days of old,
and stationed in chapels in the temples of the gods:
how their names are pronounced will never be forgotten!
The goddess Aruru, the older sister of Enlil,
for the sake of his name gave (men) offspring.[2]

The theme of descendants is expanded in the poem 'Bilgames and the Netherworld', in which his friend Enkidu's ghost comes up from the underworld and discusses his experiences with Bilgames. The basic message is that the more sons a man has, the more his family will make frequent offerings of fresh water to slake his thirst in the underworld and ease the conditions of his afterlife. For the childless dead, the opposite is true: they have no one to make offerings for them, and as a result they lead an even more miserable existence in the underworld:

'Did you see the man with seven sons?' 'I saw him.' 'How does he fare?'
'Among the junior deities he sits on a throne and listens to the proceedings' ...
'Did you see the shade of him who has no one to make funerary offerings?' 'I saw him.' 'How does he fare?'
'He eats scrapings from the pot and crusts of bread thrown

away in the street.'[3]

The Old Babylonian version of the epic of Gilgamesh, written in the eighteenth century BCE, continues the themes of fame and children. Gilgamesh sets out to kill Huwawa:

I will establish for ever a name eternal![4]

On another tablet of the same date, the tavern keeper explains to him that the task of a man is to enjoy life, cherish his wife and produce children:

Gaze on the child who holds your hand,
let your wife enjoy your repeated embrace!
For such is the destiny [of mortal men].[5]

It is worth noting that this theme of the importance of children does not survive in the extant portions of the later standard version of the epic of Gilgamesh, although it cannot be excluded that it appeared in the missing sections (indeed, part of the episode with the tavern keeper is missing on tablet X of the standard version). The punch line of the standard version is Gilgamesh's recognition that he can never attain true immortality, and instead he proudly shows off the city walls of Uruk that will be his memorial and legacy:

O Ur-shanabi, climb Uruk's wall and walk back and forth!
Survey its foundations, examine the brickwork!
Were its bricks not fired in an oven?
Did the Seven Sages not lay its foundations?[6]

Gilgamesh's faith in this memorial may not have been misplaced. In the nineteenth century BCE, a king of Uruk claimed he had reconstructed the city wall which Gilgamesh had built, supposedly hundreds of years previously; and later Babylonian tradition preserved the memory that Gilgamesh built the walls of Uruk.

Heroes and heroines: from myth to remembrance

The same themes of eschewing immortality in favour of eternal fame and family are found in the later Homeric epics. Earlier, we encountered Odysseus rejecting Calypso's offer of immortality and eternal youth, in Book 5 of the *Odyssey*. Instead, he is desperately homesick for his wife and son. Calypso tries to persuade him to change his mind and stay with her, warning him of the perils he faces on his voyage home:

> But if you understood
> how glutted you will be with suffering
> before you reach your home, you would stay here
> with me and be immortal – though you might
> still wish to see that wife you always pine for.[7]

But Odysseus explicitly rejects the offer of immortality in favour of home:

> But even so, I want to go back home,
> and every day I hope that day will come.[8]

As Martha Nussbaum remarks,

> ... he chooses the life of a human being, and a marriage to a woman who will... age and die... He chooses... not only risk and difficulty, but the certainty of death...[9]

In the *Iliad*, Achilles too makes a considered choice. He knows he is destined for a short life, but hopes for fame in recompense. His mother, Thetis, has warned him that, if he goes to Troy, he will win eternal fame but his life will be short; on the other hand, if he stays at home, his life will be long but inglorious:

> For my mother Thetis the goddess of the silver feet tells me
> I carry two sorts of destiny toward the day of my death.
> Either,
> if I stay here and fight beside the city of the Trojans,
> my return home is gone, but my glory shall be everlasting;
> but if I return home to the beloved land of my fathers,
> the excellence of my glory is gone, but there will be a long life
> left for me, and my end in death will not come to me quickly.[10]

At first, though, mindful of the prophecy, Achilles feels that his life is not worth any riches he might gain, and decides to leave the Trojan War and sail home:

> For not
> worth the value of my life are all the possessions they fable
> were won for Ilion...
> ... a man's life cannot come back again...[11]

He changes his mind, choosing renown on the battlefield and eternal fame, but only as a result of his anger – the key theme of the *Iliad* – at the killing of his friend Patroclus by the Trojan Hector and his wish for vengeance. He does this in the full knowledge that he will die soon after Hector:

> Now I shall go, to overtake that killer of a dear life,
> Hector; then I will accept my own death...
> ... Now I must win excellent glory...[12]

In these myths, and that of Gilgamesh, it is men who are concerned about achieving immortality, whether real or through fame. In Greek mythology, mortal women had less opportunity to achieve the sort of fame and glory that men like Achilles could aspire to. Deborah Lyons, in her *Gender and Immortality*, has proposed that, paradoxically, women – far more than men – could instead achieve immortality through the sorts of transformations that we saw in Chapter 5 in animist societies. Women tended to translate into the animal, vegetable or natural world, for example Arachne transformed into a spider for challenging Athena to a weaving contest; Byblis consumed by her own tears and changed into an inexhaustible stream or fountain; Cassiopeia turned into a constellation for boasting of her beauty; or Daphne transformed into a laurel tree to save her from Apollo (in fact, quite a few women – and men – are turned into trees of different kinds).

In most cases, these transformations were not through their own agency, in contrast to those we saw in Chapter 5. Instead, they are usually transformed by the gods, not as a reward, but as punishment, through vindictiveness, or occasionally to save them from an even worse fate (as with Daphne, many of the transformations are associated with actual or attempted rape and abduction by male gods). Nevertheless, it must be acknowledged that such transformations were not limited to women. Even a cursory glance at, for example, the Greek myths retold in Ovid's *Metamorphoses* shows that both women and men were regularly transformed into trees, stones and stars by the gods.

But these are all mythical heroes and heroines. How were the deeds of real, mortal heroes and heroines glorified and memorialised, and did the heroes and heroines themselves have a realistic expectation that, like Achilles, their names would reverberate through all eternity?

It is interesting to note that the rise of hero cults in Greece coincides with the rise of city-states in the eighth century BCE, at about the same time as the Homeric epics were immortalising the mythical heroes – although it is disputed whether the Homeric idealisation of the hero actually influenced the development of hero cults. The purpose of a hero cult was public immortalisation of the hero after death, a way of ensuring their name lived forever. A hero cult was characterised by some sort of public religious focus after the death of the hero that extended beyond the immediate family. Heroes were worshipped by all levels of society and had a similar role in Greek religion as the gods, which separated them from the cults of the ordinary dead.

Hero cults comprised gifts, rituals and sacrifices (often followed by communal dining) in locations ranging from small, walled-in precincts to proper sanctuaries with temples, many continuing for hundreds of years. It is true that most of the heroes so commemorated were male figures of myth, but real people had hero cults too: founders of cities and colonies; ancestors of prominent families; soldiers killed in battle; historical figures; there were even child and baby heroes, some with a specialised function, such as healers. There were hero cults for women, too, such as young women who sacrificed their lives to save a city at war. Often, these hero cults were localised and linked to the grave of the hero or heroine, but mythical heroes such as Achilles, Odysseus and particularly Herakles had a wider cult across much of Greece.

From the fourth century BCE on, however, there was a practice in many parts of the Greek world to depict the ordinary dead as heroes, and for their living relatives to establish a hero cult complete with a priesthood to service and maintain it. Despite this, real heroes could still be publicly glorified in different ways. The annual public burials of the Greek war dead in collective tombs in the Kerameikos, the ancient cemetery of Athens, were important political occasions, and the funeral orations both celebrated the memory of the dead and explicitly proclaimed the immortality of the city through their deaths. The Athenian statesman Pericles gave the most famous of all war orations in 431 BCE, connecting the greatness of Athens to the dead heroes:

... for the Athens that I have celebrated is only what the

heroism of these and their like have made her...[13]

These ideas have proved remarkably enduring and influential, adapted, consciously or unconsciously, particularly by those familiar with the Greek originals. The Greek tradition is echoed to this day in the ways we remember our heroes, in the annual ceremonies of Remembrance Day and similar national days of mourning. Laurence Binyon's poem, 'For the Fallen', regularly recited at these memorial events, similarly links patriotism, the heroic dead and remembrance, an association with ancient Greek funeral orations which would not have been lost on Binyon, an Oxford classics graduate:

> With proud thanksgiving, a mother for her children,
> England mourns for her dead across the sea...
>
> They shall grow not old, as we that are left grow old:
> Age shall not weary them, nor the years condemn.
> At the going down of the sun and in the morning
> We will remember them.[14]

Similarly, this link between patriotism and immortality was arguably central to the rise of the modern nation state in the nineteenth century. The German philosopher Johann Gottlieb Fichte (1762-1814) wrote his *Addresses to the German Nation* between 1807 and 1808 to support the resistance against Napoleon at a time when Berlin was under French occupation, and helped shape the idea of a unique German national identity. Fichte had a thorough knowledge of the classics and, like the ancient Greek orators, he connected the heroic war dead to the immortality of the nation and the importance of handing this posterity on to one's children. Gregory Moore has summed up Fichte's concept of the nation:

... the nation, like religion, answers a basic human need: the desire for transcendence, for eternity... Through the nation we can achieve immortality; it is the kingdom of heaven on earth.[15]

'History remembers kings, not soldiers'[16]

Who writes history, and who is recorded by it? According to the sociologist Zygmunt Bauman, immortality is about 'making history', about being *made* immortal through being recorded. It's all very well living a life less ordinary, being somehow distinguished by standing out from the crowd, but if there is no one to record these deeds then they will not be immortalised. Even when these histories are written down, we have no idea how durable or transient the recorded 'famous' deeds will be. Gilgamesh is only famous again today because of the accident of archaeological discovery in the nineteenth century, otherwise he would have been forgotten by the first century CE.

In the pre-modern world, the only people who had the resources to have their deeds recorded and recounted for posterity were the kings, law-givers, generals and popes who 'made history':

To assure princes and generals and prime ministers of their immortality, history must be first written in terms of dynasties, battles and legislative acts. Future immortality will grow out of today's recordings. Tomorrow's immortals must first get hold of today's archives.[17]

Those future immortals have always relied on scribes to tell their story, to record, amplify and sometimes fabricate their deeds of glory. From earliest times, rulers had themselves portrayed as all-powerful and all-conquering, with an eye to both their contemporaries and to posterity. In ancient Egypt, where reading and writing were the domain of professional scribes and most of the population was illiterate, the effect was achieved mostly through representations in sculpture and relief, usually though not always with accompanying text. One of the earliest known depictions of the Egyptian king is on the Narmer Palette, dating to c. 3000 BCE, now in the Egyptian Museum in Cairo. This shows a crowned figure smiting a foreigner on one side, and on the other taking part in a possible victory procession towards decapitated prisoners. It is now thought that this does not depict a particular or even any military campaign, but is a metaphor for the role of the Egyptian king.

This metaphor reappears later on with the traditional enemies of Egypt, referred to as the Nine Bows, who were represented either as rows of bows or of bound captives. They regularly decorated bases of thrones or footstools, so that the pharaoh was seen symbolically treading his enemies underfoot. These depictions are not to be interpreted as historical documents. They represented, instead, a key symbolic and cosmic function of the pharaoh. The pharaoh's job was to maintain harmony and order in Egypt, and an important part of that was to protect it from its enemies. The pharaoh was therefore constantly depicted – *had* to be depicted – as defeating the enemies of Egypt, irrespective of whether or not he actually defeated them in practice. In that sense, it did not matter what the pharaoh did: the depictions, for his contemporary audience and for posterity, concerned his wider role, not his specific actions.

This becomes even clearer in the accounts of the battle of Qadesh in c. 1274 BCE, the first major conflict in the ancient world to be depicted in detail. There are 13 surviving accounts of the battle, on papyri and on temple walls in Egypt and Nubia, written as poems, bulletins and captions to sculptural reliefs. The battle took place at Qadesh in northern Syria, between the Egyptian pharaoh Ramesses II and the Hittites. In the accounts of Ramesses II's campaigns, he is always called 'victorious': every foreign country 'trembles' before him, their chiefs present tribute, and rebels bow down before him. In reality, this was not necessarily the case.

At Qadesh, Ramesses II is described as being surrounded by the Hittites. He charges the enemy from his chariot, kills vast numbers and fights his way out after being deserted by all of his troops. He is depicted as a superhero. It is impossible to know how much of this actually happened as described, as the whole account of the battle is extremely euphemistic. It is quite clear from the outcome that he did not win a victory – at best, the result was a stalemate. But, in the ancient Egyptian worldview, that was not the point: the task of the scribes and artists was not to portray mundane facts but the deeper reality of Ramesses II – indeed, of any pharaoh – as the superhuman, godlike protector of Egypt, always victorious. Otherwise, there would be chaos.

Although the Assyrians did not have quite as developed an understanding of the cosmic role of their kings as their Egyptian neighbours, we see a similar process of the glorification of Assyrian kings by scribes and artists. The activities of Assyrian kings, mostly concerning their military campaigns, were depicted in reliefs on palace walls, with captions in cuneiform script, and described in detail in the annals, which were the narratives of royal exploits, written on clay tablets and prisms. These were created to glorify the god Ashur and his regent, the Assyrian king, and so, as in Egypt, they never present reverses or defeats.

The Assyrian royal annals were being constantly edited by scribes to make way for new information, and it is in the process of editing that the king's personal role is gradually amplified. One example of this editing and amplifying process are the accounts of the Assyrian king Ashurbanipal's war against Arab tribes in c. 660 BCE – the same king whose scribes copied out the standard version of the epic of Gilgamesh. The earliest edition of the annals records that the king of Qedar, a powerful confederation of Arab tribes, was captured by the king of Moab, an Assyrian vassal. A later edition no longer ascribes the capture to an individual, but to the collective kings of Syria. In his own Letter to Ashur, Ashurbanipal claims he captured the Qedarite king himself. This letter was addressed to the god Ashur, to the people of Ashur and to the city itself. If, as has been suggested, the letter was read aloud during a public victory ceremony, his claim would enhance his role and reputation as the all-conquering king.

This process is not unusual in the Assyrian annals, and shows how, in succeeding editions, the original agent of the victory becomes less individual and eventually his actions are attributed to the Assyrian king himself, who was not always present, but on whose behalf and in whose name the actions were performed. In the same way, the Assyrian king is always shown leading the battle on palace reliefs, whether or not he was there. The important fact for the Assyrian scribes and artists, as for their Egyptian counterparts, was that the Assyrian king defeated his enemies; the means mattered less. So it is the king who is glorified and 'makes history', not the actual actors in the events.

The Egyptian and Assyrian kings laid the groundwork for all future rulers who had an eye to their contemporaries as well as to posterity, history and immortality: the lesson that words speak louder than actions. To control the narrative you must control (and have access to) the scribe. But the ultimate model for rulers seeking immortality through the written word was created a few centuries later by the Roman emperor Augustus: no one ever did it better.

Octavian (63 BCE-14 CE), who took the name Augustus in 27 BCE, understood the importance of the arts for the purposes of both propaganda and the acknowledgment of future generations. The Romans regarded poets as immortalisers. Most poets of the time relied on patronage in order to make a living, although as their social status rose they became less reliant economically on that patronage. What the patron got from the poet was not merely perpetuation of their fame and glory, but what the Romans greatly valued as *memoria sempiterna*, 'being remembered for ever'. Accordingly, Augustus was a great patron of writers and poets, initially alongside his advisor Gaius Cilnius Maecenas (68-8 BCE), whose name has become the eponym for a patron of the arts.

According to Sextus Propertius (c. 50/45-15 BCE), another of the many poets patronised by Augustus and Maecenas, the emperor specifically commissioned the *Aeneid* from Virgil, who had a track record of praising him in earlier poems. We also know that Maecenas tried to persuade Virgil and other poets to write an epic on Augustus in order to immortalise his heroic deeds and, through him, the Augustan state, its policies and its image.

Virgil's purpose in the *Aeneid* was to produce a mythological work about the origins of Rome, linking the city and Augustus himself to the Trojans. The legend of Rome's Trojan origins had been known earlier, but Virgil expanded it into a foundational epic. The story follows the adventures of Aeneas, who is entrusted with transporting the House of Troy from one land to another at the end of the Trojan War, carrying the ancestral gods of his family to a new home. He becomes the mythical founder of Rome, and Virgil made Augustus his direct descendant, providing the emperor with a glorious ancestry. In the historian Jasper Griffin's words, the *Aeneid* presented the history of Rome as a 'crescendo' leading up to Augustus, a thousand years after the Trojan War.[18]

Augustus appears on several occasions in the *Aeneid*, the first time when Jupiter prophesies that Aeneas' direct descendant will conquer the world and bring peace:

From that noble blood will arise a Trojan Caesar.[19]

Later, when Aeneas visits the underworld (see Chapter 3), Augustus appears as the bringer of a golden age in the pageant of the spirits of great future Romans, most of whom are of his own family, the Julians. It is therefore largely a procession of Aeneas' heroic descendants, culminating in Augustus:

Here is the man, he's here! ... Caesar Augustus!
Son of a god, he will bring back the Age of Gold.[20]

Augustus is also represented in Book 8 on the shield forged for Aeneas by the smith-god, Vulcan, portraying his defeat of Antony and Cleopatra at Actium and his subsequent triumph at Rome, with all the defeated moving slowly in front of him, reminiscent of the earlier depictions of Egyptian and Assyrian kings on reliefs.

Unsurprisingly, Augustus was deeply interested in how Virgil was getting on with his commission, and impatiently followed the progress of the *Aeneid*; Virgil even read portions of it to him. Virgil did not manage to finish it before his death and, loath to leave behind an incomplete work, he even asked his friends to burn it. But this wish was countermanded by Augustus. The emperor's support of the project brought its hoped for rewards both in his lifetime and for posterity, as the *Aeneid* was not only very popular in antiquity but it became influential too, used as an oracle and consulted in temples. Random passages from the *Aeneid* were picked to foretell the future in this Virgilian lottery, the *Sortes Virgilianae*, a practice which continued into the Middle Ages, reminiscent of tarot cards which largely superseded it. Rulers from Hadrian to Charles I consulted the *Aeneid* to learn of their futures.

Nevertheless, scholars are divided on whether the *Aeneid* celebrates Augustus or subtly subverts him, although on balance its message seems to be that Augustus, and Rome in general, will impose peace and civilisation on a barbaric world. Virgil was certainly very successful in keeping Augustus happy. Others were not so fortunate.

Virgil's contemporary, Ovid (Publius Ovidius Naso, 43 BCE-17 CE), was an irreverent poet with a tendency to parody his varied targets. His irreverence was also aimed at Augustus, although in his *Metamorphoses* he took great care to lavish flattery on the emperor. The book ends with the prediction that Rome will rise to become the greatest city in the world, with all lands and the sea under the sway of Augustus. All this praise, though, did not prevent Augustus from expelling Ovid from Rome, possibly for suggesting adultery in his poetry at a time when Augustus had made it criminal, and he died in exile.[21]

Augustus had created what amounted to a template for the ruler-as-patron seeking immortality through art: a system of reward and punishment to ensure the loyalty of writers, consisting of financial support, including bestowal of land and property, balanced by the threat of exile and confiscation of property. He was not a man to get on the wrong side of: he had a reputation for ruthlessly executing political opponents, and had systematically tracked down every one of the conspirators against his adoptive father, Julius Caesar. And yet, even though his reputation has waxed and waned, in general Augustus is now regarded as the man who brought peace and security to Rome. His system worked well for him.

In many ways, Augustus was the most dominant leader the world has ever seen, and his system of patronising and controlling artists to glorify and immortalise him is essentially that used by many future authoritarian rulers, including the Medicis and Sforzas in Renaissance Italy and the Sun King Louis XIV in France. Classical scholars have even been tempted to cite similarities between him and more recent totalitarian leaders such as Stalin, though usually in Augustus' favour:

Augustus killed a lot of people, but he inflicted on the world nothing like the misery of a Hitler or a Stalin.[22]

There are certainly parallels in the ways both Augustus and Stalin ruthlessly secured power, ruled with absolute personal authority over a long period, were treated as gods in their lifetimes, and demanded glorification from the artists they supported to create and maintain their image. In both cases, this became a cult of personality.

Under Stalin, writers were not allowed to be politically neutral. They were required to lavish inordinate praise on Stalin as a wise leader and symbol of freedom and national pride, and on the victorious onward march of Stalinist industrial and agricultural policies. Optimism about everything Soviet was compulsory; Stalin's world had to be portrayed as the best of all possible worlds. This is all reminiscent of Virgil's and Ovid's praise of the climax of Roman civilisation and peace under Augustus, and of the symbolic depictions of Egyptian pharaohs as all-conquering maintainers of harmony and order against the forces of chaos.[23]

Something very similar to the Augustan system of rewards and punishments for poets was in operation in the Soviet Union under Stalin; while still dependent on the whim of Stalin and often random, as under Augustus, the system and its punitive measures had become bureaucratised and certainly more extreme. The incentives for conformist Soviet writers consisted of publication of their works, fees, housing, medical care, travel, privileged shopping, access to country cottages (dachas), and lucrative literary prizes. The punishments for the non-conformists who did not praise Stalin and the Soviet system ranged from taking away their livelihood and material welfare, psychological warfare and criminal proceedings, to exile and death.

Officially sanctioned criticism of Stalin only started to appear after his death, which brings us full circle to the *Aeneid* with the bizarre parody of Aeneas' journey to the underworld in Aleksandr Tvardovsky's poem 'Tyorkin in the Other World' –

perhaps to be considered as an addendum to the journeys to the underworld in Chapter 3.[24] Tvardovsky (1910-1971) began this poem immediately after Stalin's death as an outspoken satire of the Stalinist era. The hero, like Aeneas, visits the underworld, and finds that it is similar to life under Stalin. All the elements of Stalinist life are present in this hell: an elaborate security police, absurd bureaucracy and red tape, spirits of victims of concentration camps, and even unsmokeable tobacco. The poem was first recited in 1963 on the orders of Nikita Khrushchev, Stalin's successor, and was part of the post-Stalin on-off liberalisation. It was the sort of work that would have been completely unacceptable under Stalin.

From ancestor cults to the cult of the celebrity
While the pharaohs, Augustuses and Stalins of the world had the resources to be immortalised and 'make history', what about ordinary people? Not everyone can be a hero whose deeds reverberate down the centuries. Bauman claims that rulers' biographies become history, while the lives of ordinary mortals become depersonalised statistics,[25] but this has never been entirely true. Although they may not have been able to 'make history' while they were alive, from earliest times even the ordinary dead were commemorated with a view to being remembered by future generations.

There is widespread evidence from ancient Mediterranean societies of the commemoration of family ancestors, especially in the home. Admittedly, this mostly concerned dead parents and grandparents, that is, people within living memory who could be remembered and identified by name. Like those in animist societies (see Chapter 5), such ancestors were often a source of guidance and custodians of traditions, and were believed to be responsible for fertility and health – or the lack of it – in crops, animals and people.

A good example is the commemoration of the dead in ancient

Ugarit on the Syrian coast between the fourteenth and twelfth centuries BCE. Rituals and commemorative cults sustained the memory of the deceased in the minds of the living. But there was a public element to this. The names of the dead were recited publicly, which perpetuated the deceased's memory and the maintenance of their genealogical ties with living family ancestors. This type of commemoration ensured that one's names and deeds were not forgotten. When performed publicly and on family property, these rituals were also an important element in legitimising the living's claims to birthright and land ownership.

Similar considerations were at play in later Greek burials, which tended to be family affairs, using family plots in extramural cemeteries. As at Ugarit, there was a considerable interest in inheritance, and often the person organising the burial was regarded as the heir.

A rather different function was performed by ancient Egyptian stelae – commemorative tablets of stone or wood. These were inscribed with the name and titles of the dead person, and depicted the deceased seated before an offering table. They were usually set up near the front of the tomb in a place accessible to the living, so that they could leave offerings. Although stelae preserved the name of the deceased, this was not so much about commemoration and remembrance, as in the ancient Near East and Greece or on modern gravestones, but more about true immortality, preserving the name and likeness of the deceased so that they would magically survive into the afterlife (see Chapter 1). It was extremely important that the name be preserved. For a name to be lost – or, worse still, to be deliberately defaced and obliterated – was tantamount to the destruction of the memory and entire existence of the dead person.

The later memorials to the Roman dead were about a different kind of immortality, and about more than family. Sarcophagi and tombstones were deliberately accessible to the wider public and passers-by, who were expected and encouraged to read aloud the texts which recorded the good deeds and fine reputation of the deceased. Occasionally, these memorials ask a traveller to stop and read what is written:

Friend, I have not much to say: stop and read it.

There follows a description of the virtues of the deceased, and at the end:

That is all. You may go.[26]

In this way the Romans, like the Greeks, hoped to be remembered in perpetuity after death, by strangers as well as family. The Roman dead did not become ancestors who fulfilled a role among the living, as those in Chapter 5: this was about commemoration through durable memorials, just as the Roman poets immortalised their wealthy patrons through their verses.

As Philippe Ariès has demonstrated, from the Middle Ages until the eighteenth century, in the West, cemeteries were located in the middle of population centres or near family homes, and so, like the Romans, the living were in constant contact with the dead.[27] Death was thus 'tamed' and 'domesticated', treated with equanimity as a normal part of everyday life. The incorporation of inscriptions on gravestones did not become widespread until the end of the eighteenth century. In the Christian world, the epitaphs on gravestones were far less expansive and informative than their Roman predecessors, usually recording no more than the deceased's name, dates, relationships, and perhaps a brief religious or sentimental quote. The vast majority of these dead did not 'make history', but equally, through being integrated into the daily life of their communities, they were not completely forgotten.

From the early nineteenth century, in the West, cemeteries

were deliberately located outside towns and cities, away from centres of population. As a result, the dead, with their brief epitaphs, were no longer part of everyday life. Remembrance of the dead as an everyday occurrence has instead been taken over by the phenomenon of memorial benches, which are found in public places, parks and along woodland walks. These include dedications to the deceased, who usually had a special connection with that location. The oldest extant memorial bench may be at Osborne House on the Isle of Wight, dated to 1883 and dedicated to John Brown, an attendant to Queen Victoria, but it is possible that there were earlier ones which have not survived. In a way, these memorial benches return to the spirit of the Roman epitaphs by calling on the attention of passers-by and strangers to remember the dead.

Bauman has observed that, in modern times, being recorded, and having one's name and deeds preserved, is no longer limited to the chosen few among the rulers and heroes. Immortality has now been deconstructed into fame, public attention and celebrity. We have our modern equivalent of the ancient heroes:

> ... 'history is made' by footballers, tennis-players, pop-singers, murderers, painters, wine-growers, inventors, film actors, scientists.[28]

Their immortality is formally recognised and secured by Olympic medals and Nobel prizes, or more mundanely by appearances in popular soap operas and reality shows and being the subject of gossip in celebrity magazines. They too have their modern equivalents of the ancient scribes recording their deeds: the publicity, marketing, sports, literary and show business agents.

And yet, of course, immortality as fame is nothing new: it was always about fame, as Gilgamesh and Achilles would testify. The difference today is that heroic deeds are no longer a requirement of fame, and the mechanisms to achieve that fame are more easily accessible. Communications technology now allows ordinary people equal opportunity to achieve fame, celebrity or notoriety. But the ordinary person no longer requires an intermediary to make them famous, or a celebrity, or notorious: they do not need a scribe, a poet, a surviving child, or a publicist to commemorate them. Social media – Twitter, Facebook, Instagram, YouTube or whatever the current trend is – allows you to do it on your own. You can never predict what achievement (or non-achievement) will 'go viral' and make you famous – 'a celebrity' – and no longer anonymous. Although Bauman was writing before the social media explosion, his words are prescient:

> It is not the great deeds which are immortalized; the deeds become great the moment they are 'immortalized' by having been forced – for a brief, elusive, but never fully erasable moment – into the centre of public attention.[29]

Today's technology provides an improved and more equitable mechanism for memorialisation. Anyone can now memorialise and commemorate themselves through social media. The messages are not so different from those on Roman epitaphs or the public reciting of the names of the dead at Ugarit: they usually depict an idealised form of our real selves, they keep us in people's minds, but now we can write them ourselves without the bother of first having to be dead.

While the ancient heroes and rulers became immortal through being memorialised in epics and on public monuments, ordinary people in antiquity had their own more modest strategies to commemorate and immortalise their dead. In modern times, becoming immortalised has become different, easier, and accessible to anyone. The pursuit of immortality through fame is just as important today as it was for Gilgamesh and Achilles, but you no longer have to be a hero.

Part 4

Reflections on Immortality

Chapter 8

Science and philosophy v. immortality

*'You see,' Max explained as he pumped, 'there's different kinds of
dead: there's sort of dead, mostly dead, and all dead.'*
– William Goldman, *The Princess Bride*

This chapter considers what modern science and philosophy have
to say about the different forms of immortality covered in Parts
1 and 2 of this book.[1] By 'modern science' is meant materialism,
the prevailing scientific and philosophical orthodoxy: the theory
that matter alone exists, which implies a denial of anything non-
material, including minds, souls, spirits and divine beings (see
longer definition at the end of Chapter 2).

To a large extent, therefore, immortality and materialist
science are essentially incompatible worldviews, and most
scientists and philosophers discount all types of immortality
other than through fame (to which they themselves are not
immune). For materialist science, there can be no immortality:
the death of a human being is the end of the human being. It
is absolute nothingness, an existence without thought, the
end of consciousness and of all experience. As we will see, the
materialist argument against immortality often comes down
to one key point: the contention that all consciousness and
experience are dependent on the material brain, which excludes
the existence of a soul or spirit that can survive independently.

The chapter explores the ways scientific and philosophical
arguments are used to discount all the possible states
of immortality in turn: resurrection, the immortal soul,
reincarnation, and animistic transformation. For each form of
immortality, the key scientific and philosophical critiques are
provided, followed by a brief rejoinder on behalf of the defenders

of that immortality. In order to provide balance, we then apply a similar critique to materialist science itself, especially its key claim concerning the dependence of the mind on the brain, and to explore if it provides a convincing alternative explanation for what drives human beings – in the absence of a soul or spirit – and what happens to them at death.

The purpose of this chapter is not to prove one view over another, or to discount any of them, but to demonstrate that there is genuine uncertainty and debate, even among scientists, and that each view, including the materialist one, falls very far short of proof and has serious explanatory gaps.

The case against resurrection

The scientific and philosophical critiques acknowledge that resurrection, along with its contingent concepts of heaven and hell, require the existence of a supreme being – God – to work. Some scientists and philosophers believe in God, and some do not. Their critiques are not concerned with whether or not God exists, but essentially highlight the difficulties that God would have in physically resurrecting humans on the day of judgment and ensuring that their resurrected selves were identical with their selves while alive.

The four key objections to resurrection are largely philosophical rather than based on scientific evidence, and most of them are centuries old, having been argued by opponents of Christianity right from its beginnings two millennia ago. They are usually referred to by some variant of the following names: the Age Problem, the Interregnum Problem, the Cannibal Problem and the Replica Problem.

The Age Problem: What age are people when they are resurrected? If they were very old when they died, do they revert to middle age after death – and, if so, do they continue to have the consciousness, experiences and memories accumulated in old age, or do they lose those memories and character

222

development? Thomas Aquinas (see Chapter 2), in the thirteenth century CE, had maintained that the resurrected person would be transformed so that they were in their prime, assumed to be around 30 years of age. Modern philosophers argue that such a transformation is not, strictly speaking, a resurrection, but a replica or a copy of an earlier version of that person.

Similarly, what happens to an infant who died suddenly before becoming mature, or an aborted foetus – what form of resurrected person will they be in heaven (or hell)? Do they in fact continue to grow and mature in heaven until they reach their 'prime'? In the late fourth and early fifth centuries CE, Augustine had proposed that children who died young would be transformed by God into adults after resurrection. But this creates a problem. A child develops into an adult through a series of experiences and interactions with other people. How can these experiences and interactions be bypassed to create a mature, resurrected adult?

An analogous point concerns how people recognise each other in heaven or hell. As we saw in Chapter 3, the more modern versions of heaven are based on friends and family in a perfected version of life on earth. If the resurrected person is so transformed, how will infants, children, parents and grandparents recognise each other, especially if they are all in an artificial 'prime'?

The Interregnum Problem: Many – though not all – religious doctrines concerning resurrection believe that there is a gap between the moment of death and resurrection. If all the dead are to be resurrected together on the day of judgment, some time in the future, then what happens to them in the meantime? In particular, what happens to their minds? Scientists and philosophers, who equate the mind with the physical brain, point out that there is a problem with explaining exactly how a disembodied mind survives years, centuries or millennia in the grave where the brain has turned to dust. Of course, this interregnum problem does not arise for those who believe that resurrection occurs immediately after death, or that, as Aquinas maintained, the soul goes straight to heaven or hell after death and is reunited with the physical body on the day of judgment (although see below for objections to the immortal soul).

The Cannibal Problem: If John eats Mark, as a result the body parts of Mark physically become an integral part of John. How can God then separate the particles within John that originally belonged to Mark while still leaving John complete, and resurrect both John and Mark whole and unchanged on the day of judgment? Or, if we assume hypothetically that animals too might be resurrected – and some modern versions of heaven contain pets – then the animals that human meat-eaters consume become part of them: how can God then reassemble and resurrect the whole of the original animal, which has become fully integrated into one or several of the human beings who ate it, each of whom also has hopes of being resurrected whole? The French writer and philosopher Voltaire (1694-1778), a witty polemicist and satirist who derided and caricatured the idea of resurrection in his various writings, liked to take the Cannibal Problem to its limits:

> A soldier from Brittany goes into Canada; there, by a very common chance, he finds himself short of food, and is forced to eat an Iroquois whom he killed the day before. This Iroquois had fed on Jesuits for two or three months; a great part of his body had become Jesuit. Here, then, the body of a soldier is composed of Iroquois, of Jesuits, and of all that he had eaten before. How is each to take again precisely what belongs to him? And which part belongs to each?[2]

The Replica Problem: Many Christian proponents of resurrection have argued that the process does not involve the actual resuscitation of corpses, but the creation of an exact replica of the dead body: God's re-creation or reconstitution of the human individual, essentially Paul's 'spiritual body' (see Chapter 1). In this way, resurrection can even occur if the original body has been completely destroyed (and therefore overcomes both the Interregnum and Cannibal Problems above). But this solution creates further problems: is the resurrected replica identical to the pre-mortem individual – are you identical with your future resurrected self? – and is this replication any sort of resurrection at all? Some philosophers also argue on moral grounds that, if either heaven or hell are to be the destiny of the resurrected replica, then to reward or punish a replica for the virtues or sins of the original is unfair and unethical.

The Replica Problem has spawned the related Duplication Problem, which is a prime example of an objection that is little more than a philosophical puzzle, created by philosophers for other philosophers as a theoretical game. The Duplication Problem proposes that, in theory, God has the ability to resurrect more than one version of the same human being, an older and a younger version. Which version would then be the 'real' person, identical with their living self? This is a problem for philosophers because it breaches the law of logic by allowing, in principle at least, multiple versions of the same person to exist at the same time. Philosophers cannot resist imaginative and often bizarre flights of fancy on this problem, such as Edwards' imagined replica of a great singer appearing on stage with the real singer, or Cave's fictional malfunctioning 'future immortality factory', which accidentally creates a replica of a person named Frank while he is still alive, or alternatively produces multiple replicas of him after his death, all of whom believe they are Frank.[3] But these are puzzles just for philosophers: one would sincerely hope that a supreme, omnipotent being would be omnipotent enough to avoid such a logical disaster.

Brief rejoinder: The usual response to these scientific and philosophical objections is that a supreme being – an omnipotent creator God – would be capable of solving the problems: for example, addressing the Cannibal Problem, that God has the power to collect all the particles of the consumed body and reassemble them. Many often cite Paul's statement in 1 Corinthians 15 on the 'spiritual body', pointing out that the expectation of some kind of a transformation from a mortal body to an immortal one has been an integral part of the belief in resurrection right from the beginning of Christianity. The concept of time has also been challenged, originally by Augustine and Aquinas: everyday time is a human construct, but post-mortem existence (including heaven and hell) is outside of time and therefore the same rules about the passage of time do not apply.

But there are also some extremely creative and fanciful theories that try to deny that human bodies decay after death, claiming that they are fakes put there by God while our real ones are stored elsewhere in preparation for the day of judgment. Unsurprisingly, these are not generally accepted even by most proponents of resurrection.

The case against the soul

The belief that a human being is a composite of a physical body and an immaterial soul that will continue to exist after death is a form of philosophical dualism. As we saw in Chapter 2, the Greek philosophers Democritus and Epicurus had already challenged Plato's dualist view of the body and soul, and believed that the mind as well as the body consisted of atoms. They were the forerunners of today's materialists who conclude that dualism is false and that there is no soul and therefore no prospect of its survival after death.

Some of the objections to the soul are relatively straightforward questions. Where was the soul before the body was born, and what happens to it when the body dies? Does it have its own memory and does it remember anything and, if so, where is this memory located since it is immaterial? If the soul is immaterial, how can it sense anything? These points were already made by the Roman philosopher Lucretius in the first century BCE:

> Besides, if the soul's nature is immortal, and can have sensation, sundered from the body, then we must, I think, suppose it furnished with five senses; and in this way only can we picture to ourselves the souls below roaming in Acheron. And so the painters and the writers of past times have introduced souls thus equipped with senses. But by themselves souls can have neither eyes, nor nose, nor tongue, nor even hands, nor can the ears exist and have the sense of hearing by themselves (in soul apart from body) ... Besides, if the soul's nature is immortal, and finds entrance to the body at our birth, why can we not remember bygone time as well as present?[4]

There are four key scientific or empirical objections: the failure to locate the soul, the Causal Interaction Problem, the Neural Dependency Problem, and, most crucially, the dependence of the mind on the brain.

Failure to locate the soul: Although dualists define the soul as immaterial, there have been many attempts to find it or at least locate it within the body. In the seventeenth century, Descartes believed that the soul was related to the pineal gland in the brain: willing an action led to movement of the pineal gland which produced additional movements and eventually caused the relevant limbs to move. His suggestion has since been disproved, as it is possible to remove the pineal gland entirely without any effect on mental functioning.

More recently, the Nobel prize-winning neurophysiologist Sir John Eccles (1903-1997) proposed that the interaction between the soul (or mind – for him, as for Descartes, they were the same thing) and the brain occurred only in the cerebral cortex, with the firing of neurons as a result of electricity. Although it has since been proved that such transmissions are chemical, not electrical, Eccles stuck to his dualist position on the interaction of soul/mind and brain to the end of his life.

In 1907, an American doctor, Duncan MacDougall, in a now notorious experiment, claimed that souls have physical weight. He placed the beds of six of his terminally ill patients on extremely sensitive scales to record if, as they died, there was a loss of weight. Only one of his patients lost weight – 21.3 grams – coinciding with the moment of death, which MacDougall attributed to the soul leaving the body. The experiment was rejected by scientists due to the small sample size, that a clear result was found in only one of six patients while he ignored the other results, and that there were other explanations for any loss of weight. The *New York Times* reported in 1911 that MacDougall hoped to carry out experiments to photograph souls, but apparently he did not get around to it before his death in 1920.

Nevertheless, his experiment popularised the notion that the soul has weight and prompted renewed speculation concerning when it leaves the body. In 1957, Pope Pius XII addressed an international congress of anaesthetists about the medical and moral problems of resuscitating patients. He expressed concern regarding the exact moment at which, in the intensive care unit, the soul actually leaves the body: clearly, he was worried about resuscitating patients whose soul had already departed and was winging its way to heaven. Scientists have since failed to locate the soul in the body, and, as we shall see below, have concluded that they will never locate it because it is not there, and that human beings function perfectly well without one.

The Causal Interaction Problem: How can an immaterial soul cause a physical body to do something? Most scientists accept that the physical world is causally closed: that is, only physical events can cause other physical events. For example, if you want to raise your arm, your arm goes up. The movement is caused by neurons in the brain firing and sending nerve signals to your arm: this is all physical and unconnected with an immaterial soul. Scientists argue that one cannot explain the movements of a human body in terms of a soul's purposeful action: an immaterial soul wishing to do something cannot activate neurons or move muscles.

The Neural Dependency Problem: If the soul is separate from the body, and is responsible for reasoning, emotion, values and purposes, why is the mental almost completely dependent on the physical?

> If there really is a distinct entity in which reasoning, emotion, and consciousness take place, and if that entity is dependent on the brain for nothing more than sensory experiences as input and volitional executions as output, then one would expect reason, emotion, and consciousness to be relatively invulnerable to direct control or pathology by manipulation or damage to the brain.[5]

Yet the opposite is true. Our awareness of the world is affected by damage to, or manipulation of, the brain, for example by physical force, chemicals, or the effects of ageing. Brain damage can cause loss of memory and a change in personality: how can this happen if our soul is the seat of our personality and holds all our memories? If there is a soul, and it can be so seriously affected by damage to the brain, then how could it survive the trauma of the physical death of the brain? Even if it does survive, it is likely that the personality of the dead individual would be completely changed. The only plausible explanation, scientists suggest, is that all mental phenomena, conscious or unconscious, are actually physical and are caused not by an immaterial soul but by processes going on in the brain. This is the core of the next, and most serious, objection.

Dependence of the mind on the brain: This objection is very simple:

what some people regard as the workings of an immaterial soul or mind are in fact the workings of the physical brain. Current neuroscience research associates more and more of the faculties once attributed to a soul or mind – such as thoughts, consciousness and emotions – with the functions of specific regions or systems of the brain, and concludes that the brain itself performs these functions. Research correlates localised brain activity with the performance of specialised cognitive and physical tasks, such as language in the left hemisphere, memory in the hippocampus, or equilibrium and coordination in the cerebellum. This leaves no room for the soul or any argument for its existence, since the supposed job of the immaterial soul is being done by the physical brain. Everything that we regard as our mental life is actually caused by the physical brain and neurons. The brain is not immortal, and eventually dies. At that point, all mental life, consciousness and experience cease.

There are other more philosophical and conceptual objections, mostly based on arguments about the primary importance of the physical body in determining personal identity, humanity and being distinguished from others: for example, how might one identify disembodied souls in the next life with human beings who once lived on earth? According to these arguments, only continuity of bodily identity is a secure foundation of personal identity, rather than mental continuity, since memories can be false and unreliable.[6]

Brief rejoinder: Although Plato's notion of the soul did not involve a supreme creator being, most contemporary understandings of the soul, in Christianity, Judaism and Islam, believe that the immaterial soul is created by God. Since God is believed to be omnipotent, it is argued that He/She has the power to create a soul that is immaterial, incapable of being detected and measured, and yet contains the mind, identity and memories of an individual human being and can interact with the physical body in ways undiscoverable by science. Clearly, such a response is not satisfactory to materialists or atheists.

The most serious objection, that the mind is totally dependent on the brain, is countered by the argument that the mind is not *identical* with the brain, merely that mental events are *correlated* with events in particular regions of the brain. Correlation is not the same as identity, and there is no evidence to exclude that any causal action willed by the soul takes place, physically, through the brain – hence the near total dependence of mental processes upon bodily processes – but it is not, ultimately, caused by the brain. Dualists reject the assumption that the physical world is causally closed, an assumption for which there is no proof. They argue that there is nothing in the nature of neurons, or other physical entities, which means they can only be moved by other physical entities – nothing that excludes that they can be moved by an immaterial soul making a choice. Returning to the example of moving an arm, cited above, it is your soul that causes your arm to move by causing neural events in a part of the brain which ultimately lead to the movements of the limb. Thus the movement is purposeful, not reflexive. Below, when we consider objections to materialist science, we will also encounter the argument that only a soul can provide reasons or purposes, otherwise any movement is caused by a random firing of neurons.

The case against reincarnation

The most comprehensive critique of reincarnation by a materialist philosopher is *Reincarnation: A Critical Examination*, by Paul Edwards, published in 2002. This section largely draws from that work, partly because Edwards has both a systematic approach to evaluating reincarnation, but also a very personal bias informed by his utter faith in materialism. Edwards' approach is to examine the evidence for reincarnation, argue that it is worthless, and offer reasons for rejecting it. His arguments are a mixture of empirical evidence and more philosophical arguments. The objections can be divided into general ones about reincarnation as a whole, and specific ones evaluating the evidence of individual cases. There are seven general objections: the Age Problem, the Problem of Evolution and the Recency of Life, the Population Problem, the Absence of Memories, the Interregnum Problem, the *Modus Operandi* problem, and the dependence of the mind on the brain.

The Age Problem: A different version of the age problem than the one cited above under resurrection, Edwards calls this problem Tertullian's Objection, as it was first stated by the Church father Tertullian in the early third century CE in his *Treatise on the Soul*. How is it possible for someone who dies in old age to be reincarnated as an infant, rather than at the age they had reached in their previous life? This objection to reincarnation argues that babies are not born with adult egos, as one might expect if they were direct continuations of dead adults.

The Problem of Evolution and the Recency of Life: Edwards claims that reincarnation is inconsistent with the theory of evolution. Many – though not all – forms of reincarnation are based on an infinite series of past incarnations in human bodies, whereas evolution is based on humans descending from non-humans at a time when humans did not exist. Moreover, materialist evolutionary theory argues that consciousness gradually developed along with the brain and nervous system, whereas reincarnation believes that there was no such development and the same soul, regarded as the seat of consciousness, has always migrated from body to body. Furthermore, life only emerged fairly recently in the history of the universe, whereas most forms of reincarnation believe in an infinite series of incarnations stretching back to the past without limit.

The Population Problem: This objection does not apply to all forms of reincarnation, but Edwards believes it to be conclusive. If all souls have always existed, and every birth is a rebirth with no new souls ever added to the world, then this rules out any population increase. Yet the facts are that the world's population is steadily growing. The two positions are therefore incompatible. Indeed, if, as in most Eastern forms of reincarnation, souls are eventually liberated from the cycle of birth, death and rebirth and merge with the infinite beyond death and life, then the expectation would be of a population decrease over time, rather than the increase that actually occurs.

The Absence of Memories: If reincarnation is a fact, we should remember our memories of past lives, but (mostly) we do not. This is an objection that dates back to the Roman philosopher Lucretius in the first century BCE. If person A is reborn as person B, but has no memories of person A, then Edwards argues that they are not the same person, since there is no sense of continuity or persisting personal identity. Of course, there are case studies of spontaneous memories of previous lives, and of memories brought to the surface through hypnosis, but Edwards dismisses such evidence as spurious and illusory.

The Interregnum Problem: This is a slightly different version of an interregnum problem than that cited above as an objection to resurrection. This one is concerned with what happens in the periods between incarnations. Most forms of reincarnation believe that there is an interval between the time of death and the beginning of life in a new body, an interval that Edwards calls the interregnum. The Tibetan Book of the Dead, the *Bardo thödol* (literally, 'liberation through hearing in the in-between state'), concerns descriptions and instructions about the intermediate state between death and rebirth, called *bardo*. The length of this interregnum varies across different beliefs in reincarnation: it can be six or seven days, 49 days (in Tibetan Buddhism), six months, a few years, a thousand years (in Plato), and a figure of ten thousand years has also been reported. Edwards asks:

... just where and how do people spend the interregnum and, more specifically, what are they like between incarnations?[7]

Edwards thinks there are just two possibilities: a disembodied or pure mind, and some sort of astral body. He questions whether statements about pure minds are intelligible and asks – much as with the Causal Interaction objection to the soul, cited above – how a pure mind, without sense organs, can find and choose its next incarnation. The astral body solution is the one preferred by most believers in reincarnation. An astral body is an exact duplicate of the human body, and is separated from it at death. This astral body can go anywhere instantaneously and pass through all material objects. It can see and hear, and contains a person's consciousness. Edwards raises problems with how the concept of an astral body might work in practice, such as querying why astral bodies are usually reported as clothed rather than naked, as one might expect; how astral and regular bodies and brains are synchronised with regard to memories and bodily changes; whether it can be identical with the person whose life it is supposed to continue; and that, if it is an exact duplicate of the regular body, it must, logically, die along with the regular body. He also calls on the lack of explanation concerning how a soul can enter the womb of a prospective mother to produce a new incarnation (though in a sense this is the *modus operandi* problem which we deal with below). In his view, such reincarnation claims about what he calls womb invasions are 'empirically vacuous',[8] on the grounds that he cannot find a scientific explanation or any evidence or proof that they actually occur.

Of course, there are people who have claimed detailed memories of their interregnum existence, often through hypnosis, but Edwards rejects any hypnotically obtained memories on the basis that they are unreliable and worthless as evidence. In his view, such interregnum memories are not genuine memories at all, but 'cultural artefacts', shaped by a person's worldview, education and religion.

The Modus Operandi *Problem*: This objection is essentially about practical, believable mechanisms of transmission from one incarnation to another. Evidence of reincarnation is often claimed on the basis that wounds, illnesses, birthmarks or special knowledge have been transmitted from the dead person to a child or embryo. The *modus operandi* objection is that there is no conceivable way in which such a transmission could take place:

> How are the scars picked up, how are they going to be stored for a period of varying length, and how are they going to be imprinted on the successor body?[9]

The *modus operandi* problem encompasses alleged telephone calls and tape recordings from the dead, which we encountered in Chapter 3: it is impossible to find a credible explanation for how they could have been transmitted by the dead. Edwards regards the *modus operandi* problem as fatal to the entire reincarnation theory, which he concludes is 'deluded' and an 'absurd nonsense'.[10] He extends the argument to God, arguing that God, if he exists, is a pure mind, and as such cannot interfere in the world – in this way responding to those believers in resurrection and the immortal soul who argue that God, as an omnipotent creator, can do and solve anything.

Dependence of the mind on the brain: This is, of course, the same objection as applied above to the existence of the soul, but extended to reject the astral or other duplicate body:

> If my mind is finished when my brain dies, then it cannot transmigrate to any other body. Similarly, if God created a duplicate of my body containing a duplicate of my brain, *my* mind would not be able to make use of it since it stopped existing with the death of my original body.[11]

For Edwards, this objection is the weightiest argument against reincarnation and all other forms of physical immortality: it rules out the survival of a disembodied mind, and rules out reincarnation altogether, because the mind depends for its survival on the physical and mortal brain.

Edwards also investigates individual cases of alleged reincarnation, and in general relies on four types of objection. Often, he resorts to two of the objections already cited – the *modus operandi* problem and the dependence of the mind on the brain – but he also cites proof of bad data in the cases recorded, and the possibility of alternative explanations other than reincarnation in other cases.

Proof of bad data: One of the most famous – and controversial – of all reincarnation cases is that of Bridey Murphy. It was also one of the earliest in which details of a past life were brought out through hypnosis, a technique called past life regression. In 1956, Morey Bernstein published his book *The Search for Bridey Murphy*, in which he reported on his hypnotic regression of a young American woman, later identified as Virginia Tighe, born in 1923. Under hypnosis, Virginia regressed to a past life in which she claimed to be an Irish woman, Bridey Murphy, who lived between 1798 and 1864 in County Cork in Ireland. She gave details of the people and places of this past life, spoke in a pronounced Irish accent, and was able to perform an Irish jig, despite being a poor dancer in her present life. Notoriously, the *Chicago American* newspaper attempted to discredit the story by reporting on Virginia's Irish aunt and the 'real' Bridey Murphy – Mrs Bridie Murphy Corkell – who lived across the street from Virginia, from both of whom it claimed Virginia could have learned all the facts of her alleged past life. Subsequent investigation revealed that the newspaper reporters had invented, or at least seriously distorted, most of these 'facts' which contradicted her story – an early instance of 'fake news'.

Edwards' own critique of the case is based on checking Bridey's memories against extant Irish records, which produced overwhelmingly negative results. Edwards lists all the key facts that Bridey claimed about her life, which are not corroborated in those records. He therefore rejects her recollections as having no evidential value. He concludes that this is a case of cryptomnesia, in which subjects obtain their knowledge through normal daily channels, such as overheard conversations, but are unable to recall them consciously. In his view, hypnotically obtained memories cannot be relied on, and he rejects them as evidence for reincarnation.

Edwards devotes a whole chapter of his book to discrediting Ian Stevenson, who we encountered at the end of Chapter 4 as the leading figure in presenting case studies, especially of children's spontaneous memories of past lives, as evidence for reincarnation. It is important to note that Edwards starts out with an initial presumption against reincarnation and therefore fierce scepticism about Stevenson's evidence. It is probably not going too far to state that Edwards would not accept any evidence of any sort that pointed to reincarnation. The following passage leaves no doubt at all about where he stands:

> ... the question before a rational person can be stated in the following words: which is more likely – that there are astral bodies, that they invade the wombs of prospective mothers, and that the children can remember events from a previous life although the brains of the previous persons have long been dead, or that Stevenson's children, their parents, or some of the other witnesses and informants are, intentionally or unintentionally, not telling the truth: that they are lying, or that their very fallible memories and powers of observation have led them to make false statements and bogus identifications.[12]

Edwards reports on the claims of methodological flaws in Stevenson's research by his former assistant, Champe Ransom, who accused Stevenson of asking leading questions of his subjects; a questioning period too brief to achieve any depth; a long time lapse, often many years, between the alleged event and its investigation; lack of investigation of the subject's friends and the extent of their knowledge of the events; embellishing stories to make them complete; unreliability of details; and witness bias.

The philosopher C.T.K. Chari has also dismissed Stevenson's evidence by suggesting that the cases he collected occur mostly in cultures which have a deeply ingrained belief in reincarnation, and that the type of reincarnation claimed in any particular case fits in with the specific form of reincarnation believed in that area. Chari concludes that, in these cultures, it is normal for young children to play at a 'reincarnationist fantasy', which is then encouraged by the conscious or unconscious beliefs, attitudes and responses of family members. Edwards draws attention to the huge disparity in numbers between Stevenson's reincarnation case studies in India, where there is widespread belief in reincarnation, and in the West. He attributes this to the lack, in the West, of

a host of witnesses with an ardent belief in reincarnation who will manufacture the necessary 'proofs' ...[13]

Alternative explanations: We saw above that Edwards has an initial presumption against reincarnation, and will always look for the possibility of an alternative explanation. Reviewing certain case studies, he offers little or no evidence of bad data or methodological flaws, but simply presents an alternative explanation that would dispense with the need for reincarnation. A prime example is one of Stevenson's case studies, Jagdish Chandra, born in 1923 (coincidentally the same year that Virginia Tighe aka Bridey Murphy was born) in the Indian city of Bareilly.[14] Aged three and a half, he claimed to have lived before as Jai Gopal in Benares, and his memories were published by his father in a newspaper before any contact was made with the previous family in Benares. Those memories of the place and his previous family were extremely detailed and very precise, including what family members wore, how they died, what music they listened to, and most of what he said was found to be true. Edwards dismisses this story as having gaping holes, and accuses the father of twisting the child's innocent remarks into reincarnation memories. He creates a hypothetical scenario which explains how all the facts could have been obtained by the father, learned by rote by the young Jagdish, and fraudulently published as a reincarnation scenario. For Edwards, this is a better explanation of the events than any reincarnationist assumption, although he acknowledges it as speculation.

Brief rejoinder: Not surprisingly, proponents of reincarnation have answers to all these objections, although many of them are impossible to test and verify. They include assertions that what survives and is eventually reincarnated is a transcendental, unageing soul; that in the distant past humans could have been incarnated in non-human bodies; theories of astral worlds, whereby the populations of this world and the astral world are always in balance; or that reincarnation occurs only in certain cases. Hypnotically obtained memories are defended on the grounds that often they are so detailed, extensive and obscure that cryptomnesia or even dishonesty are insufficient as explanations.

The philosopher Robert Almeder has systematically answered each of Edwards' objections, and himself objects to what he calls Edwards' 'dogmatic materialism', accusing him of using circular arguments that presuppose materialism to be self-evidently true. He also objects to Edwards' dismissive use of sarcasm in place of objective argument, which is 'unworthy of a reasoned response', and highlights Stevenson's transparent efforts to detect fraud and identify flaws in each of his case studies.[15] Almeder himself is a dualist, who believes that minds are not reducible to brain states, and clearly the dependence of the mind on the brain is the strongest argument for Edwards and the lynchpin of all his objections, which he expects anyone rational and with common sense to believe in as a self-evident truth:

> It is difficult to reason with people whose entire mental frame is so different from that of science and common sense.[16]

Ironically, the mirror argument to that is found more than two and a half thousand years earlier in the Mundaka Upanishad, which divides knowledge into lower and higher levels: intellectual knowledge is lower, while realisation or enlightenment is higher. Science, from this perspective, concerns itself solely with lower knowledge, which is why some conclude that it has little of value to say about immortality, reincarnation or the nature of being:

> Ignorant of their ignorance, yet wise
> In their own esteem, these deluded men
> Proud of their vain learning go round and round
> Like the blind led by the blind.[17]

Clearly, what we have here is not primarily an issue about evidence or proof for or against reincarnation, but a clash of worldviews with completely different understandings of how the world works and little common ground for rational and respectful dialogue. The philosophy behind reincarnation and most of the Eastern religions and theosophy is called idealism, the view that everything that exists is mental and immaterial: material objects and their properties are reduced to mind and states of mind. In its extreme version, absolute (or monist) idealism, the nature of ultimate reality is spirit or pure consciousness, and the world of matter is an illusion: this is *maya* in Hindu tradition, as we saw in Chapter 4 – the illusion of a separate, phenomenal world, masking the reality that everything is one.

Idealism as a philosophy is the polar opposite of materialism. In the history of Western philosophy, it goes back to George Berkeley (1685-1753), who attempted to refute materialism and coined the term 'immaterialism', an alternative name for idealism. It has gained in popularity in recent years, and among others the theoretical quantum physicist Amit Goswami argues that the problems of quantum physics – which describes nature at the smallest scales of atoms and subatomic particles – can only be solved through idealism, a recognition that an absolute mind or soul is the only thing in the universe.[18] One of the key quantum problems Goswami refers to is that the material world seems to require a conscious observer to become definite and fixed, and therefore it is in effect the mind that creates matter. In the Upanishads, this absolute mind is called Brahman, and union with the infinite is the ultimate goal of the cycle of reincarnations.

The case against animism

In Chapter 5, the belief that the dead (and sometimes the living) transform into other beings, some of whom are treated as ancestors, was linked intimately with animist cultures. As we saw, in recent years animism has been redefined as being about relationships between persons, human and non-human, alive and dead, but it is still not well understood and is often misrepresented. Some objections can be simplistic and misinformed, harking back to the 'old' animism which is dismissed as a primitive and childlike belief in spirits, ghosts and fairies, in which objects such as rocks, trees and clouds have a rational human-like personality and language. It is necessary first to clarify our terms, and then select objections that are valid and relevant.

Animism and panpsychism: The most extensive exposition of contemporary animism from a philosophical perspective is Emma Restall Orr's *The Wakeful World: Animism, Mind and the Self in Nature*. Her definition of animism as the idea that mind and matter are not distinct and separate substances, but an integrated reality within all aspects of nature – that nature's essence is minded, everything in nature perceiving its environment and having a sense of its own being – is nearly identical to the philosophy known as panpsychism.[19]

Panpsychism goes back to the Greek Stoics in around 300 BCE, and the term itself derives from the Greek for 'all soul' or 'all mind'. Although there is a lack of agreement on the basic definition of panpsychism, it is the view that all forms of matter have some form of mental property – mind, experience, sentience or consciousness – whether or not they are parts of living organisms and 'alive' by scientific definition. It is important to emphasise that panpsychism does not ascribe fully developed, fully aware, human-like consciousness to all forms of matter, such as mountains, rocks, molecules and elementary particles, but acknowledges that there are different types of mental awareness. David Skrbina has proposed a panpsychist hierarchy of terminology to clarify this issue, from the most human-like to inanimate objects:

> humans: self-consciousness, cognition
> all animals: thought, consciousness
> animals and plants: sense, awareness, sentience, emotion
> all animate and inanimate: experience, mind, mental state, what-it-is-like, qualia, nous, psyche.[20]

In recent years there has been an increase of interest in panpsychism as an alternative to materialism, resulting in a plethora of new alternative terms. The psychologist Max Velmans coins the phrase 'continuity theory', on the grounds that consciousness co-emerged with matter and co-evolves with it, as opposed to a discontinuity theory like materialism which claims that consciousness emerged at a particular point in evolution. The neuroscientists Giulio Tononi and Christof Koch propose the term 'integrated information theory', on the basis that mind and matter are completely integrated. The philosopher David Ray Griffin uses 'pan-experientialism', since experience and a capacity for feeling permeate all levels and types of being, from human brains to subatomic particles. Some forms of panpsychism, such as the philosopher Philip Goff's 'cosmopsychism', essentially morph into idealism, arguing that the whole universe is one big experiential subject that can be divided into various experiential parts. In contemporary quantum physics, there is a variety of theories that ascribe some form of mentality to the quantum level, whether in the form of idealism, as we saw above under objections to reincarnation, or as panpsychism, arguing that quantum theory implies that elementary particles have certain mind-like qualities.[21]

Like animism, panpsychism is not well understood and is often easily dismissed as a belief that everything is conscious in the same way that humans are conscious. So, for example, if it is equated with a belief that 'rocks are conscious', it can easily be dismissed as ludicrous. Just as with animism, the language we use is important, and Skrbina has noted that terms like 'consciousness', 'soul' (or 'spirit') and 'thought' are particularly troublesome when used in relation to panpsychism, because they imply and impose a human framework of mind. So objections that simply assume that panpsychism equates to human-like consciousness are a misrepresentation.

Animism and panpsychism are not identical, however. Firstly, the terms tend to be used in different contexts: 'animism' is used within religion and anthropology, while 'panpsychism' is more common in philosophical and scientific discourse. Secondly, animism is a way of life, a way of actively engaging with and relating to the world, while panpsychism is a philosophical theory about how the world works.

The objections below encompass both the 'new' animism and

panpsychism, which to a certain extent can be taken together, with the caveats noted above. Some of the objections will by now be familiar, and are variations of what we have already seen as objections to resurrection, the soul and reincarnation. Discounting objections which are based on misinformation and misrepresentation, there are four substantive objections: the Combination Problem, the Behaviour Problem, the Causality Problem, and the now familiar dependence of the mind on the brain.

The Combination Problem: This problem concerns how to account for mental unity. If, as animists and panpsychists argue, all matter has an element of mind, how can a single mind, composed of many elementary particles of matter – for example, a human mind or the mind of a fish – be composed of many minds? In the philosopher Thomas Nagel's words, how could a single self be composed of many selves? There is no good explanation for how simpler minds, such as those of atoms, could combine into complex, unified, self-conscious minds such as those of humans. The philosopher William Seager asks how those unified minds relate to their constituent minds: is it some sort of sum of all the minds, or a synthesis, or a super-hierarchy? Nagel raises the further difficulty that they would have to be re-combinable into many different minds and types of mind, since matter can be re-combined to form other organisms, animate and inanimate. Therefore, the mental properties of all matter could not be species-specific, but universal, since they would underlie all possible forms of mind, sentience and consciousness. While such a scenario fits in with the sorts of transformations we saw in Chapter 5, animists and panpsychists have produced no explanation of how such combinations and re-combinations work in practice to produce a unified mind.

The Behaviour Problem: The philosopher Colin McGinn objects that things like rocks and atoms (and, by extension, the dead) exhibit no signs of mind-like qualities or mental properties.

Inanimate objects, like rocks, tables, aeroplanes and the dead, instead exhibit behaviour which can be predicted according to the laws of physics, and this precludes the presence of mind. Paul Edwards uses the example of the proverbial dead doornail. The doornail does not behave like beings whom we regard as having emotions and thoughts. It is not composed of the kind of organic or biological material of which plants and animals are composed, and it does not have a brain or a nervous system. He therefore rejects the idea that it can have any sense of 'what it feels like to be a doornail'.

The Causality Problem: This is similar to the Causal Interaction problem we encountered above as an objection to the soul. If matter has both physical and mental properties, Nagel asks how the mental properties cause physical events. He cannot understand the causal connections, and animists and panpsychists have provided no explanation.

Dependence of the mind on the brain: The all-time favourite response of materialists, we have already met this argument above as the strongest objection against the soul and reincarnation. The mind is a creation of the physical brain, not something separate, and it dies along with the brain. It cannot transform into any other being or ancestor, since the brain is dead and it cannot think or possess any sentience or mind-like quality at all. It is just dead, and there can be no sense of 'what it feels like to be dead', as being dead is the end of all sentience and experience.

Brief rejoinder: There is a range of views within animism and panpsychism, and many forms avoid the Combination Problem by distinguishing between true individuals, like animals and possibly elementary particles, which are capable of experience, and aggregates, like rocks, plants, mountains and man-made objects like telephones, which do not have experiences or anything like a collective 'self'. Many of the objections are anthropocentric, and it is misleading to use human analogies to understand the inner lives of other creatures: the subjective experience of simple minds may be like nothing that we, as humans, can comprehend, and may well appear to us as law-like. As we will see below under objections to materialist science, there is evidence for experience and cognition without brains, for example in plants and bacteria.

If mind is not dependent on the physical brain, but co-evolved with matter, then death is the process of dissolution of both body and mind, and of change into other entities. The issue of death reveals another difference between animism and panpsychism. While panpsychist philosophers are silent on the implications of death, their animist colleagues have followed through the logical conclusion that, as the body decomposes and its constituent parts transform, so too the mental experiences, memories, thoughts and emotions lose their coherence and individuality and become parts of something else. This is not a cessation of mental life, but a re-combination into other forms of minded being – a transformation.[22]

The case against (materialist) science

In a critique of materialist science, it is important to distinguish between the practice and aims of science as a whole, and the materialist assumptions of the vast majority of scientists working today; though, as we will see, they are closely interconnected historically, and even the practice has problematic issues which, as scientists themselves acknowledge, can undermine confidence in results.

The founders of the scientific method were the contemporaries René Descartes and Francis Bacon (1561-1626). Descartes' philosophical approach, as we saw in Chapter 2, was based on systematic doubt about what it is possible to know, while the empiricist Bacon aimed to reconstruct all human knowledge based on experiments, working gradually from the particular to the general. Together, their objective was a science that gave a complete account of the universe – described as a machine or a clockwork mechanism – in which everything could be explained by physical causes, without recourse to mind or soul:

> There exists nothing in the whole of nature which cannot be explained in terms of purely corporeal causes devoid of mind and thought.[23]

This hypothetical and elusive 'theory of everything', which the philosopher Sir Karl Popper has called 'a day-dream of omniscience' and an 'inescapable nightmare',[24] remains the goal of science today. In the words of the late Stephen Hawking:

> And our goal is nothing less than a complete description of the universe we live in.[25]

That is the first fundamental assumption of materialism and, indeed, of science: the belief that everything that exists can be measured and quantified, and 'reduced' to mathematics and physics. The second assumption of materialism, with huge implications for belief in immortality, is that 'mind' is physical, a product of physical processes in the brain. The third is that mind and consciousness emerged in certain animals at some point in evolution, and that all non-living things, and even most living things, are fundamentally devoid of mental qualities. It cannot be emphasised too strongly that these are all assumptions, which have not been proved: they may well turn out to be true, although the first may be an assertion that is incapable of proof. Materialist science is only 'unbiased' insofar as it accepts those assumptions uncritically as a starting point; but it cannot be truly objective and unbiased unless it also examines the assumptions themselves objectively.

This mechanistic worldview is deeply embedded as a dominant orthodoxy – what the philosopher Mary Midgley calls the 'church of academic orthodoxy', likening it to a religious faith.[26] She further points out that scientists today, unlike their nineteenth-century predecessors, mostly refuse on principle to publish or even consider research outside a materialist framework. It is virtually impossible to get funding for scientific research that does not accept the materialist orthodoxy, to persuade a laboratory or university to host such research, and to get the results published in a reputable journal. As Midgley comments, there may be good reasons for this – which eventually may well turn out to be correct – but the reasons operate before considering the evidence. They are based on the assumption that the worldview of materialism is self-evidently true and cannot be challenged.[27] The objections below challenge this view, and demonstrate that, on the contrary, materialism faces problems in nearly every aspect. Worries about materialist science's inability to provide convincing and coherent explanations, particularly for the mind-body problem, are pushing some scientists and philosophers towards other solutions, as we saw in the earlier sections in this chapter.[28]

The Replication of Results Problem: An integral element of the scientific method is that experimental findings should be replicated by other researchers before they can be regarded as verified and accepted. But, in recent years, what scientists are referring to as a 'replication crisis' has been unearthed, which throws doubt on the reliability of scientific work. A survey in 2016 in the science journal *Nature* showed that more than 70 per cent of scientific researchers have tried and failed to reproduce another scientist's experiments, and more than half have failed to reproduce their own.[29] The most popular explanations for this failure were selective reporting and cherry-picking of data to obtain a desired outcome. But an astonishing 40 per cent of researchers thought that fraud was always or often a contributory factor, and 70 per cent thought it was a possible factor. This is backed up by another survey in which up to 72 per cent of researchers believed that their colleagues were engaged in questionable research practices, such as selective reporting, and over 14 per cent thought they deliberately falsified results.[30] These findings underline the perhaps obvious point made by the neuroscientist Christof Koch, that

> research is done by flesh-and-blood creatures with less than pristine motivations and desires.[31]

While this does not mean that we should dismiss the results of all scientific research – and scientists, on the whole, still tend to trust the published results of other scientists – it does mean that scepticism regarding claims by scientists is both healthy and warranted. It is a salutary reminder that the practice of science is not a selfless quest for knowledge and truth: the day-to-day practice involves intensive competition for research grants, quick publication of results, careers, money and prestige. In the light of these findings, it would be unwise to regard the practice of science as value-free and objective.

The Mind-Brain Problem: A key argument of materialist scientists and philosophers against most forms of immortality is that the mind is created by the physical brain. If the mind dies along with the brain, then it no longer exists and cannot be immortal in any way. There are two objections to this argument. The first is that we still know very little about the brain. We do not know how consciousness is created in humans or other animals, what the physical and chemical interactions are, what sort of neuronal system is necessary to support consciousness, and whether it is confined to brains. Even the largest ever international research project to explore how the brain makes decisions, called the International Brain Laboratory, is restricted in its focus on simple, responsive, perceptual decisions, such as reactions to sights or sounds in mice, and is incapable of investigating complex decision-making. Scientists have not been able to explain how the brain makes such purposeful decisions.

One of the neuroscientists involved, Matteo Carandini, admits that:

What people often don't realise is that we have no clue how the brain works.[32]

Given this limited range of knowledge about the brain, it is hard to see how materialists can defend the claim that the dependence of the mind on the brain has been proved beyond reasonable doubt. The second objection is that there is evidence for experience and cognition both outside brains and without brains. Some neuroscientists and psychologists do not discount that the human body might contain several autonomous minds, unaware of each other, subservient to the brain, which lose their separate identities when they are integrated into higher-order entities, like human beings.[33] If that is the case, then consciousness is not confined to brains. The neuropsychologist Paul Pearsall and his colleagues have carried out research on the phenomenon of organ transplant recipients who claim that they have inherited the memories, experiences and emotions of the deceased donors.[34] They conclude that heart transplant recipients seem most susceptible to personality changes, which are more strongly associated with the donor's history. Pearsall and his colleagues suggest that this evidence indicates the existence of cellular memory. This is the theory that all living cells possess memory, which is therefore not confined to the brain, and is transplanted along with the organ if it is kept alive. Most scientists remain sceptical, and suggest that there are psychological explanations for the changes in transplant recipients. Such scepticism is not unexpected, since the existence of cellular memory would undermine one of the key tenets of materialism regarding the dependency of the mind on the brain, so their scepticism is not so much an issue of assessing evidence as of conflicting worldviews. However, some of the heart transplant case studies do not seem amenable to a psychological explanation, including one where the recipient's 'new' memory was so vivid and detailed that it led to the arrest and conviction of the murderer of the donor, who was unknown to the recipient.

Moreover, there is also evidence for experience, awareness, communication and cognition in plants, without the complex brains and neural networks of humans and other animals. Even bacteria, which are among the planet's oldest life forms, have been described as having rich social lives, with collective memory, shared knowledge, group identity and decision-making. This is based on complex chemical communication, in the form of 'chemical tweets' that keep all bacteria in a group updated all of the time. Some scientists conclude that it resembles the basic grammatical structures of human language, and that there must be a seamless transition from this bacterial sentience to that of humans.[35]

If the mind is not restricted to the brain, but is dispersed among cells and non-neural networks (or, potentially, exists as a soul), then the hypothetical futuristic hope, and staple of science fiction, of immortality through uploading or copying brains to a computer is fatally undermined. Even if the considerable technical complexities of reconstructing neurons, their connections and the electrical and biochemical signal exchanges between them could be overcome, the result might be akin to copying all the files from your old computer to a new one, and expecting to have all the same data and functionality as before, only to find that all you have is the hardware of the new computer: no data, and (possibly) not even any software.

The Emergence Problem: We saw above that one of the assumptions of materialism is that mind 'emerged' at some point in complex animals, and that most forms of existence are devoid of mind, which excludes the animist form of immortality as transformation. The objection is that it is inconceivable that mind, sentience or consciousness could ever emerge or evolve from wholly insentient physical matter. As the neuroscientist Christof Koch, a former proponent of the emergence theory, points out:

> This sort of emergence is at odds with a basic precept of physical thinking – *ex nihilo nihil fit*, or nothing comes from nothing... Subjectivity is too radically different from anything physical for it to be an emergent phenomenon. A kind of blue is fundamentally different from electrical activity in the cone photoreceptors of the eyes...[36]

Moreover, where and how does this emergence happen: how, in practice, did mind emerge from a world in which no mind existed? Materialists cannot explain the criteria for this emergence or how the qualities of mind or consciousness are linked to biological or functional complexity. In his last book, *Invariances*, philosopher Robert Nozick attempted to address this by proposing that consciousness emerged because it had evolutionary usefulness. He distinguished seven gradations of conscious behaviour that create increasing capacity to fit actions to the world, from an organism simply registering an external object or situation, to fully concentrating on it. But he was still unable to explain how this development happens.

Others tend to draw an arbitrary line between what has capacity for mentality and supposedly mindless objects; so, in their view, mind and consciousness cease somewhere down the evolutionary scale, but they disagree on where on that scale, and cannot explain why and how it happens in the first place. Todd Feinberg and Jon Mallatt, in *The Ancient Origins of Consciousness*, argue that consciousness appeared much earlier in evolutionary history than is generally assumed, and conclude that complex brains produced consciousness 520 to 560 million years ago. Among conscious entities they include mammals, fish, reptiles, amphibians and birds, as well as many invertebrates and insects.

But they do not explain why and how such an emergence occurred: like most materialists, they simply assume that consciousness naturally arises when the neural system reaches a certain level of complexity, which explains nothing, and merely perpetuates the assumption of emergence. Different researchers draw the line in different places, or, more often, avoid drawing a line at all, merely arguing the principle of emergence.

The philosopher Galen Strawson is dismissive of the whole approach:

> Does this conception of emergence make sense? I think that it is very, very hard to understand what it is supposed to involve. I think that it is incoherent, in fact, and that this general way of talking of emergence has acquired an air of plausibility...[37]

For some, the solution for where mind comes from lies in the soul or spirit. Others offer a continuity argument in place of emergence: mind did not emerge, but always existed in all matter, even in the simplest of structures. The argument runs that, if mind and consciousness evolved from a physical brain, then the basic forms of mental being must have been present at the outset of the evolutionary process.

The Explanatory Gaps Problem: This objection is that materialist views offer only a partial description of the world. There is no explanation for how the brain converts bioelectrical activity into subjective states. At present, science cannot account for how the brain generates phenomenal experiences that make humans conscious of themselves and of others, of colours, of the past and future, and of pain and pleasure. There is a lot of data that shows specific correlations between the physical parts or processes of the brain and specific mental phenomena, but so far there is no explanation for how, and whether, the physical brain actually produces a single belief or purpose. The late neurologist Volker

Henn criticised the hypothesis that neurons firing in a rhythmic manner generate the sensation of seeing red as no different from Descartes' proposal to locate the soul in the pineal gland.[38] According to Christof Koch,

> ... experience, the interior perspective of a functioning brain, is something fundamentally different from the material thing causing it and that it can never be fully reduced to physical properties of the brain.[39]

Materialism offers only electrochemical impulses and neurons firing randomly, and cannot explain the things humans value most: love, freedom, beliefs, desires and purposes. The philosopher Thomas Nagel explains the problem:

> The concepts of physical science provide a very special, and partial, description of the world that experience reveals to us. It is the world with all subjective consciousness, sensory appearances, thought, values, purposes, and will left out; what remains is the mathematically describable order of things and events in space and time.[40]

There are too many aspects that a materialist view cannot explain, perhaps suggesting that physics cannot be the theory of everything. This leaves the field open to other approaches, explanations and worldviews, which we have been encountering throughout this book. To take just one example, according to Goetz and Taliaferro the only plausible view is that neurons do not fire randomly but because of the causal input of a mind or soul choosing to act for a purpose.[41] Otherwise, where do purposes come from? Materialism, at least, has not provided a persuasive answer.

Brief rejoinder: There are three types of rejoinder that focus on the key materialist claim of the dependency of the mind on the brain. The first is that, although it might not amount to conclusive proof, there is already sufficient evidence that makes the dependency of the mind on the brain the most likely solution. For Paul Edwards, if a certain brain state or physical condition is always accompanied by a certain mental state, then that mental state has been explained and accounted for to his satisfaction.[42] Moreover, experimental evidence shows that movement of a part of the body starts before there is any conscious decision to move it. This implies that the brain acts before the mind decides to act, and that therefore the mind is dependent on the brain rather than the mind causing the brain to act; although it is still unknown how the feeling of agency is created. The defence, then, is that materialism is not dogmatism but a simple, economical default working hypothesis that best fits the current empirical evidence.

The second rejoinder is often labelled 'the promissory note' or, in Mary Midgley's phrase, 'post-dated cheques for the future':[43] it is an admission that, as current knowledge stands, science cannot resolve all the problems, but it works on the assumption that it is close to finding solutions in the near future. This approach has total and utter faith that science will explain the problems of how and why the brain produces mind and consciousness, as it has explained other so-called mysteries. Indeed, Midgley notes that, from Descartes' time, it has been constantly claimed that science is on the verge of producing complete explanations (the 'theory of everything'), and the belief that it will is 'a part of what is held to be a scientific attitude'.

The third rejoinder comes from the philosopher Colin McGinn, who suggests that we can never solve the mind-body problem, and how it is possible for conscious states to depend on brain states, because the human mind is not capable of understanding itself and is limited as to the kinds of thoughts it can entertain. It is a deep fact about our own conscious nature that is necessarily hidden from us, and we can never understand our own consciousness.[44]

'The courtroom was adjourned, no verdict was returned'[45]

This chapter has considered scientific objections to immortality through resurrection, the immortal soul, reincarnation and transformation, as well as objections to materialist science itself, particularly its key argument of the dependency of the mind on the brain. The one thing that stands out from this survey of objections, arguments and counter-arguments is that there is no conclusive proof for any of the views, including the materialist scientific view. Each has major explanatory problems and gaps, but these arguably fall short of proving the views to be false. So we have no alternative but to conclude that, while none of them can be conclusively proved, equally none of them can, at present, be excluded. We must keep open the possibility that any one of these views might be true, but, with the lack of proof, we have no way of knowing which one. The implications of this will be examined further in the Epilogue.

Chapter 9

Is immortality a curse?

Why did he grant me life eternal – rob me of our one privilege, death?
– Virgil, *Aeneid*

The awful prospect that hard-won immortality might turn out to be a curse rather than a blessing because it could become tedious or unfulfilling, or be too high a price to pay for the individual or for society, has been extensively explored across the centuries in myth, fiction and philosophy.

Most discussions of whether or not immortality is worth achieving have suggested that being in heaven for all eternity might become dreary and monotonous, or that the actual experience of living forever in this life and on this earth too might become repetitive, dull, sterile and purposeless. These will be the main focus of this chapter.

Less has been written about the downsides of reincarnation and virtually nothing about those of animistic transformation. One of philosopher Bernard Williams' conditions for immortality to be attractive to us now, while we are alive, which we will explore in more detail below, is that personal identity must be preserved. Many of the examples of animistic transformation that we saw in Chapter 5 would seem to satisfy that condition, since the ancestral dead, though transformed, remain intimately and actively connected with their societies and landscapes: they remain persons with an individual identity.

Regarding reincarnation, which Williams calls 'an indefinite series of lives', he concludes that the various forms fail his condition because the lack of memory of the previous existence in most forms of reincarnation means that you may as well have been born as a new person with a new personal identity:

> they get nowhere near providing any consideration to mark the difference between rebirth and new birth.[1]

He then considers whether some form of bodily continuity would be minimally sufficient for personal identity, or whether memory of previous lives is necessary, and leaves these questions largely open. Of course, as we saw in Chapter 4, there are many different beliefs in reincarnation, and in its Eastern forms reincarnation is not actual immortality but a path to immortality, which itself is not about the survival of personal individuality, the ultimate goal being to break out of the cycle of birth, death and rebirth. In Buddhism, life, and the endless cycle of rebirths, is experienced as suffering, and achieving nirvana is a means of ending that suffering. Likewise, in Hinduism, the goal of the cycle of incarnations is to get rid of individuality and the feeling of separateness to reach a state of union with the infinite. Williams acknowledges that these beliefs look forward to release from life, and comments that

> Such systems seem less interested in continuing one's life than in earning one the right to a superior sort of death.[2]

Will heaven be boring?

In Chapter 3, we encountered many descriptions of heaven across the millennia. They are so different that, in order to assess whether or not they might be tedious, we have to specify which heaven we are referring to.

In the thirteenth century, Thomas Aquinas wrote:

> Final and perfect happiness can consist of nothing else than the vision of the divine essence.[3]

This was his idea of heaven: the Beatific Vision, a face-to-face relationship with God for all eternity. While this version persisted through the medieval period, concerns that this sort of heaven might be boring can be traced to the eighteenth and nineteenth centuries, eventually leading to the alternative visions of Swedenborg and *The Gates Ajar*. In his last, satirical story, published in 1909, Mark Twain made clear that he considered this sort of heaven a waste of time:

> Singing hymns and waving palm branches through all eternity is pretty when you hear about it in the pulpit, but it's as poor a way to put in valuable time as a body could contrive.[4]

Philosopher Geoffrey Scarre assumes that one's primary heavenly 'activity' would be the worshipping of God, and admits that it is hard to conceive of this now as an attractive way of spending eternity, unless our desires and notion of time also undergo some profound changes. He concludes that, for an existence in heaven to be fulfilling, one would have to be active rather than passive, and he wonders if there are any opportunities for development and a sense that one's existence was going somewhere.[5] Similarly, Bernard Williams cannot imagine any model of an unending existence that will not, ultimately, prove boring:

> Nothing less will do for eternity than something that makes boredom *unthinkable*[6]

– but he is unable to suggest what that might be.

Of course, the social heaven of Swedenborg and *The Gates Ajar* answered these objections and became popular among late nineteenth-century Christians, who imagined a heaven of activity, progress, family, friends and pets, with little or no mention of the Beatific Vision and little opportunity for tedium.

Yet, in modern fundamentalist Christianity, there has been a renewed and deliberate emphasis on the Beatific Vision. God, largely missing from the social heaven of the eighteenth and nineteenth centuries, has once more become central, and the human family has been excluded. This is the easily satirised heaven of contemporary cartoonists, where people lie on clouds with harps, angels open the pearly gates, and nothing much else happens as time seems to stand still. Scarre's and Williams' questions therefore remain pertinent.

The sensual and luxurious heaven of Islam, with its pleasure garden motif, despite differences in interpretation of details and especially questions about gender bias, remains a key part of contemporary Muslim belief. It is also a very potent symbol and an important, though by no means the only, part of the appeal of Islam to certain groups, mainly fundamentalist and predominantly young and male. Far from being boring, as Alan Segal has pointed out this vision has a reality through the promise of heavenly rewards for martyrdom which address economic and social hardship in this life. As well as the supposed virgins of paradise, which are certainly a motivation (with martyrs' funerals often celebrated as weddings to the heavenly virgins), disenfranchised youths can aim to provide for their families in heaven compared with their powerlessness on earth, and many have given their lives to achieve this version of heaven sooner.[7]

The problem of living forever: from classical myth to modern fiction

The earliest and greatest classical myth about the downside of immortality is the story of Tithonus. This concerns the problem – or curse – of old age, and of immortality without eternal youth. It first appeared in the Homeric Hymn to Aphrodite, the goddess of love, one of 33 anonymous Greek songs of praise to individual gods, attributed to Homer in antiquity and sharing the same style as the *Iliad* and *Odyssey*. The hymn is usually dated to the seventh or sixth century BCE, contemporary with or a little after Homer, but its dating is contested and some argue that it is even later.[8]

Eos, the goddess of the dawn, whose mythology focuses on her role as a predatory lover, falls in love with the handsome mortal Tithonus. She asks Zeus to make Tithonus immortal, but forgets to ask for eternal youth. So while Eos remains unchanged, Tithonus grows older until she loses interest in him sexually. Once he can no longer move or lift his limbs, she locks him into a room:

> There he babbles endlessly, and no more has strength at all, such as once he had in his supple limbs.[9]

In later versions of this story, once Tithonus' old age has become unendurable, Eos changes him into a cicada, a winged insect with a shrill voice – an echo of Tithonus' 'endless babble'. The first mention of the cicada theme is by Hellanicus of Lesbos (c. 480-395 BCE), after which it was taken up by many other writers from the fourth century BCE onwards. According to Hieronymus of Rhodes in the third century BCE, by transforming Tithonus into a cicada Eos got continual pleasure from hearing his voice; other sources recount that Eos carried the aged Tithonus around in a basket like a baby in a cradle.

Some scholars argue that the cicada story was not an addition to the Tithonus myth, but was already known to the author of the Homeric hymn, who deliberately suppressed it because it contradicted the moral of his story, that there can be no remedy for old age. The ancient Greeks believed that cicadas had a kind of immortality, since it was thought that by sloughing off their old skin periodically, like a snake, they rejuvenated themselves. The Greek word used for the insect skin was the same as that for 'old age', the wordplay suggesting that this too could be shed. The message of the cicada theme was therefore quite different from the original version, in which there is no salvation for the ever-ageing Tithonus, who is locked away.[10]

When Alfred, Lord Tennyson (1809-1892) wrote his poem 'Tithonus', first published in 1860, he returned to the original theme of the Homeric hymn and ignored the cicada, because it also undermined the moral of his poem. Tennyson's Tithonus yearns for death, and questions why a man should wish to avoid it and be different from other mortals:

> Me only cruel immortality
> Consumes: I wither slowly in thine arms...
> Immortal age beside immortal youth...
> Release me, and restore me to the ground...[11]

The Greeks also explored the idea that the state of immortality might be tedious. Lucian (c. 125-after 180 CE), originally from Samosata, a town on the Euphrates River, now in Turkey, wrote satirical dialogues modelled on those of Plato, comic rather than philosophical, but still dealing with serious themes. Many of his *Dialogues of the Dead* centre on the Cynic philosopher Menippus, who had lived in the third century BCE, in which Menippus mocks the rich and powerful who have lost more by death than he has. They ask the serious question: what do you lose by death, and who loses more?

One of the dialogues is a conversation in the underworld between Menippus and Chiron, the most famous and wisest of the Centaurs, half-man and half-horse, who was often depicted on Greek painted vases. Chiron had been born an immortal, and had brought up Achilles after his mother Thetis deserted him. During a battle between the Centaurs and Heracles, Chiron was wounded by Heracles' arrows. When the wounds would not heal, Chiron begged to be made mortal, and died. Menippus asks Chiron why he voluntarily relinquished immortality and is in love with death, that most people try to avoid:

CHIRON: There was no further satisfaction to be had from immortality.

MENIPPUS: Was it not a pleasure merely to live and see the light?

CHIRON: No; it is variety, as I take it, and not monotony, that constitutes pleasure. Living on and on, everything always the same; sun, light, food, spring, summer, autumn, winter, one thing following another in unending sequence, – I sickened of it all. I found that enjoyment lay not in continual possession; that deprivation had its share therein.[12]

For Chiron, immortal life had become tedious and repetitive, and he concluded that he could do without it. Menippus further asks if eternal existence in the underworld might not also become monotonous, to which there is no satisfactory answer:

MENIPPUS: Why, if the monotony of the other world brought on satiety, the monotony here may do the same. You will have to look about for a further change, and I fancy there is no third life procurable.

CHIRON: Then what is to be done, Menippus?

MENIPPUS: Take things as you find them, I suppose, like a sensible fellow, and make the best of everything.

As well as his satirical dialogues, Lucian is best known for more or less inventing the genre of science fiction in the form of imaginary and fantastic voyages, and introducing the idea of alien beings by describing the manners and customs of inhabitants of other planets. His *A True Story* describes his own voyage to the Moon, a war between the Moon and the Sun, and details of how life on the Moon is different to life on Earth. On his return to Earth, he visits the Isles of the Blessed, where he meets Homer and Pythagoras – an example we can add to the list of voyages to the underworld in Chapter 3 – and then delivers a letter to Calypso from Odysseus. In Chapter 7, we saw how Odysseus chose to leave Calypso to return to his wife and family, but in the letter delivered by Lucian he explains that he now wishes he had stayed with Calypso and accepted her offer of immortality.

Lucian's satirical approach and themes of fantastic voyages were hugely popular and influential once they became available again in print in 1499, having been forgotten during the Middle Ages. The *Dialogues of the Dead* were especially popular, while *A True Story* inspired Sir Thomas More's *Utopia* of 1516 and Jonathan Swift's *Gulliver's Travels* of 1726. It is known that Swift owned a copy of Lucian's works in a Latin translation and was a great admirer. In Part III of *Gulliver's Travels*, the eponymous hero sails to the Kingdom of Luggnagg, encounters the Struldbrugs or Immortals, and explicitly explores Lucian's theme from the *Dialogues of the Dead* of whether or not immortality is worth having.

The Struldbrugs were rare births in Luggnagg society – marked by a spot on the forehead – who never died. Gulliver is so excited that the Luggnaggians can benefit from the wisdom of these immortals, free from the 'continual apprehension of death', that he is asked to describe how he would live his life were he born a Struldbrug. He lists the benefits of immortality: he would procure wealth and learning, keep a record of changes in society, instruct the young, but mostly fraternise and philosophise with fellow immortals and advise society against corruption and degeneracy.

In response, the Luggnaggians are amused by his optimism concerning the advantages of immortality. In contrast, and unlike most human societies, by having the Struldbrugs as a living example, the Luggnaggians are inoculated against a desire to live forever. In reality, the immortal Struldbrugs become increasingly melancholy and dejected after the age of 30. Like Tithonus, they do not have eternal youth, but grow old and infirm, vain and opinionated, incapable of friendship, affection and pleasure, all exacerbated by the dreadful prospect of never dying; indeed, they envy the mortals who can die. Swift describes them as essentially developing dementia:

> In talking they forget the common Appellation of things, and the names of Persons, even of those who are their nearest Friends and Relations.[13]

Once they reach the age of 80, Luggnaggian society takes precautions against any havoc these incompetent and avaricious immortals might cause: any marriages are dissolved, they are pronounced legally dead, and their estates pass to their heirs. At 90 they lose their teeth, hair, taste and appetite, are subject to constant illness, and cannot even amuse themselves by reading because they are so forgetful. As a result, Gulliver's attitude towards death and immortality is irrevocably changed:

> ... my keen Appetite for perpetuity of Life was much abated. I grew heartily ashamed of the pleasing Visions I had formed, and thought no Tyrant could invent a Death into which I would not run with pleasure from such a Life.[14]

Since living forever remains a fantasy possibility, it is not surprising that its implications have been most extensively explored through fantasy and science fiction. One hundred and sixty years after *Gulliver's Travels*, Henry Rider Haggard's *She* – inspired, as we saw in Chapter 6, by Gilgamesh, classical myths and Zulu folklore – described a journey in search of the secret of immortality. Yet its narrator, Horace Holly, rejects Ayesha's offer of immortality on much the same grounds as Lucian's Chiron, that eternal life would be tedious, but also full of bitterness and sorrow:

At any rate I was very sure that *I* would not attempt to attain unending life. I had had far too many worries and disappointments and secret bitternesses during my forty odd years of existence to wish that this state of affairs should be continued indefinitely... Who would endure this for many lives? Who would so load up his back with memories of lost hours and loves, and of his neighbour's sorrows that he cannot lessen, and wisdom that brings not consolation?[15]

While this offer comes with eternal youth, Holly rejects the argument – the same one initially assumed by Swift's Gulliver – that immortality would bring wealth and beneficial wisdom:

Does not wealth satiate and become nauseous, and no longer serve to satisfy or pleasure, or to buy an hour's ease of mind? And is there any end to wisdom that we may hope to reach it? ... Would not our wisdom be but as a gnawing hunger calling our consciousness day by day to a knowledge of the empty craving of our souls?[16]

With modern science fiction, which at its best deals with 'what if?' scenarios, we move beyond the largely philosophical and individual implications of immortality to its potential impacts on society.[17] Robert Heinlein (1907-1988) was an influential writer whose work often dealt with social themes. In *Methuselah's Children*, first published in 1958, he follows through the concern with immortality and eternal youth of the classical myths by exploring the impact on society when one group finds the secret of eternal youth and longevity through a genetic experiment. The discovery results in social tension and violence, as everyone demands a share of the secret. But this leads to discussion among politicians that immortality may need to be restricted to an elite so as not to exacerbate the population problem. Heinlein explores the jealousy of mortals in the face of the new immortals:

He does not plan for the future; you blithely undertake plans that will not mature for fifty years – for a hundred. No matter what success he has achieved, what excellence he has attained, you will catch up with him, pass him – outlive him.[18]

He suggests that immortality changes the nature of social and family relationships – an aspect not acknowledged by Swedenborg or *The Gates Ajar* with their pictures of eternal happy families. When you live indefinitely, it is not feasible to maintain family relationships over long periods and with so many children. Heinlein's immortals lack filial affection, and even friendships are temporary and shallow:

He suddenly envied normal short-lived people – at least they could go make nuisances of themselves to their children.[19]

Robert Silverberg is another award-winning science fiction writer who has shown considerable interest in the implications of immortality and the afterlife, for example in *Gilgamesh the King* (1984), a retelling of the Gilgamesh epic in novel form. His *Recalled to Life*, originally published in the same year as Heinlein's book but revised in 1971, examines the social implications if everyone – not just one group – has the opportunity of resurrection, through a discovery that brings the recently dead back to life. How would society react and how would it need to change? Silverberg explores the practical implications – political, social, religious, ethical and moral – of this type of resurrection. Concepts of death are based on its being irreversible, so if that is no longer the case, new laws and codes of medical ethics would be required around the redefinition of death. If you kill someone, or commit suicide (which is still a crime in some parts of the world), can these any longer be called crimes, subject to punishment, since the dead person can be reanimated? The book presents the reanimation process as complex and expensive, so not immediately available to everyone – not dissimilar to modern cryonics – and poses the question: who decides who lives and who stays dead? Many people worry that reanimation will become the property of an elite that would perpetuate itself, leaving the common people to die. Silverberg also hypothesises that the Catholic Church might not officially approve such a process: since its theological position is that the soul leaves the body at death, unless the process has provision for restoring the soul, then the revived human beings would be without souls and therefore no longer human. His message is: if immortality were ever to become a reality, it would require major practical changes in society, which would then be unrecognisable from the current model:

> This was a new era – an era in which death, the darkest fact of existence, had lost much of its dread finality. Staggering tasks awaited mankind now. A new code of laws was needed. A new ethics of life and death.[20]

While these are fantasy, 'what-if?' possibilities explored through the imaginations of science fiction writers, as we will see in the last section of this chapter the reality of people living longer and the possibility of revival through cryonics raise some of the same issues, and have potential social and legal implications.

The problem of living forever: philosophical perspectives

Philosophers have also been fond of 'what-if?' scenarios, taking fictional works dealing with the problems of immortality and exploring their implications. The two key texts, which have spawned a lively debate among other philosophers, are by Bernard Williams (1929-2003) and Jorge Luis Borges (1899-1986), both of whom conclude that immortality would be a bad thing.

Williams' essay, 'The Makropulos case: reflections on the

tedium of immortality', is based on the play *The Makropulos Case* (sometimes translated as *The Makropulos Affair* or *Secret*) by the Czech playwright Karel Čapek, first performed in 1922. It was adapted a few years later by Leoš Janáček into an opera of the same name. Čapek also wrote science fiction – he was the first to use the word 'robot', coined by his brother – and his play was inspired by scientific work on ageing. The story concerns the psychological effects of an extended life. Born in 1585, at the age of 16 Elina Makropulos is forced to test a potion ordered by the emperor, which would give him 300 years of youth. It is successful, and she then lives an itinerant life for just over 300 years, taking various names all with the initials EM. The action takes place in 1913, when under the name of Emilia Marty, a famous singer, she is now 327 years old[21] and involved in a lawsuit to recover the document with the formula for the potion. The dialogue discusses the implications of an extended life, employing arguments similar to those rehearsed by Swift and others: that an extended life would allow humans to accomplish great deeds, but on the other hand it would disrupt the social system; who should be granted such a life; and whether it would result in happiness. As the potion wears off, Emilia realises, like Lucian's Chiron, that life has grown to be an intolerable burden, with every pleasure hopelessly stale and no new experiences – everything that could happen to her had already happened. She chooses not to renew the effects of the potion to gain another 300 years; the other characters – rather unbelievably, according to critics – also refuse the opportunity, and the document with the formula is burnt.

Čapek was aware of the coincidence that George Bernard Shaw's series of plays *Back to Methuselah*, first performed in the same year as his own play, also acknowledged the age of 300 as a significant number, but had come to very different conclusions. In Shaw's plays, once certain humans reach the age of 300 they have developed spiritual wisdom but, like Elina Makropulos, have to live out their longer lives clandestinely as different characters among normal people and pretend to die. Eventually, they become immortal, pure energy and wanderers throughout the universe – in effect, the totally opposite message of Čapek's, which is that immortality is undesirable.

Williams sets out his stall right at the beginning of his essay based around Čapek's play:

Immortality, or a state without death, would be meaningless, I shall suggest; so, in a sense, death gives the meaning to life.[22]

He proposes two conditions for immortality to be appealing to us and worth pursuing. The first condition, noted at the beginning of this chapter, is that personal identity must be preserved; it should clearly be *me* who lives for ever. This condition was satisfied for Elina Makropulos. The second, rather vaguer, condition is that the form or experience of immortality which one looks forward to should be adequately related to one's current aims in wanting to survive at all; that is, that endless life should give me things I want *now*, and there should be something interesting to look forward to. This condition failed for Elina Makropulos, because endless repetition was boring, and Williams concludes that death is necessary and welcome before you get to the point of having too much of a life with no further meaning, purpose or enjoyment.

Both of Williams' conditions have been challenged by other philosophers, and his paper and conclusions are still frequently referred to as the starting point for a discussion around immortality.[23] A common argument is that the state of immortality would be such a novel situation that a great many things would be different, and might include changes to human psychology that make us better able to deal with boredom. Some challenge the claim that repetition is always tedious and argue that there are repeatable pleasures (though not, as far as we know, based on Elina Makropulos' personal experience of having repeated the same things for 327 years: repetition may be tolerable within a normal human lifespan, but it may be unendurable for eternity); on the other hand, infinitely long life may not involve repetition and boredom at all, as there may always be possibilities for compelling new experiences and activities, including ones not yet invented. Other philosophers suggest that immortality might change our characters and inspire new interests and desires, and this would give us a reason for wishing to live forever. That last point also excludes Williams' first condition, since personal identity and character might change so much over a period of thousands of years that the immortal 'I' would seem a very different person from the 'I' living now; indeed, just as personality, values and interests can change drastically over the course of a normal human life.

But Geoffrey Scarre disagrees with these challenges. We might be alarmed at any future changes to our personality (what he calls a potential Jekyll to Hyde situation); and we would need to have more powerful memories than we have now in order to recall our own distant pasts, and even to remember our own childhood, parents or children – in essence, the point made above by the science fiction writer Robert Heinlein, concerning immortality's potential to destroy family bonds. So Scarre agrees with Williams that immortality could not be made attractive to us, because death gives a sense of structure and direction, and perhaps also of purpose, to life.

Repetitiveness and lack of purpose as the result of an immortal life are also the focus of the short story 'The immortal' by the Argentinian writer Jorge Luis Borges, which has been used as a stimulus for reflections on immortality by many philosophers, notably Zygmunt Bauman and Geoffrey Scarre. 'The immortal', first published in 1947 in Spanish, presents the autobiography of a Roman soldier, Marcus Flaminius Rufus, who goes in search of the City of the Immortals and a river that bestows immortality.

He encounters the troglodytes, who live in caves and sandpits, have forgotten how to speak, are lifeless, and eat snakes. It turns out that these are the fabled Immortals, one of whom is Homer. They had destroyed the City of the Immortals, bored with its repetitive life, and replaced it with an irrational, confusing and chaotic city of labyrinths with dead ends, inverted staircases leading nowhere, and bizarre uninhabitable buildings, which they had long since abandoned. Immortality for them has come to mean that everything is tedious, purposeless, lacking new experiences, and no one is different or distinguished in any way because given an infinite amount of time everyone will do everything that can be done – good, bad and indifferent – probably several times over:

> There are no moral or intellectual merits. Homer composed the *Odyssey*; if we postulate an infinite period of time, with infinite circumstances and changes, the impossible thing is not to compose the *Odyssey*, at least once... Nothing can happen only once, nothing is preciously precarious.[24]

So now, they find there is no point doing anything at all, and they eke out a dismal, trance-like existence, indifferent to themselves and to others. The narrator, Rufus, drinks from the immortal river – now a polluted stream – thus gaining immortality, but comes to regret it. Centuries later, they learn of another river which has the power to remove that immortality, and all scatter in search of it, desperate to end their futile and sterile eternal lives. After many adventures, and many more centuries, Rufus finds the river, and eventually dies in 1929, leaving the manuscript describing his experiences.

Borges is unambivalent that immortality is a curse. Scarre comments that the story identifies three distinct downsides of living forever.[25] The first is that fragile and passing things, including human lives, are valued at a premium, while immortality removes that sense of preciousness. The second is the now familiar theme that immortality involves mind-numbing repetition and loss of any sense of novelty, and there is no reason to value time, so everything can be deferred indefinitely. The third is that creativity has no place in a world of immortals, largely because there is nothing transient, lost, or lamented to respond to creatively – as Borges puts it, there is nothing 'preciously precarious' that might stimulate creativity.

Zygmunt Bauman's essay 'Immortality, Postmodern Version' takes Borges' story as a starting point for his reflections on immortality, some of which were incorporated into Chapter 7. Bauman comments that the rebuilt city in the story was a city not just of immortals, but of immortals who first went through the experience of being mortal, and so needed to express, architecturally, their realisation that everything they had learned while mortal was suddenly useless and devoid of meaning. It is a point that brings us back full circle to issues raised in the Prologue: the idea that everything in human life counts only because humans know they are mortal. If death is defeated, there is no more sense or purpose:

> That human culture we know – the arts, politics, the intricate web of human relations, science or technology – was conceived at the site of the tragic yet fateful encounter between the finite span of human physical existence and the infinity of human spiritual life.[26]

His conclusion is that only the dream of immortality fills life with meaning. Immortality, if ever achieved in practice, would bring the death of meaning, which is precisely what happens in Borges' story.

The problem of living forever: social implications
So far, this chapter has largely concerned the philosophical

and psychological implications of an extended or eternal life, and how an individual person might deal with the daunting prospect of living forever. But, as science fiction writers have pointed out, there are wider social implications too. It isn't just about how an individual might cope with immortality; it's about how society would cope, with massive implications for the law, population increase, and pressure on resources, how to divide them and who to prioritise. Two areas in particular have been explored: the legal and moral implications of cryonics, and the major impact of a rising global population that is already ageing, let alone becoming immortal.

John Harris imagines a future in which reviving the dead who have been cryonically preserved has become a reality. Just as Robert Silverberg did in fiction, he considers the legal problem of the reversibility of death.[27] If cryonically frozen people, who are legally dead, are ever successfully revived, what will that mean for the legal definition of death, since it is based on an assumption that it is irreversible? Do they remain officially alive while cryonically preserved, and if so for how long – decades, centuries? Meanwhile, can their families inherit their estate; do they remain on the voting register?

In this imagined future, the advances in medical knowledge and technology that can save lives – on which the hope of cryonics is based – create a potential problem of how to allocate resources and decide who takes priority for benefiting from the new procedures. Imagining a new programme for cleaning coronary arteries that has only 100 places, and 100 non-frozen, 'alive' or 'fresh' people, and 100 cryonically frozen people, all of whom could benefit, Harris asks:

On what basis would the fresh be preferred to the frozen, or vice versa?

Who has priority on scarce resources: the living or the frozen?

Who makes the decision and on what basis? The situation could become complex and contentious:

> ... the fresh citizens may have more presently useful skills and be better able to contribute to society as a whole if they are preserved. To counter-balance this, the frozen have also frozen assets – they have invested sums of money to accumulate at compound interest and which thus hugely magnified, can only be thawed to benefit their new world when the owners are thawed and cured.

If preference is always given to contemporaries who are still legally alive, they will always use up all available resources, and the frozen will therefore never be revived and cured. Harris concludes that this is tantamount to deciding that some sorts of lives are more valuable than others, and that what are characterised as less valuable lives (i.e. the cryonically frozen) will not be further lived at all. He suggests that the most likely outcome would be that the number of contemporary 'fresh' people who require medical help will far outstrip the resources available to save them; and so they will always be given priority, and the revival and curing of the frozen will always be postponed indefinitely.

This leads us to the impact of a globally ageing population, since we are already at the stage where the needs of the living outstrip resources, or at the very least put a severe strain on them. Were human lives to be extended further, or even indefinitely, it is highly unlikely that economic, social and health systems could cope. As we saw in Chapter 6, there are few prospects of ageing being stopped, and most scientific opinion agrees that it is biologically impossible.

What happens when people age, what resources do they need to support them, and therefore what might the implications be if human life were to be extended even further? Bodies change as we age. Bone density decreases with age, so bones become weaker and can break more easily; muscles shrink and lose mass; tissues become softer and less able to tolerate stress; heart muscles become less able to pump blood, so we tire more quickly and take longer to recover; joint motion becomes more restricted and flexibility decreases; there is loss of bladder control; eyesight and hearing diminish. Dementia – defined as a broad category of brain diseases, with Alzheimer's the most common, that cause long-term decrease in the ability to think and remember and affect daily functioning including difficulties with language – becomes more common with age, and there is no known cure. Nearly half of those over 85 years of age have dementia, which has been termed an epidemic of our time:

> In most countries around the world, especially wealthy ones, this 'old old' population will continue to grow, and since it accounts for the largest proportion of dementia cases, the dementia epidemic will grow worldwide. The combined effects of longer lives and the dramatic bulge of baby boomers reaching old age will magnify the epidemic in future decades.[28]

No wonder the ancient myths sought eternal youth as well as eternal life. Life expectancy over the last few decades worldwide has increased by almost 20 years, according to Age International, due to improved healthcare and lifestyles. But as we live longer, our bodies weaken and their systems collapse. Virtually every country in the world is experiencing growth in the number and proportion of older persons in their population. Globally, the number of persons aged 80 or over is projected to triple by 2050, from 137 million in 2017 to 425 million in 2050; by 2100, it is expected to increase to 909 million, a sevenfold increase since 2017.[29] In the United Kingdom the population aged 90 or over has grown more rapidly than younger groups in recent years.

As a result, long-term care of the elderly is rapidly becoming a major political, economic and healthcare challenge. Systems have had to change to cope. Many countries have reformed pension systems, increased retirement age, limited benefits, and reduced resources allocated to health and social care. Were a solution to ageing ever to be found – the fabled elixir of youth – they would have to do exactly the same: current systems would not cope with extended lives. An ageing population also creates an unsustainable burden at the household level, in terms of the physical and emotional burden of providing care to an ageing loved one: as Eos learned with Tithonus, finally locking away his withered, babbling wreck of a body.

The main challenges to the healthcare system of an increasingly ageing population will be cancer, dementia, and increase in number of falls, obesity and diabetes. In the USA, the Office of Disease Prevention and Health Promotion estimates that more than 60 per cent of those born between 1946 and 1964 (the baby boomers) will be managing more than one chronic condition as they age, and it expects twice as many hospital admissions and doctor visits by 2030. In the UK, two-fifths of the National Health Service budget is already spent on over-65s, and the costs are set to rise as people live longer. An 85-year-old man costs the NHS about seven times more on average than a man in his late thirties, and health spending per person increases steeply after the age of 50.[30] And as we have seen, we are looking forward to a world in which, by 2100, about 450 million of those aged 80 or over are likely to have dementia – and this without further increases in longevity or magical elixirs which confer immortality.

The lesson is stark: society could not cope with immortality – or even with lives extended much further. Quite apart from the legal and moral issues highlighted earlier, healthcare systems would most likely collapse under the pressure of unsustainable demand. Who would want such an immortality, with our bodies and minds shutting down, potential boredom and lack of purpose, and unobtainability of effective healthcare because of pressure on resources? Immortality without eternal youth and health does begin to look like a curse. Tellingly, this is the message of the ancient myths and legends made real: that immortality is either unachievable or comes at too high a price.

Epilogue

The ethics of immortality

This book has explored different types of immortality, and a running theme throughout has been how interpretations, choices and preferences – of one type of immortality over another, or of none, or of one particular vision of heaven over another – are profoundly conditioned by culture, religion and worldview. Before we consider the ethical implications of that, it may be useful to sum up where we have got to.

Summing up

The theme of resurrection is found in ancient Near Eastern myth, connected with the cycle of the seasons. It was a central part of ancient Egyptian belief, where it was similarly linked with fertility and growth, with the first appearance of the idea that immortality is conditional on living a good life. The idea of bodily resurrection for the righteous developed in early Judaism as a response to persecution, and was later incorporated into Christianity and Islam, although there was – and still is – much debate about whether this resurrection is truly bodily or more spiritual.

Most human cultures have had a belief in some sort of 'soul', from the ancient Near East and Egypt onwards. The Greek philosophers were the first to systematically explore the nature of the soul. In Christianity, and to a lesser extent in Judaism and Islam, there was tension between belief in physical resurrection and the immortal soul, with frequent attempts to reconcile physical resurrection with the Greek philosophy of the soul. Modern materialism, however, denies the existence of a soul.

Where do those who hope for physical resurrection and/ or an immortal soul expect that they will end up? Human societies have imagined many different types of heaven and hell, influenced by religion, how they understand their universe, and cultural factors. Many details of early Jewish, Christian and Islamic heavens, and of the Celtic Otherworld, were derived from the pleasure garden motif of classical Elysium – itself possibly borrowed from the ancient Egyptian Field of Reeds. In many modern versions of heaven, friends and family seem to have taken the place of God, who is no longer the prime focus as he was in early and medieval times.

Reincarnation was a popular belief in Greece and Rome, and remains central to all the major Eastern religions, in which there are significantly different understandings of what becomes immortal once liberated from the cycle of reincarnations. There have been minority strands of reincarnation belief even in Christianity, Judaism and Islam, and it is a hugely popular subject today, with forests-worth of books concerning memories of past lives.

In animist societies, reincarnation is one of several different types of transformation. Humans, dead or alive, are believed to transform into other humans, animals, plants and spirits, connected with the continuing involvement of ancestors in their communities and the preservation of traditional social structures.

Not all hope of immortality involves life after death, though. Failed searches for earthly immortality in myth and legend date back to Gilgamesh, the world's oldest story, which has been continuously adapted and retold, and they became important themes in the ever-popular legends of Achilles and in the Arthurian tales of the Holy Grail. In modern times, cryonics continues the search, taking its place alongside the mythical magical elixirs and plants, sacred fires and holy vessels that confer immortality on this earth.

The simplest, and perhaps the only, way to achieve immortality is to be remembered forever, to achieve fame of some kind, to leave behind something of lasting value, or to beget children. In ancient times, heroes and rulers had the resources to ensure that they were immortalised in epics and on public monuments, but ordinary people had their own modest strategies to be remembered and to commemorate their dead. In modern times, communication technologies have made it easier to pursue a form of immortality through fame and celebrity, without the inconvenience of having to be a hero.

The materialist worldview rejects all the different types of post-mortem immortality – resurrection, the immortal soul, reincarnation and transformation – but materialism itself has many explanatory gaps and is not beyond critique. Ultimately, there is no conclusive proof for any of these beliefs, including the materialist conclusion that there can be no immortality; equally, though, none of them can be excluded.

The final chapter considered if immortality is worth having, or if it might be a curse. From ancient Greece to the present, concerns have been expressed that any form of immortality could become tedious and unfulfilling, especially if the problem of ageing is not solved, and that heaven might be boring. The implications of immortality for the individual and for society, and the legal and moral issues it would throw up, have been taken up by modern philosophers. With a growing ageing population already putting a strain on health services worldwide, it is likely that society could not cope with immortality.

Reflecting on the history of immortality, it is remarkable how many of the ideas that still concern us today have their origins in the ancient Near East and Greece. Did those cultures 'invent' immortality? One possible interpretation is that the ancient Near East's ritual memorialisation of the dead, and the human drive to leave a legacy, combined to create a unique cultural tradition that vainly sought immortality, stimulating speculation on whether death was restful or restless, whether the dead were sentient or not, and whether the living could encounter the dead.

Or perhaps it is not so remarkable. Although it is in

these cultures that we first find ideas around immortality recorded, they are, arguably, universal preoccupations and not something that could be 'invented', like writing or the wheel. An alternative interpretation is that this was not so much a unique cultural response, as a generic human one to the fact of death, attempting to minimise it and make it acceptable. The dismal early underworlds of the ancient Near East, Sheol and Hades were strikingly similar, offering at least some sort of continued existence and sentience, however dreary, that was better than nothingness; and they offered the reassurance that the dead could still be communicated with. Indeed, every culture since then, probably in every period, has had its seers, shamans, mediums and witches who have, or claim, the ability to communicate with the dead. Within every culture, they are the carriers of the possibility that some sort of sentience persists after death. In some societies, they are valued and honoured, in others they are marginalised and persecuted, in still others they are ignored and laughed at – but they are always present, providing an alternative narrative around death.

Nevertheless, it was in the ancient Near East that human concerns about immortality were first incorporated into myths, legends and stories, and were deemed important enough to be preserved in writing on clay tablets and stored in libraries, for reading, reference and scribal training. Although the Hindu Sanskrit texts predate Greek philosophical speculation, they were sacred texts largely concerned with spiritual instruction and ritual; it was in Greece that philosophers first began, seriously and systematically, to explore the nature and meaning of the soul and of immortality – although, fascinatingly, the earliest Upanishads, the Homeric epics and the standard version of Gilgamesh were all being produced at about the same time, an extraordinarily inventive period across different geographical and cultural regions. Those ancient ideas and writings have come down to us through the legacy of Arabic culture brought into Europe via medieval Spain, which reintroduced the thinking of the Greek philosophers to the West, through medieval and Renaissance learning, and through the accident of discovery, and they continue to influence how we think about what happens after – or possibly instead of – death.

Ethical implications

Reflecting on the implications of the final chapter, one possible conclusion is that it would be selfish for individuals to extend their lives indefinitely because of the stress it would put on society and their families. An unlikely and unforeseeable solution to the problem of ageing would address some of these problems, but would raise others.

But there are other kinds of ethical issues which have practical implications now, not in some fantasy world in which humans are no longer mortal, and these concern our attitudes to alternative worldviews. As we saw in Chapter 8, there is no conclusive proof for any of the forms of 'real' immortality, through resurrection, an immortal soul, reincarnation or transformation, or for the materialist argument that the mind depends on the brain, which would exclude all these forms of immortality. Each has major problems and explanatory gaps. None can be proved, but equally none can be dismissed. We do not know, for certain, which view is correct; or, as Alan Segal suggests, they may all be merely approximations of what awaits us.[1]

Materialists often dismiss most of these beliefs about immortality as irrational and unintelligible.[2] They may have unsolved (and possibly unsolvable) problems, but it must be emphasised that all of the thought behind them is rational. They are all grounded in perfectly legitimate metaphysical philosophies about the nature of reality and how the world might work. The issue for materialists is that they do not fit into the materialist framework, which is only one of several possible worldviews (and which, of course, might turn out to be correct).

Mockery of other worldviews is not limited to materialists: as we saw in Chapter 8, the Mundaka Upanishad hit back pre-emptively, more than two and a half thousand years ago, by dismissing intellectual knowledge as 'lower' knowledge that is ignorant and deluded. The destruction of Native American and Australian Aboriginal cultures also has its roots in misunderstanding and persecution of alternative worldviews – essentially, an attempt to 'civilise' by imposing other (mostly Christian) worldviews and values.

The question of immortality, then, is not a clash of evidence, but of worldviews and of interpretation. David Skrbina, in assessing the materialist attitude to panpsychism, makes points that are true for any worldview:

Two individuals, each observing nature from the perspective of different worldviews, will reach different conclusions about the meaning of reality... there is great difficulty in properly assessing other worldviews. All judgments are colored by one's own perspective, especially one's judgment *about* one's perspective, or another's perspective... The materialist... has no unbiased standpoint from which to make a judgment. Thus, a ruling of 'unintelligible' or 'false' is meaningless.[3]

Although this is largely a clash of worldviews, nevertheless I would argue that the tensions around immortality are not an example of relativism, in which all the views might be true in their own cultural, religious or philosophical context: it is genuine uncertainty about whether or not there can be any form of immortality and, if there is, what form (or lack of form) it might take.

This is not to deny the depth of conviction people have about whether or not they have an immortal soul, will go to a particular heaven, reincarnate or transform into ancestors. Already in 1902, in *The Varieties of Religious Experience*, William James defended our right to believe ahead of the evidence, concluding that some things cannot be settled by the rational procedures of common sense or science: we feel and believe things to be true regardless of any objective evidence. We tend to be led by instinct, not evidence, often dismissing or ignoring evidence that is contrary to those beliefs, and embracing evidence that supports them:

> ... something in you absolutely *knows* that the result must be truer than any logic-chopping rationalistic talk, however clever, that may contradict it... If a person feels the presence of a living God... your critical arguments, be they never so superior, will vainly set themselves to change his faith.[4]

But, however deeply felt one's own views, whatever worldview informs them, and however enthusiastically we embrace the evidence that supports them, it should not be an excuse for mockery, ridicule and dismissal of other views as irrational, unintelligible and worthless fantasies. Ultimately, as we have seen, every single one of these positions about immortality or its impossibility has some element of incoherence; none is capable of explaining all the problems. There is always the possibility that the other person may be right.

Whatever beliefs we were brought up with, have adopted or seem 'common sense' to us, as Mary Midgley points out in *The Myths We Live By*, we always have a choice about the perspective from which we look. Of course we can disagree with other views, and stick to our own chosen beliefs. Trouble arises when we dogmatically universalise our own assumptions, perspective and worldview and promote them as laws of nature and as the one and only way to explain the world. With the lack of conclusive proof for any of the views about immortality examined throughout this book, highlighted in Chapter 8, no one is in a position to be dogmatic about their assumptions and perspective. No alternative belief or worldview is irrational, and our own chosen belief and worldview, whichever it might be, is chock-full of problems and explanatory gaps. We are all in the same position of having to admit the possibility that explanations and beliefs about what happens to us after death, other than those we might hold dear, may be correct or at least deserving of respect and open to investigation rather than outright dismissal.

It is salutary to note just how many traditions about immortality were borrowed between cultures and religions: not only from the ancient Near East and Greece, but especially between Judaism, Christianity and Islam. These three had a mutual indebtedness in their approaches to the afterlife, and this obvious and well-worn point bears repeating in a world gripped by rising religious hate crime, Islamophobia, anti-Semitism, and persecution of Christian communities especially in Muslim countries. They drew on the same traditions concerning physical resurrection, the immortal soul and the nature of the afterlife that developed in Palestine in the centuries between c. 300 BCE and c. 300 CE, each adapting those traditions in distinctive ways over the next few hundred years. All three religions had similar debates concerning whether a human is a physical body, an immortal soul, or both, do they reunite after death, what aspect of a person goes to heaven, and all attempted to reconcile their doctrines with the philosophies of the soul of Plato and Aristotle. The idea of heaven for the virtuous and a fiery hell for the wicked in all three religions originated in early Jewish thinking about physical resurrection – possibly borrowed from Zoroastrianism in Persia – in response to persecution and a hope for a blessed afterlife. They all had similar early traditions of ascents to heaven and descents to hell, with multiple heavens, a guide, encountering the same angels and prophets, heaven imagined as a temple or palace, and a single deity seated on a throne.

Segal, closing his magisterial study of the afterlife in these three religious traditions, brings us full circle to the arguments presented in the Preface to the present book by concluding that the forms of the afterlife reflect any particular culture's social goals:

> ... our 'immortal longings' are mirrors of what we find of value in our lives. They motivate our moral and artistic lives.[5]

Indeed, it has become customary – a sort of developing mini-tradition – for books on immortality and the afterlife to end with a meaningful comment on life after death that provides a revealing insight into the authors' worldview. The materialist arch-sceptic Paul Edwards, concluding his introduction to readings on immortality, raises what for him are insurmountable problems and difficulties around the practicalities of immortality:

> The history of theology undoubtedly contains some ingenious answers, but perhaps it would be wise to wait for the solution until we ourselves reach the hereafter – provided of course that there is a hereafter and that we are among those who will reach it.[6]

His fellow materialist Stephen Cave likens life to a book that has a beginning and an end, and argues that we should all accept that life ends, with no sequel:

> The book's characters know no horizons; they, like we, can only know the moments that make up their lives, even when the book is closed. They are therefore untroubled by reaching the last page. And so it should be with us.[7]

Jeffrey Burton Russell's overtly Christian history of heaven ends poetically, focusing on the eternity of God's love:

> So shall every love every love more enkindle, until the cosmos

coruscates with loving light, living more and ever more.[8]

Not dissimilar in sentiment are the final lines of Philip Almond's history of the afterlife in Western thought, which acknowledges human desire for life beyond the grave and the hope that life has some eternal meaning and purpose. It ends with a passage from Paul's letter to the Romans promising a better life to come:

> For I reckon that the sufferings of this present time are not worthy to be compared with the glory that shall be revealed to us.[9]

The conclusion of David Fontana's review of the evidence for the afterlife also raises questions about the meaning of life:

> If your answer is that you are more than a biological accident whose ultimately meaningless life is bounded by the cradle and the grave, then I have to say I agree with you.[10]

The present short history of immortality has attempted to trace where particular ideas about the afterlife originated, whence they were borrowed, and how and why they were adapted to fit in with different worldviews, religions and cultural traditions. It has highlighted historical disputes concerning, among others, resurrection, the immortal soul or its absence, the types of heaven and hell and who goes there, or what happens when the cycle of reincarnations is broken. Historically, there has been plenty of uncertainty around those issues, and no definitive proof for any of the interpretations.

So, on what basis do we choose which interpretation to believe, if any? And do we remain open to other perspectives, recognising their potential validity? Looked at that way, our attitude to immortality is an ethical choice: it is a window on to our soul (if we have one).

Notes

Prologue. An urge to immortality?

1. Camus, *The Myth of Sisyphus and Other Essays*, p. 2.
2. Freud, Thoughts for the Times on War and Death, p. 152.
3. See Magee, *The Philosophy of Schopenhauer*, pp. 52-3.
4. Plato, *Symposium* 208d-e.
5. Plato, *Symposium* 209c-d.
6. Lucretius, *De Rerum Natura* 3: 830-842, translated by T. Jackson, in Clark, *Selections from Hellenistic Philosophy*, pp. 27-8.
7. For the existentialists on death, see Cooper, *Existentialism*, pp. 133-39. The analytic tradition of philosophy, which included most of British philosophy, paid little attention to the meaning of life until the end of the twentieth century: see the historical survey in Seachris (ed.), *Exploring the Meaning of Life*, pp. 1-20.
8. Heidegger, *Being and Time*, section 53, p. 308.
9. Heidegger, *Being and Time*, sections 46-53. For an analysis, see Mulhall, *Heidegger and* Being and Time, pp. 114-20. *Being and Time* was first published in German in 1927.
10. Becker, *The Denial of Death*, p. xvii.
11. Solomon, Greenberg and Pyszczynski, *The Worm at the Core*.
12. Pyszczynski, Solomon and Greenberg, *In the Wake of 9/11*.
13. I am indebted to the analysis of this book in Beilharz, *Zygmunt Bauman*, pp. 146-52.
14. Bauman, *Mortality, Immortality and Other Life Strategies*, p. 31.
15. Bauman, *Mortality, Immortality and Other Life Strategies*, p. 7.
16. Cave, *Immortality*, p. 2.
17. See Ucko, Ethnography and archaeological interpretation of funerary remains.
18. Anderson, Chimpanzees and death.

19. Scarre, *Death*, pp. 51 and 155, note 12; Simpson, *Death, Dying, and Grief*.
20. Ecclesiastes 9:5.

Chapter 1. Resurrection from the ancient Near East to Jesus
1. For more on this, see Smith, *Drudgery Divine*.
2. For translations of poems about Baal, see Pritchard, *Ancient Near Eastern Texts*, pp. 129-42.
3. Assmann, Resurrection in ancient Egypt.
4. Lichtheim, *Ancient Egyptian Literature Volume 1: The Old and Middle Kingdoms*, p. 230.
5. From Ishtar's Descent to the Underworld, translated by S. Dalley, *Myths from Mesopotamia*, p. 155.
6. *Aeneid* 6: 373-4, translated by R. Fagles. The line numbers here and throughout this book refer to the Fagles translation of the *Aeneid*, where the line numbers of the Latin text are found at the top of every page.
7. Pliny, *The Letters of the Younger Pliny*, p. 203 (Book 7, Letter 27).
8. Davies, *Death, Burial and Rebirth in the Religions of Antiquity*, p. 122.
9. Luke 24:39.

Chapter 2. The immortal soul
1. 2009 survey by Theos, and World Values Surveys 1981-2002.
2. Homer, *Odyssey* 11: 219-24, translated by E. Wilson.
3. Virgil, *Aeneid* 2: 984-86, translated by R. Fagles.
4. Quoted in Runes, *Treasury of Philosophy*, p. 495.
5. Whitehead, *Process and Reality*, p. 39.
6. *Phaedo* 80A: Plato, *The Last Days of Socrates*, translated by H. Tredennick, p. 132.
7. *Phaedo* 106: Plato, *The Last Days of Socrates*, translated by H. Tredennick, p. 169.
8. From his Letter to Herodotus, in Book 10 of Diogenes

Laertius' *Lives of the Eminent Philosophers*.

9. Tertullian, *On the Resurrection of the Flesh* I, translated by P. Holmes, p. 545.

10. *Catechism of the Catholic Church*, revised edition, Burns & Oates, 2002.

11. Aquinas, *Commentary on the First Epistle to the Corinthians*, para. 924.

12. From the *Summa Theologica*, in Edwards (ed.), *Immortality*, p. 98.

13. From Descartes' letter to Isaac Beeckmann, the Dutch mathematician, in 1619, quoted in Descartes, *Discourse on Method and the Meditations*, translated by F.E. Sutcliffe, p. 8. For an analysis of this letter, see Bos, *Redefining Geometrical Exactness*, pp. 231ff.

14. Sixth Meditation: Descartes, *Discourse on Method and the Meditations*, translated by F.E. Sutcliffe, p. 156.

15. From the Discourse on the Method: Descartes, *Discourse on Method and the Meditations*, translated by F.E. Sutcliffe, p. 76.

16. Hickson, The Moral Certainty of Immortality in Descartes.

17. Kant, Refutation of Mendelssohn's proof of the permanence of the soul, and Hume, Of the immortality of the soul, both in Edwards (ed.), *Immortality*, pp. 139 and 156.

18. Segal, *Life After Death*, p. 608.

19. Quoted in Segal, *Life After Death*, p. 628.

Chapter 3. Journeys to heaven and hell

1. Pew Research Center, U.S. public becoming less religious.

2. https://yougov.co.uk/news/2016/03/26/o-we-of-little-faith/

3. A good introduction to wide-ranging cross-cultural writings about heaven is Carol and Philip Zaleski's anthology, *The Book of Heaven*.

4. Translation by S. Dalley, *Myths from Mesopotamia*, pp. 184-88.

5. For the story of Etana, see Dalley, *Myths from Mesopotamia*,

pp. 189-202.

6. Homer, *Odyssey* 4: 561-7, translated by E. Wilson.
7. Homer, *Odyssey* 6: 42-6, translated by E. Wilson.
8. Virgil, *Aeneid* 6: 313-20, translated by R. Fagles.
9. Virgil, *Aeneid* 6: 741-42, translated by R. Fagles.
10. Virgil, *Aeneid* 6: 779-80, translated by R. Fagles.
11. Assmann, *Death and Salvation in Ancient Egypt*, p. 392.
12. Wright, *The Early History of Heaven*, p. 171.
13. Wright, *The Early History of Heaven*, p. 174.
14. Quoted in Wright, *The Early History of Heaven*, p. 179.
15. See below in this chapter, and Zaleski, *Otherworld Journeys*, p. 28.
16. Luxenberg, *The Syro-Aramaic Reading of the Koran*.
17. Ibn Warraq, Virgins? What virgins? *The Guardian*, 12 January 2002.
18. Quoted in Wright, *The Early History of Heaven*, p. 212.
19. Segal, *Life After Death*, pp. 658-81.
20. Smith and Haddad, *The Islamic Understanding of Death and Resurrection*, pp. 158-68.
21. In C. and P. Zaleski, *The Book of Heaven*, p. 321.
22. In C. and P. Zaleski, *The Book of Heaven*, p. 329.
23. In Gardiner, *Visions of Heaven and Hell before Dante*, pp. 83-4.
24. Severin, *The Brendan Voyage*.
25. Usefully collected in Gardiner, *Visions of Heaven and Hell before Dante*.
26. Segal, *Life After Death*, p. 190.
27. Zaleski, *Otherworld Journeys*, p. 38.
28. McDannell and Lang, *Heaven*, pp. 119-24.
29. Phelps, *The Gates Ajar*, pp. 93-4.
30. Phelps, *The Gates Ajar*, p. 130, footnote.
31. Jürgenson, *The Voices from Space*; Raudive, *Breakthrough*; Brune, *Les morts nous parlent*.
32. Similarly, NDEs among Native Americans record their own culture and customs, with a focus on ancestors of the

tribe. See, for example, a Hopi tale of an NDE in Voth, The traditions of the Hopi; also Chapter 5, for Native Americans and ancestors.

33. For the Sumerian version, see Pritchard, *Ancient Near Eastern Texts*, pp. 52-7; for the Akkadian version, *ibid.* pp. 106-09 and Dalley, *Myths from Mesopotamia*, pp. 154-62.
34. Virgil, *Aeneid* 6: 647-48, translated by R. Fagles.
35. Virgil, *Aeneid* 6: 712-14, translated by R. Fagles.
36. Bremmer, The Golden Bough.
37. Translation by Charlesworth, *The Old Testament Pseudepigrapha*.
38. Virgil, *Aeneid* 6: 724-27, translated by R. Fagles.
39. Apocalypse of Paul, fourth redaction, quoted in Zaleski, *Otherworld Journeys*, p. 28.
40. For an overview of these 'test-bridges', see Zaleski, *Otherworld Journeys*, pp. 65-9.
41. Quoted in Lange, *Locating Hell in Islamic Traditions*, p. 17.
42. Goodrich, *Chinese Hells*. The Chinese hells are not everlasting, but sufferings between one incarnation and the next. Other cultures, too, portray ice as a form of punishment in the afterlife; for example, a story of the Cochiti tribe of Native Americans in New Mexico has ice-cold water running over sinners' bodies as punishment, as they sit on ledges on an ice mountain after death. See Benedict, Tales of the Cochiti Indians.
43. See Barolini, Inferno 11.
44. Russell, *A History of Heaven*, pp. 151ff.

Chapter 4. Reincarnation and the eternal spirit
1. From Rigveda Book 1, Hymn 164, line 30, translation by S. Radhakrishnan, cited in the introduction to his *Principal Upanishads*, pp. 43-44, as evidence for his claim that elements of reincarnation are to be found in this text.
2. Rigveda Book 1, Hymn 164, line 30, translation by Jamison

and Brereton, *The Rigveda*, Volume 1.

3. See Doniger O'Flaherty (ed.), *Karma and Rebirth in Classical Indian Traditions*, pp. 3-11.

4. Shvetashvatara Upanishad I.6.⁵ All translations from the Upanishads are by Easwaran, *The Upanishads*, unless otherwise noted.

5. Brihadaranyaka Upanishad IV.4.6-7.

6. Amritabindu Upanishad 12.

7. Amritabindu Upanishad 15.

8. Katha Upanishad II.1.10.

9. Shvetashvatara Upanishad V.11-12.

10. Katha Upanishad II.2.7, and see associated note in Easwaran, *The Upanishads*, p. 351.

11. Katha Upanishad II.3.13.

12. Prashna Upanishad Question VI.5.

13. Quoted in Vetter, *The Ideas and Meditative Practices of Early Buddhism*, p. 41, note 11.

14. Dhammapada 279, translation by Buddharakkhita in his *The Dhammapada*, p. 65.

15. See, for example, Katulkar, Rethinking Rebirth.

16. *Majjhima-Nikaya* 63, in Warren, *Buddhism in Translations*, p. 122. The Pali version consists of 152 sutras, while the Chinese translation of the lost Sanskrit version has 222, with 97 common to both.

17. Translation by Osborne, from *Dumb Beasts and Dead Philosophers*, p. 47.

18. Shakespeare, *As You Like It*, Act 3, scene 2; see also *The Merchant of Venice*, Act 4, scene 1; and Marlowe's *Doctor Faustus*, Act 5, scene 4.

19. Diogenes Laertius, *Lives of the Eminent Philosophers*, Book 8, chapter 1.

20. Diogenes Laertius, *Lives of the Eminent Philosophers*, Book 8, chapter 2.

21. *Phaedo* 72: Plato, *The Last Days of Socrates*, translated by H.

Tredennick, p. 119.

22. Virgil, *Aeneid* 6: 821-4, translated by R. Fagles.

23. Virgil, *Aeneid* 6: 865-9, translated by R. Fagles.

24. Brihadaranyaka Upanishad II.4.14.

25. Plotinus, *Ennead* V.III.5: 44-5, in Clark, *Selections from Hellenistic Philosophy*, p. 245.

26. Mundaka Upanishad III.2.9, translation by Mascaró, *The Upanishads*, p. 81. An alternative translation of this line is: 'Those who know the Self become the Self', by Easwaran, *The Upanishads*, p. 195.

27. Plotinus, *Ennead* V.III.7: 2-3, in Clark, *Selections from Hellenistic Philosophy*, p. 247.

28. Plotinus, *Ennead* VI.IX.10: 1-4, in Clark, *Selections from Hellenistic Philosophy*, p. 266.

29. The Anathemas are conveniently reproduced in Head and Cranston, *Reincarnation: An East-West Anthology*, pp. 321-5. Note that the status of the council, and whether the Anathemas were issued properly and were formally binding, are the subject of much discussion.

30. Quoted in Ogren, *Renaissance and Rebirth*, p. 256.

31. Pico, *On the Dignity of Man*.

32. Quoted in Ogren, *Renaissance and Rebirth*, p. 220.

33. Pew Research Center, Many Americans mix multiple faiths.

34. Zohar 3: 99b, in Sperling and Simon, *The Zohar*.

35. The actual incarnation of the divine spirit in humans is called *hulul* in Arabic. Nine extreme Shia sects and five others, including the Druze and Sufi sects, are known to be believers in this process, rejected by mainstream Islam: see *Shorter Encyclopaedia of Islam*, 'Hulul', p. 141.

36. Lessing, *Education of the Human Race*, quoted in Head and Cranston, *Reincarnation: An East-West Anthology*, p. 176.

37. Poe, *Selected Tales*, p. 22.

38. Magee, *The Philosophy of Schopenhauer*, p. 15.

39. Blavatsky, *The Secret Doctrine*, quoted in Head and Cranston,

Reincarnation: An East-West Anthology, p. 65.

40. Besant, *Reincarnation*, quoted in Head and Cranston, *Reincarnation: An East-West Anthology*, p. 68.

41. Blavatsky, *Isis Unveiled*, quoted in Head and Cranston, *Reincarnation: An East-West Anthology*, p. 63.

42. Some accounts are described briefly in Head and Cranston, *Reincarnation: The Phoenix Fire Mystery*, pp. 395-416; in Edwards, *Reincarnation: A Critical Examination*, pp. 59-105; and in Wilson, *Mind Out of Time*.

43. Besterman, *Mrs. Annie Besant*, pp. 214-21.

Chapter 5. Immortal ancestors: death as transformation

1. Harvey, *Animism*, p. xi.

2. Hogan in Harvey, *The Handbook of Contemporary Animism*, p. 22.

3. Harvey, *The Handbook of Contemporary Animism*, p. 4.

4. Nowadays, Christianity in parts of this region contends with the resilience of traditional beliefs. As Swain and Trompf report in *The Religions of Oceania*, p. 209, Trobrianders sometimes say that their dead go first to Tuma and later to the Christian heaven.

5. Most of this has not been systematically collated, but for a dated overview see Moss, *The Life After Death in Oceania and the Malay Archipelago*. The book was Rosalind Moss' Bachelor degree thesis in anthropology. Her later specialism was actually Egyptology.

6. Terminology is problematic for the indigenous peoples of North America. This book uses the term Native Americans, which includes the Inuit, the native peoples of the North American Arctic, formerly known as Eskimos. Other terms frequently used are American Indians, Amerindians, and – in Canada – Aboriginal peoples.

7. Oceania is the geographic term for Australasia and the Pacific Islands. Ninety-five per cent of people in this area

now regard themselves as Christian in some way: statistic quoted in Swain and Trompf, *The Religions of Oceania*, p. 192.

8. The Yukaghirs of Siberia have similar rebirth beliefs to the Inuit: see Willerslev, *Soul Hunters*.

9. Census figure quoted in Swain and Trompf, *The Religions of Oceania*, p. 102.

10. Frazer, *The Belief in Immortality and the Worship of the Dead*. Frazer's understanding of Central Australian reincarnation beliefs was based largely on the work of Spencer and Gillen, *The Northern Tribes of Central Australia*, pp. 145-76.

11. Besterman, Belief in rebirth among the natives of Africa. Besterman did more or less the same job of compiling existing accounts for Africa as Moss did for Oceania (see note 5). See also Onyewuenyi, *African Belief in Reincarnation*, who argues, on philosophical grounds, that African connections to ancestors are mistakenly interpreted as belief in reincarnation.

12. Seabrook, *The Magic Island*, p. 99.

13. Seabrook, *The Magic Island*, p. 101.

Chapter 6. From Gilgamesh to cryonics: the search for the everlasting body

1. The First Emperor's search for immortality is recorded as historical fact in the later *Historical Records* of Sima Qian, but many scholars now suspect this is either folklore or deliberate fabrication to undermine the reputation of a ruler regarded by later tradition as an unhinged tyrant. Certainly the quest for the immortals and the elixir of everlasting life reads like myth: they are to be found in the spirit mountains, where all the flora and fauna are white, and the palaces and gates are made of gold and silver (see Sima Qian, *The First Emperor: Selections from the* Historical Records, pp. 98-9). Elixirs with various wonderful properties were a staple theme of Chinese and Japanese mythology.

2. George, *The Epic of Gilgamesh*, pp. 70-72.

3. George, *The Epic of Gilgamesh*, p. 98.

4. George, *The Epic of Gilgamesh*, p. 124.

5. George, *The Epic of Gilgamesh*, p. 199.

6. George, *The Epic of Gilgamesh*, p. 200.

7. George, *The Epic of Gilgamesh*, p. 198.

8. George, *The Epic of Gilgamesh*, p. 77.

9. Homer, *Odyssey* 5: 156-8, translated by E. Wilson.

10. Admittedly the Siduri episode, by then at least 500 years old, does not appear on any of the fragments of the Gilgamesh story so far found in Syria and Palestine, but what has been found through the accident of discovery are just disjointed parts of the story, suggesting that originally there was more.

11. See Dalley, Gilgamesh in the Arabian Nights.

12. Quoted in George, *The Epic of Gilgamesh*, p. xxiii.

13. Most of these are now in the collections of National Museums Liverpool, where they used to be curated by the author.

14. Ziolkowski, *Gilgamesh Among Us*, p. 197.

15. George, *The Epic of Gilgamesh*, p. 160.

16. Homer, *Iliad* 1: 1-2, translated by R. Lattimore.

17. Apollonius Rhodius, *Argonautica* 4: 869-72, translated by R.C. Seaton. This story is retold in the *Library* ascribed to Apollodorus of Athens, dated to the first or second century CE (Apollodorus, *The Library of Greek Mythology* III.13).

18. Statius, *Achilleid* 1: 269, translated by J.H. Mozley.

19. Hyginus, *Fabulae* 107, translated by M. Grant. See Grant, *The Myths of Hyginus*.

20. An account of the Achilles' heel story does appear in the commentary on the *Aeneid* by Maurus Servius Honoratus, a late fourth/early fifth-century CE Italian scholar who wrote a set of commentaries on Virgil, which might be slightly earlier than Fulgentius; but the surviving manuscripts of the expanded commentary date much later, to the tenth and eleventh centuries, and contain many additions which

were almost certainly not by Servius. See Fowler, The Virgil commentary of Servius.

21. Fulgentius, *Mythologiae* 3: 7, translated by L.G. Whitbread. See Whitbread, *Fulgentius the Mythographer*.

22. The earliest written reference to this tendon being named after Achilles is by the Flemish surgeon and anatomist Philip Verheyen (1648-1710) in his *Corporis Humani Anatomiae*, a survey of the current knowledge of anatomy published in 1693, in which he records that the tendon was commonly called the 'cord of Achilles'. For background, see Suy, Philip Verheyen (1648-1710) and his *Corporis Humani Anatomiae*.

23. Reprinted in Rooke (ed.), *The Collected Works of Samuel Taylor Coleridge: The Friend, Volume 4*: volume I, p. 311, volume II, p. 357.

24. Ovid, *Metamorphoses* 12: 615-19, translated by M.M. Innes.

25. Wolfram von Eschenbach, *Parzival*, Book IX, section 469 (p. 198), translated by C. Edwards.

26. Malory, *Le Morte Darthur*, Vol. 3, Book XI, Chapter XIV, p. 213.

27. Malory, *Le Morte Darthur*, Vol. 3, Book XIII, Chapter VII, p. 254.

28. A slightly earlier oddity, seemingly unconnected to the other Grail traditions, is *De schismate libri III* by Dietrich von Niem (c. 1345-1418), completed in 1410, a personal history of events, which records that the Grail is a round hill in the Italian countryside where men live until the day of judgment – arguably a form of immortality.

29. In *Der Parcival* by Friedrich de la Motte Fouqué (1777-1843), completed in 1832 and inspired by Wolfram von Eschenbach's *Parzival*, the Grail too sustains life and can prevent death. But this book was only published in 1997, and so did not contribute to the development of the Grail immortality theme during the nineteenth and twentieth centuries. Wolfram's *Parzival* was also a key source for

Richard Wagner's last opera, *Parsifal*; Fouqué was a friend of Wagner's uncle, and his Nibelung trilogy was one of many sources for Wagner's *Ring* cycle.

30. In the novelization of the film, the knight explains that this is because he did not drink from the Grail every day: he aged a year for every day he did not drink. See MacGregor, *Indiana Jones and the Last Crusade*.
31. The history of attempts to prolong life is entertainingly described in Haycock's *Mortal Coil* and Boia's *Forever Young*.
32. Bauman, *Mortality, Immortality and Other Life Strategies*, p. 138.
33. The thousand-years claim was made in a TV programme, *Aux frontières de l'immortalité*, on the ARTE network, 16 November 2008.
34. Weon and Je, Theoretical estimation of maximum human lifespan.
35. Nelson and Masel, Intercellular competition and the inevitability of multicellular ageing.
36. Ettinger, *The Prospect of Immortality*, p. 11.
37. Ettinger, *The Prospect of Immortality*, p. 15.
38. Ettinger, *The Prospect of Immortality*, p. 15.
39. Ettinger, *The Prospect of Immortality*, p. 63.
40. Ettinger, *The Prospect of Immortality*, p. 16.
41. 2014. See Moen, The case for cryonics.
42. Cryonics is of course a staple of science fiction, and the cryonic preservation of heads is a theme in the science fiction animated series *Futurama* (1999-2013), with the heads of historical figures and celebrities preserved in jars.
43. Harris, *The Value of Life*, pp. 250-51.
44. Harris, *The Value of Life*, p. 244. Harris goes on to develop a fanciful example of a world in which people are endlessly revived and refrozen as they await the cure for their next ailment, postponing death in perpetuity. 'They might well have to stay frozen a long time – but then you're a long time

dead' (p. 245).

Chapter 7. 'I will establish for ever a name eternal!'

1. From the poem 'Bilgames and Huwawa', in George, *The Epic of Gilgamesh*, p. 151.
2. From the poem 'The Death of Bilgames', in George, *The Epic of Gilgamesh*, p. 207.
3. George, *The Epic of Gilgamesh*, pp. 188-9. This is the poem that was translated into Akkadian and formed tablet XII of the standard version of the epic of Gilgamesh (see Chapter 6).
4. George, *The Epic of Gilgamesh*, p. 112 (Yale tablet).
5. George, *The Epic of Gilgamesh*, p. 124 (Sippar tablet).
6. George, *The Epic of Gilgamesh*, p. 99.
7. Homer, *Odyssey* 5: 206-10, translated by E. Wilson.
8. Homer, *Odyssey* 5: 219-20, translated by E. Wilson. In his 1833 poem, 'Ulysses', Alfred, Lord Tennyson reinvented Ulysses/ Odysseus as ageing, restless, discontented and seeking further adventures in which 'Some work of noble note, may yet be done'. Tennyson's portrayal was influenced by that of Dante, who consigned Ulysses to hell for his unnatural thirst for knowledge.
9. Nussbaum, *Love's Knowledge: Essays on Philosophy and Literature*, p. 365.
10. Homer, *Iliad* 9: 410-16, translated by R. Lattimore.
11. Homer, *Iliad* 9: 400-08, translated by R. Lattimore.
12. Homer, *Iliad* 18: 114-21, translated by R. Lattimore.
13. Thucydides, *History of the Peloponnesian War* 2.42.2, translated by R. Crawley.
14. R.L. Binyon, 'For the Fallen', published in *The Times* newspaper, 21 September 1914.
15. Moore, introduction to Fichte, *Addresses to the German Nation*, pp. xxvii-xxviii.
16. Agamemnon, played by Brian Cox, in the 2004 film *Troy*.

17. Bauman, *Mortality, Immortality and Other Life Strategies*, p. 57.

18. Griffin, in Boardman, Griffin and Murray (eds.), *The Oxford History of the Classical World*, p. 627.

19. Virgil, *Aeneid* 1: 344, translated by R. Fagles.

20. Virgil, *Aeneid* 6: 913-15, translated by R. Fagles.

21. Some scholars argue that Ovid was never banished, and that his tales of exile are the product of his imagination.

22. Goldsworthy, *Augustus*, p. 8. For other parallels with Stalin, see Linderski's paper Mommsen and Syme: Law and Power in the Principate of Augustus, p. 49.

23. Griffin protests that Augustan pressure on poets and writers was civilised, in contrast to the world of Stalin, in Boardman, Griffin and Murray (eds.), *The Oxford History of the Classical World*, p. 626 (see also Griffin's *Virgil*).

24. Selections translated into English by A. Rudolf have been published in Tvardovsky, *Tyorkin and the Stovemakers*.

25. Bauman, *Mortality, Immortality and Other Life Strategies*, p. 58.

26. Lattimore, *Themes in Greek and Latin Epitaphs*, p. 271.

27. Ariès, *The Hour of Our Death* and *Western Attitudes toward Death from the Middle Ages to the Present*.

28. Bauman, *Mortality, Immortality and Other Life Strategies*, p. 58.

29. Bauman, *Mortality, Immortality and Other Life Strategies*, p. 172.

Chapter 8. Science and philosophy v. immortality

1. A critique of the possibilities and potential of cryonics has already been included as part of Chapter 6.

2. Voltaire, *Questions sur l'encyclopédie* (1770-1772), from selection in Edwards (ed.), *Immortality*, pp. 146-7. For a historical survey of responses to the Cannibal Problem, see Almond, *Afterlife*, pp. 66-72.

3. Edwards (ed.), *Immortality*, pp. 58-9; Cave, *Immortality*, pp. 140-43.
4. Lucretius, *De Rerum Natura* 3: 624-678, translated by T. Jackson, in Clark, *Selections from Hellenistic Philosophy*, pp. 26-7.
5. Churchland, *Matter and Consciousness*, p. 20.
6. Edwards (ed.), *Immortality*, pp. 46-53; for other, largely conceptual, objections to the soul, see Velmans, *Understanding Consciousness*, pp. 12-20; Goetz and Taliaferro, *A Brief History of the Soul*, pp. 182-201.
7. Edwards, *Reincarnation*, p. 239.
8. Edwards, *Reincarnation*, p. 247.
9. Edwards, *Reincarnation*, p. 139.
10. Edwards, *Reincarnation*, p. 140.
11. Edwards, *Reincarnation*, p. 281.
12. Edwards, *Reincarnation*, p. 256.
13. Edwards, *Reincarnation*, p. 268.
14. In Stevenson, *Cases of the Reincarnation Type: Vol. 1 – Ten Cases in India*.
15. Almeder, *Death and Personal Survival*, pp. 34-5.
16. Edwards, *Reincarnation*, p. 248.
17. Mundaka Upanishad I.2.8.
18. Goswami, *The Self-Aware Universe*. For a philosophical perspective, see Foster, *The Case for Idealism*.
19. Harvey, in *Animism*, p. 17, and *The Handbook of Contemporary Animism*, p. 6, also essentially equates panpsychism with the 'new' animism.
20. Skrbina, *Panpsychism in the West*, p. 18. 'Qualia' and 'nous', derived from Latin and Greek respectively, are alternative terms for 'what it feels like' and 'mind'.
21. For these recent and alternative approaches, see Strawson, Realistic monism; de Quincey, *Radical Nature*; Velmans, *Understanding Consciousness*; Tononi, *Phi: A Voyage from the Brain to the Soul*; Koch, *Consciousness*; Griffin, *Unsnarling the*

World-Knot; Goff, *Consciousness and Fundamental Reality*; for quantum physics and panpsychism, see Skrbina, *Panpsychism in the West*, pp. 188-206.

22. Restall Orr, *The Wakeful World*, pp. 222-7. Harvey, *Animism*, pp. 115-20.
23. Descartes, in Alquie (ed.), *Oeuvres Philosophiques de Descartes*, p. 502 note.
24. Popper, *Objective Knowledge*, p. 222.
25. Hawking, *A Brief History of Time*, p. 13.
26. Midgley, *Science and Poetry*, abridged in Midgley (ed.), *The Essential Mary Midgley*, p. 334.
27. Midgley, *Science as Salvation*, p. 58.
28. For a collection of philosophical critiques of materialism, see Robinson (ed.), *Objections to Physicalism*.
29. Baker, 1,500 scientists lift the lid on reproducibility.
30. Fanelli, How Many Scientists Fabricate and Falsify Research?
31. Koch, *Consciousness*, p. 8.
32. Quoted in Ian Sample, Ambitious neuroscience project to probe how the brain makes decisions. *The Guardian*, 19 September 2017.
33. Tononi and Koch, Consciousness.
34. Pearsall *et al.*, Changes in Heart Transplant Recipients that Parallel the Personalities of Their Donors; Pearsall, *The Heart's Code*.
35. See Velmans, *Understanding Consciousness*, Chapter 14, and the chapters by S. Harding and M. Hall in Harvey (ed.), *The Handbook of Contemporary Animism*, pp. 373-94; for bacteria, the papers by Ben-Jacob *et al.* in the bibliography.
36. Koch, *Consciousness*, pp. 118-19.
37. Strawson, Realistic monism, p. 12.
38. Quoted in Koch, *Consciousness*, p. 114.
39. Koch, *Consciousness*, p. 119.
40. Nagel, *Secular Philosophy and the Religious Temperament*, p. 25.

41. Goetz and Taliaferro, *A Brief History of the Soul*, p. 167.
42. Edwards, *Reincarnation*, p. 295.
43. Midgley, *Science as Salvation*, p. 89.
44. McGinn, Can we solve the mind-body problem?
45. From the 1971 song *American Pie* by Don McLean, published by the Universal Music Publishing Group.

Chapter 9. Is immortality a curse?

1. Williams, The Makropulos case, p. 92.
2. Williams, The Makropulos case, p. 94.
3. Aquinas, *Summa Theologica*, Part II.1, Question 3, Article 8.
4. Twain, *Extract from Captain Stormfield's Visit to Heaven*.
5. Scarre, *Death*, pp. 153-4, note 9.
6. Williams, The Makropulos case, p. 95.
7. Segal, *Life After Death*, pp. 679-81. Not all scholars agree that the rewards of heaven are a primary motivation for martyrdom, despite the evidence of diaries, letters and interviews. Olivier Roy, in *Jihad and Death*, argues that Islamic State, at least, is motivated largely by a fascination for death, and is in essence a death cult.
8. For dating of the Homeric Hymn to Aphrodite, see Rodda, *L'Inno Omerico ad Afrodite*.
9. Homeric Hymn to Aphrodite: 237-8, translated by Evelyn-White in *Hesiod, the Homeric Hymns and Homerica*.
10. Janko, Tithonus, Eos and the cicada.
11. Tennyson, *The Works of Alfred Lord Tennyson*, pp. 96-7.
12. Lucian, Menippus and Chiron, from *Dialogues of the Dead*, translated by Fowler and Fowler in *The Works of Lucian of Samosata*.
13. Swift, *Gulliver's Travels*, p. 267.
14. Swift, *Gulliver's Travels*, p. 269.
15. Haggard, *She*, pp. 137 and 258-9.
16. Haggard, *She*, p. 259.
17. See the various essays in Slusser, Westfahl and Rabkin (eds.),

Immortal Engines.

18. Heinlein, *Methuselah's Children*, p. 52.
19. Heinlein, *Methuselah's Children*, p. 63.
20. Silverberg, *Recalled to Life*, p. 188.
21. Williams wrongly calculates her age as 342, a mistake perpetuated by most commentators on his paper. In both the play and the opera she states her age as 327, and that she took the potion at the age of 16, not 42 as Williams claims.
22. Williams, The Makropulos case, p. 82.
23. The responses to Williams' essay are many and varied, and rather than cite individual ones, the reader is referred to the summary, with references, in Scarre, *Death*, pp. 56-60, to which this section is indebted. See also Fischer, Why immortality is not so bad.
24. Borges, The Immortal, pp. 145-6.
25. Scarre, *Death*, pp. 53-5.
26. Bauman, Immortality, Postmodern Version, p. 153.
27. For the following, including the next two quotes, see Harris, *The Value of Life*, pp. 244-52.
28. Larson, Yaffe and Langa, New Insights into the Dementia Epidemic.
29. United Nations, *World Population Prospects: The 2017 Revision*.
30. Robineau, Ageing Britain.

Epilogue. The ethics of immortality

1. Segal, *Life After Death*, p. 711.
2. For example, Edwards dismisses reincarnation as 'worthless', and panpsychism as 'meaningless', in *Reincarnation*, p. 7, and in his encyclopedia entry 'Panpsychism'. He has been criticised by many for his 'astounding' bias and ridicule of worldviews he does not share: see, for example, Skrbina, *Panpsychism in the West*, p. 235, citing quotes from other philosophers. Cave is more circumspect, but privileges a materialist view, without acknowledging its own

shortcomings, in concluding that all forms of immortality lack credibility: *Immortality*, p. 274.

3. Skrbina, *Panpsychism in the West*, pp. 259 and 269.
4. James, *The Varieties of Religious Experience*, pp. 73-4.
5. Segal, *Life After Death*, p. 731.
6. Edwards (ed.), *Immortality*, p. 70.
7. Cave, *Immortality*, p. 307.
8. Russell, *A History of Heaven*, p. 189.
9. Romans 8:18; Almond, *Afterlife*, p. 193.
10. Fontana, *Is There an Afterlife?*, p. 469.

TIMELINE

	Near East and Egypt	Classical world	Far East	Europe
2500 BCE	Earliest Egyptian funerary texts (Pyramid Texts) Sumerian stories of Gilgamesh			
2000 BCE	Old Babylonian version of Gilgamesh			Bronze Age (to c. 600 BCE)
1500 BCE	Baal Cycle from Ugarit Ramesses II	Mycenaean civilisation	Rigveda	
1000 BCE	Ashurbanipal and standard version of Gilgamesh	Homer: *Iliad* and *Odyssey*	Oldest Upanishads	
500 BCE	Persian Empire Jewish apocalyptic writings	Plato Aristotle Epicurus Virgil: *Aeneid* Augustus	Buddha Mahavira, founder of Jainism	Celtic cultures
1 BCE/1 CE	Jesus Destruction of Jerusalem Temple Augustine	Plotinus		Roman Empire
500 CE	Muhammad			Celtic Voyage of Bran
1000 CE	Crusades			Vision of Tundale *The Story of the Grail* Thomas Aquinas Dante: *Divine Comedy*
1500 CE			Guru Nanak, founder of Sikhism	René Descartes

Further Reading

General

Bremmer, J.N., *The Rise and Fall of the Afterlife*. Routledge, 2001.

Cave, S., *Immortality: The Quest to Live Forever and How it Drives Civilisation*. Biteback Publishing Ltd, 2013.

Edwards, P. (ed.), *Immortality*. Prometheus Books, 1997.

Fontana, D., *Is There an Afterlife? A Comprehensive Overview of the Evidence*. O-Books, 2005.

Segal, A.F., *Life After Death: A History of the Afterlife in Western Religion*. Doubleday, 2004.

Prologue. An urge to immortality?

Bauman, Z., *Mortality, Immortality and Other Life Strategies*. Polity Press, 1992.

Becker, E., *The Denial of Death*. Souvenir Press, 2011.

Scarre, G., *Death*. Acumen, 2007 (especially Chapter 4, pp. 65-83).

Chapter 1. Resurrection from the ancient Near East to Jesus

Davies, J., *Death, Burial and Rebirth in the Religions of Antiquity*. Routledge, 1999 (especially Parts I and II, pp. 23-124).

Mettinger, T.N.D., *The Riddle of Resurrection: 'Dying and Rising' Gods in the Ancient Near East*. Almqvist & Wiksell International, 2001.

Wright, N.T., *The Resurrection of the Son of God*. SPCK, 2003.

Chapter 2. The immortal soul

Almond, P.C., *Afterlife: A History of Life After Death*. I.B. Tauris, 2016.

Bremmer, J.N., *The Early Greek Concept of the Soul*. Princeton University Press, 1983.

Goetz, S. and Taliaferro, C., *A Brief History of the Soul*. Wiley-

Blackwell, 2011.

Martin, R. and Barresi, J., *The Rise and Fall of Soul and Self: An Intellectual History of Personal Identity.* Columbia University Press, 2006.

Chapter 3. Journeys to heaven and hell

Bernstein, A., *The Formation of Hell: Death and Retribution in the Ancient and Early Christian Worlds.* Cornell University Press, 1993.

Gardiner, E. (ed.), *Visions of Heaven and Hell before Dante.* Italica Press, 1989.

Himmelfarb, M., *The Apocalypse: A Brief History.* Wiley-Blackwell, 2010.

Lange, C., *Paradise and Hell in Islamic Traditions.* Cambridge University Press, 2015.

Le Goff, J., *The Birth of Purgatory.* University of Chicago Press, 1986.

Loffler, C.M., *The Voyage to the Otherworld Island in Early Irish Literature.* University of Salzburg, 1983.

McDannell, C. and Lang, B., *Heaven: A History.* Vintage Books, 1990.

Smith, J.I. and Haddad, Y.Y., *The Islamic Understanding of Death and Resurrection,* new edition. Oxford University Press, 2002.

Wright, J.E., *The Early History of Heaven.* Oxford University Press, 2000.

Chapter 4. Reincarnation and the eternal spirit

Christie-Murray, D., *Reincarnation: Ancient Beliefs and Modern Evidence.* Prism Press, 1988.

Edwards, P., *Reincarnation: A Critical Examination.* Prometheus Books, 2002.

Head, J. and Cranston, S.L. (eds.), *Reincarnation: The Phoenix Fire Mystery.* Julian Press/Crown Publishers, 1977.

McClelland, N.C., *Encyclopedia of Reincarnation and Karma.*

McFarland and Co., 2010.

Chapter 5. Immortal ancestors: death as transformation

Cowan, J., *Aborigine Dreaming: An introduction to the wisdom and thought of the Aboriginal traditions of Australia*. Thorsons, 2002.

Davis, W., *Passage of Darkness: The Ethnobiology of the Haitian Zombie*. University of North Carolina Press, 1988.

Harvey, G., *Animism: Respecting the Living World*. Hurst and Company, 2005.

Mills, A. and Slobodin, R. (eds.), *Amerindian Rebirth: Reincarnation Belief Among North American Indians and Inuit*. University of Toronto Press, 1994.

Chapter 6. From Gilgamesh to cryonics: the search for the everlasting body

Barber, R., *The Holy Grail: The History of a Legend*. Penguin Books, 2005.

Burgess, J.S., *The Death and Afterlife of Achilles*. Johns Hopkins University Press, 2009.

Ettinger, R.C.W., *The Prospect of Immortality*. Doubleday, 1964.

George, A., *The Epic of Gilgamesh: The Babylonian Epic Poem and Other Texts in Akkadian and Sumerian*. Allen Lane: The Penguin Press, 1999.

Ziolkowski, T., *Gilgamesh Among Us: Modern Encounters With the Ancient Epic*. Cornell University Press, 2011.

Chapter 7. 'I will establish for ever a name eternal!'

Bauman, Z., *Mortality, Immortality and Other Life Strategies*. Polity Press, 1992.

Cave, S., *Immortality: The Quest to Live Forever and How it Drives Civilisation*. Biteback Publishing Ltd, 2013 (especially Chapter 8, pp. 215-42).

Davies, J., *Death, Burial and Rebirth in the Religions of Antiquity*. Routledge, 1999 (especially Part III, pp. 125-86).

George, A., *The Epic of Gilgamesh: The Babylonian Epic Poem and Other Texts in Akkadian and Sumerian*. Allen Lane: The Penguin Press, 1999.

Stahl, H.-P., *Poetry Underpinning Power – Vergil's* Aeneid: *The Epic for Emperor Augustus*. Classical Press of Wales, 2016.

Chapter 8. Science and philosophy v. immortality

Edwards, P. (ed.), *Immortality*. Prometheus Books, 1997.

Edwards, P., *Reincarnation: A Critical Examination*. Prometheus Books, 2002.

Goetz, S. and Taliaferro, C., *A Brief History of the Soul*. Wiley-Blackwell, 2011 (especially Chapters 6-8, pp. 152-215).

Midgley, M., *Are You An Illusion?* Routledge, 2014.

Skrbina, D., *Panpsychism in the West*. MIT Press, 2005.

Velmans, M., *Understanding Consciousness*, second edition. Routledge, 2009.

Chapter 9. Is immortality a curse?

Bauman, Z., Immortality, Postmodern Version. In *Postmodernity and its Discontents* (Polity Press, 1997): 152-64.

Borges, J.L., The immortal. In *Labyrinths: Selected Short Stories and Other Writings* (Penguin, 2000): 135-49.

Scarre, G., *Death*. Acumen, 2007 (especially Chapter 3, pp. 47-63).

Williams, B., The Makropulos case: reflections on the tedium of immortality. In *Problems of the Self: Philosophical Papers 1956-1972* (Cambridge University Press, 1973): 82-100.

Bibliography

Albrecht von Scharfenberg, *Der jüngere Titurel*. G. Basse, 1842.

Almeder, R., *Death and Personal Survival: The Evidence for Life After Death*. Littlefield Adams, 1992.

Almond, P.C., *Afterlife: A History of Life After Death*. I.B. Tauris, 2016.

Alquie, F. (ed.), *Oeuvres Philosophiques de Descartes*. Gamier Frères, 1973.

Anderson, J.R., Chimpanzees and death. *Philosophical Transactions of the Royal Society B: Biological Sciences* (16 July 2018). doi. org/10.1098/rstb.2017.0257.

Apollodorus, *The Library of Greek Mythology*, translated by R. Hard. Oxford University Press, 1997.

Apollonius Rhodius, *Argonautica*, translated by R.C. Seaton. Loeb Classical Library, Heinemann, 1912.

Aquinas, T., *Summa Theologica*, translated by the Fathers of the English Dominican Province. Benziger Brothers, 1947 (republished by Catholic Way Publishing, 2014).

Aquinas, T., *Commentary on the First Epistle to the Corinthians*. Amazon Media, Kindle edition, not dated.

Ariès, P., *Western Attitudes toward Death from the Middle Ages to the Present*, translated by P.M. Ranum. Johns Hopkins University Press, 1975.

Ariès, P., *The Hour of Our Death*, translated by H. Weaver. Knopf, 1981.

Aristotle, *De Anima (On the Soul)*, translated by H. Lawson-Tancred. Penguin Classics, 1987.

Aristotle, *The Nicomachean Ethics*, translated by D. Ross, revised by L. Brown. Oxford University Press, 2009.

Assmann, J., Resurrection in Ancient Egypt. In *Resurrection: Theological and Scientific Assessments*, eds. T. Peters, R.J. Russell and M. Welker (Eerdmans, 2002): 124-35.

Assmann, J., *Death and Salvation in Ancient Egypt*. Cornell University Press, 2006.

Avery, W.T., Augustus and the 'Aeneid'. *The Classical Journal* 52 (5) (1957): 225-29.

Bacon, F., *The History, Natural and Experimental, of Life and Death: Or of the Prolongation of Life*. Forgotten Books, 2017 [1638].

Baker, M., 1,500 scientists lift the lid on reproducibility. *Nature* 533, 452–454 (26 May 2016). doi:10.1038/533452a.

Barber, M., *The Cathars: Dualist Heretics in Languedoc in the High Middle Ages*. Longman, 2000.

Barber, R., *The Holy Grail: The History of a Legend*. Penguin Books, 2005.

Barolini, T., Inferno 11: Aristotle, Pagan Authority of a Christian hell. *Commento Baroliniano, Digital Dante*. Center for Digital Research and Scholarship. New York: Columbia University Libraries, 2015. http://digitaldante.columbia.edu/dante/divine-comedy/inferno/inferno-11/

Bauman, Z., *Mortality, Immortality and Other Life Strategies*. Polity Press, 1992.

Bauman, Z., Immortality, Postmodern Version. In *Postmodernity and its Discontents* (Polity Press, 1997): 152-64.

Becker, E., *The Denial of Death*. Souvenir Press, 2011 [1973].

Beilharz, P., *Zygmunt Bauman: Dialectic of Modernity*. Sage Publications, 2000.

Benedict, R., Tales of the Cochiti Indians. *Bureau of American Ethnology Bulletin 98*, 1932.

Ben-Jacob, E.; Becker, I.; Shapira, Y. and Levine, H., Bacterial linguistic communication and social intelligence. *Trends in Microbiology* 12:8 (2004): 366-72.

Ben-Jacob, E., Shapira, Y. and Tauber, A.I., Smart bacteria. In *Chimeras and Consciousness: Evolution of the Sensory Self*, eds. L. Margulis, C.A. Asikainen and W.E. Krumbein (MIT Press, 2011): 55-62.

Berndt, R.M. and Berndt, C.H., *The World of the First Australians*.

Aboriginal Studies Press, 1992.

Bernstein, A., *The Formation of Hell: Death and Retribution in the Ancient and Early Christian Worlds*. Cornell University Press, 1993.

Bernstein, M., *The Search for Bridey Murphy*. Doubleday, 1956.

Besterman, T., *Mrs. Annie Besant: A Modern Prophet*. Kegan Paul, Trench, Trubner & Co., 1934.

Besterman, T., Belief in rebirth among the natives of Africa. In *Collected Papers on the Paranormal* (Garrett, 1968): 22-59.

Betts, R.B., *The Druze*. Yale University Press, 1988.

Bienkowski, P., Archaeological Knowledge, Animist Knowledge, and Appropriation of the Ancient Dead. In *Heritage from Below*, ed. I. Robertson (Ashgate, 2012): 29-58.

Bienkowski, P. and Coleman, E.B., Contesting 'claims' on human remains: which traditions are treated as legitimate and why? In *Global Ancestors: Understanding the Shared Humanity of Our Ancestors*, eds. M. Clegg, R. Redfern, J. Bekvalac and H. Bonney (Oxbow Books, 2013): 81-101.

Bienkowski, P. and Millard, A. (eds.), *British Museum Dictionary of the Ancient Near East*. British Museum Press, 2000.

Bienkowski, P. and Tooley, A.M.J., *Gifts of the Nile*. HMSO, 1995.

Boardman, J., Griffin, J. and Murray, O. (eds.), *The Oxford History of the Classical World*. Oxford University Press, 1986.

Boia, L., *Forever Young: A Cultural History of Longevity from Antiquity to the Present*. Reaktion Books, 2004.

Borges, J.L., The immortal. In *Labyrinths: Selected Short Stories and Other Writings* (Penguin, 2000): 135-49.

Bos, H.J.M., *Redefining Geometrical Exactness: Descartes' Transformation of the Early Modern Concept of Construction*. Springer, 2001.

Bremmer, J.N., *The Early Greek Concept of the Soul*. Princeton University Press, 1983.

Bremmer, J.N., *The Rise and Fall of the Afterlife*. Routledge, 2001.

Bremmer, J.N., The Golden Bough: Orphic, Eleusinian, and

Hellenistic-Jewish Sources of Virgil's Underworld in *Aeneid* VI. *Kernos* 22 (2009): 183-208.

Brown, P., *Augustine of Hippo: A Biography*, second edition. University of California Press, 2000.

Brune, F., *Les morts nous parlent*. Éditions du Félin, 1988.

Bruntrup, G. (ed.), *Panpsychism: Contemporary Perspectives*. Oxford University Press, 2016.

Buddharakkhita, A., *The Dhammapada: The Buddha's Path of Wisdom*. Buddhist Publication Society, 1985.

Burgess, J.S., *The Death and Afterlife of Achilles*. Johns Hopkins University Press, 2009.

Bynum, C.W., *The Resurrection of the Body in Western Christianity*. Columbia University Press, 1995.

Callicott, J.B., Traditional American Indian and Western European attitudes toward nature: an overview. *Environmental Ethics* 4 (1982): 293-318.

Camus, A., *The Myth of Sisyphus and Other Essays*, translated by J. O'Brien. Vintage International, 1991.

Cave, S., *Immortality: The Quest to Live Forever and How it Drives Civilisation*. Biteback Publishing Ltd, 2013.

Chadwick, N., *The Celts*. Pelican Books, 1970.

Chari, C.T.K., Reincarnation research: Method and interpretation. In *The Signet Handbook of Parapsychology*, ed. M. Ebon (New American Library, 1978): 313-24.

Charlesworth, J.H., *The Old Testament Pseudepigrapha*. Doubleday, 1983.

Chrétien de Troyes, *Perceval: The Story of the Grail*, translated by B. Raffel. Yale University Press, 1999.

Christie-Murray, D., *Reincarnation: Ancient Beliefs and Modern Evidence*. Prism Press, 1988.

Churchland, P.M., *Matter and Consciousness*, revised edition. MIT Press, 1984.

Clark, G.H., *Selections from Hellenistic Philosophy*. Appleton-Century-Crofts, 1940.

Coleman, G. and Dorje, G. (eds. and translators), *The Tibetan Book of the Dead: First Complete Translation*. Penguin, 2006.

Collins, S., *Selfless Persons: Imagery and Thought in Theravāda Buddhism*. Cambridge University Press, 1982.

ComRes, *BBC Religion and Ethics Survey* (2017). http://www.comresglobal.com/polls/bbc-religion-and-ethics-survey/

Conklin, B.A., *Consuming Grief: Compassionate Cannibalism in an Amazonian Society*. University of Texas Press, 2001.

Cooper, D.E., *Existentialism: A Reconstruction*, second edition. Blackwell Publishing, 1999.

Cowan, J., *Mysteries of the Dream-time: The Spiritual Life of Australian Aborigines*. Prism Press, 1992.

Cowan, J., *Aborigine Dreaming: An introduction to the wisdom and thought of the Aboriginal traditions of Australia*. Thorsons, 2002.

Dalley, S., *Myths from Mesopotamia*. Oxford University Press, 1989.

Dalley, S., Gilgamesh in the Arabian Nights. *Journal of the Royal Asiatic Society* series 3, vol. 1, no. 1 (1991): 1-17.

Damasio, A., *The Feeling of What Happens: Body, Emotion and the Making of Consciousness*. Vintage, 2000.

Damrosch, D., *The Buried Book: The Loss and Rediscovery of the Great Epic of Gilgamesh*. Henry Holt, 2007.

Dante, *The Divine Comedy*, translated by C. James. Picador, 2013.

Davies, B. and Stump, E. (eds.), *The Oxford Handbook of Aquinas*. Oxford University Press, 2014.

Davies, J., *Death, Burial and Rebirth in the Religions of Antiquity*. Routledge, 1999.

Davis, W., *Passage of Darkness: The Ethnobiology of the Haitian Zombie*. University of North Carolina Press, 1988.

Davis, W., *The Serpent and the Rainbow*. Pocket Books, 1997.

De Quincey, C., *Radical Nature: Rediscovering the Soul of Matter*. Invisible Cities Press, 2002.

Descartes, R., *Discourse on Method and the Meditations*, translated by F.E. Sutcliffe. Penguin, 1968.

Diogenes Laertius, *Lives of the Eminent Philosophers*, translated by R.D. Hicks. Loeb, 1989.

Doniger O'Flaherty, W. (ed.), *Karma and Rebirth in Classical Indian Traditions*. University of California Press, 1992.

Dundas, P., *The Jains*. Routledge, 2002.

Easwaran, E. (translator), *The Upanishads*, second edition. Nilgiri Press, 2007.

Eberl, J., *The Routledge Guidebook to Aquinas' Summa Theologiae*. Routledge, 2015.

Edwards, P., Panpsychism. In *The Encyclopedia of Philosophy*, Volume VI, ed. P. Edwards (Macmillan, 1967): 22-31.

Edwards, P. (ed.), *Immortality*. Prometheus Books, 1997.

Edwards, P., *Reincarnation: A Critical Examination*. Prometheus Books, 2002.

Edwards, W.H., *Traditional Aboriginal Society: A Reader*. Macmillan, 1987.

Ekroth, G., *The Sacrificial Rituals of Greek Hero-Cults in the Archaic to the Early Hellenistic Period*. Centre International d'Étude de la Religion Grecque Antique, 2002.

Ettinger, R.C.W., *The Prospect of Immortality*. Doubleday, 1964.

Evelyn-White, H.G. (translator), *Hesiod, the Homeric Hymns and Homerica*. Loeb Classical Library, Heinemann, 1914.

Fanelli, D., How Many Scientists Fabricate and Falsify Research? A Systematic Review and Meta-Analysis of Survey Data. *PLoS ONE* 4 (5): e5738. https://doi.org/10.1371/journal.pone.0005738

Feinberg, T.E. and Mallatt, J.M., *The Ancient Origins of Consciousness: How the Brain Created Experience*. MIT Press, 2016.

Fichte, J.G., *Addresses to the German Nation*, edited by G. Moore. Cambridge University Press, 2008.

Fischer, J.M., Why immortality is not so bad. *International Journal of Philosophical Studies* 2:2 (1994): 257-70.

Fontana, D., *Is There an Afterlife? A Comprehensive Overview of the*

Evidence. O-Books, 2005.

Foster, J., *The Case for Idealism*. Routledge and Kegan Paul, 1982.

Fouqué, F. de la Motte, *Der Parcival*. G. Olms, 1997.

Fowler, D., The Virgil commentary of Servius. In *The Cambridge Companion to Virgil*, ed. C. Martindale (Cambridge University Press, 1997): 73-78.

Fowler, H.W. and Fowler, F.G., *The Works of Lucian of Samosata*. The Clarendon Press, 1905.

Frazer, J.G., *The Belief in Immortality and the Worship of the Dead*. Macmillan and Co., 1913.

Frazer, J.G., *The Golden Bough: A Study in Magic and Religion. A New Abridgment*. Oxford University Press, 2009.

Freedman, D.N. (ed.), *The Anchor Bible Dictionary*, 6 volumes. Doubleday, 1992.

Freud, S., Thoughts for the Times on War and Death. In *Death: Philosophical Soundings*, ed. H. Fingarette (Open Court, 1996): 149-56.

Gardiner, E. (ed.), *Visions of Heaven and Hell before Dante*. Italica Press, 1989.

George, A., *The Epic of Gilgamesh: The Babylonian Epic Poem and Other Texts in Akkadian and Sumerian*. Allen Lane: The Penguin Press, 1999.

Gibb, H.A.R. and Kramers, J.H., *Shorter Encyclopedia of Islam.* Brill, 1953.

Goetz, S. and Taliaferro, C., *A Brief History of the Soul*. Wiley-Blackwell, 2011.

Goff, P., *Consciousness and Fundamental Reality*. Oxford University Press, 2017.

Goldsworthy, A., *Augustus: From Revolutionary to Emperor*. Weidenfeld and Nicolson, 2014.

Goodrich, A.S., *Chinese Hells: The Peking Temple of Eighteen Hells and Chinese Conceptions of Hell*. Monumenta Serica, 1981.

Goswami, A., *The Self-Aware Universe: How Consciousness Creates the Material World*. Putnam/Tarcher, 1993.

Grant, M. (translator), *The Myths of Hyginus*. University of Kansas Press, 1960.

Grey, A. de, *Ending Aging: The Rejuvenation Breakthroughs That Could Reverse Human Aging in Our Lifetime*. St Martin's Press, 2007.

Griffin, D.R., *Unsnarling the World-Knot*. University of California Press, 1998.

Griffin, J., *Homer on Life and Death*. Clarendon Press, 1980.

Griffin, J., *Virgil*. Oxford University Press, 1986.

Griffiths, J.G., *The Origins of Osiris and His Cult*. Brill, 1980.

Grimal, P., *The Penguin Dictionary of Classical Mythology*. Penguin Books, 1990.

Haggard, H.R., *She: A History of Adventure*. Macdonald, 1948 [1886].

Hallotte, R., *Death, Burial, and Afterlife in the Biblical World: How the Israelites and Their Neighbors Treated the Dead*. Ivan R. Dee, 2001.

Halman, L., Inglehart, R., Diez-Medrano, J., Luijkx, R., Moreno, A. and Basáñez, M., *Changing Values and Beliefs in 85 Countries: Trends from the Values Surveys from 1981 to 2002*. Brill, 2008.

Hankins, J., Marsilio Ficino on reminiscentia and the transmigration of souls. *Rinascimento* 45 (2005): 3-17.

Harris, J., *The Value of Life: An Introduction to Medical Ethics*. Routledge & Kegan Paul, 1985.

Harvey, G., *Animism: Respecting the Living World*. Hurst and Company, 2005.

Harvey, G. (ed.), *The Handbook of Contemporary Animism*. Routledge, 2014.

Hawking, S., *A Brief History of Time*. Bantam Press, 1988.

Haycock, D.B., *Mortal Coil: A Short History of Living Longer*. Yale University Press, 2008.

Head, J. and Cranston, S.L. (eds.), *Reincarnation: The Phoenix Fire Mystery*. Julian Press/Crown Publishers, 1977.

Head, J. and Cranston, S.L. (eds.), *Reincarnation: An East-West*

Anthology. Quest Books, 1990.

Heidegger, M., *Being and Time*, translated by J. Macquarrie and E. Robinson. Blackwell, 1962.

Heil, J. (ed.), *Philosophy of Mind: A Guide and Anthology*. Oxford University Press, 2004.

Heinlein, R.A., *Methuselah's Children*. New English Library, 1971 [1958].

Hickson, M.W., The Moral Certainty of Immortality in Descartes. *History of Philosophy Quarterly* 28/3 (July 2001): 227-46.

Himmelfarb, M., *Tours of Hell: An Apocalyptic Form in Jewish and Christian Literature*. Fortress, 1985.

Himmelfarb, M., *Ascent to Heaven in Jewish and Christian Apocalypses*. Oxford University Press, 1993.

Himmelfarb, M., *The Apocalypse: A Brief History*. Wiley-Blackwell, 2010.

Hingley, R., *Russian Writers and Soviet Society 1917-1978*. Methuen, 1981.

Homer, *The Iliad of Homer*, translated by R. Lattimore. University of Chicago Press, 1951.

Homer, *The Odyssey*, translated by E. Wilson. W.W. Norton & Company, 2018.

Huffman, C., Pythagoras. *The Stanford Encyclopedia of Philosophy* (Summer 2014 edition), E.N. Zalta (ed.), https://plato.stanford. edu/archives/sum2014/entries/pythagoras/

Humphreys, S.C. and King, H. (eds.), *Mortality and Immortality: The Anthropology and Archaeology of Death*. Academic Press, 1981.

Irwin, R., *The Arabian Nights: A Companion*. Tauris Parke, 2012.

Jacoff, R. (ed.), *The Cambridge Companion to Dante*, second edition. Cambridge University Press, 2007.

James, W., *The Varieties of Religious Experience: A Study in Human Nature*. Longmans, Green, and Co., 1917 [1902].

Jamison, S.W. and Brereton, J.P. (translators), *The Rigveda: The Earliest Religious Poetry of India*. Oxford University Press, 2014.

Janko, R., Tithonus, Eos and the cicada in the *Homeric Hymn to Aphrodite* and Sappho fr. 58. In *The Winnowing Oar: New Perspectives in Homeric Studies*, eds. C. Tsagalis and A. Markantonatos (Walter de Gruyter, 2017): 267-96.

Jefferson, W., *Reincarnation Beliefs of North American Indians: Soul Journeys, Metamorphoses, and Near-Death Experiences*. Native Voices, 2008.

Jürgenson, F., *The Voices from Space*. Saxon and Lindström, 1964.

Katulkar, R., Rethinking Rebirth: A Modern Buddhist Challenge to Justification of Prevailing Myth, Inequality and Social Injustice. Paper presented at the Twelfth International Buddhist Conference, Bangkok, 28-30 May 2015. https://www.academia.edu/25443690/Rethinking_Rebirth_A_Modern_Buddhist_Challenge_to_Justification_of_Prevailing_Myth_Inequality_and_Social_Injustice

Kitagawa, J.M. and Cummings, M.D. (eds.), *Buddhism and Asian History*. Macmillan, 1989.

Koch, C., *Consciousness: Confessions of a Romantic Reductionist*. MIT Press, 2017.

Lambert, M., *The Cathars*. Blackwell, 1998.

Lange, C., *Paradise and Hell in Islamic Traditions*. Cambridge University Press, 2015.

Lange, C. (ed.), *Locating Hell in Islamic Traditions*. Brill, 2015.

Larson, E.B., Yaffe, K. and Langa, K.M., New Insights into the Dementia Epidemic. *New England Journal of Medicine* 369 (2013): 2275-77. DOI: 10.1056/NEJMp1311405.

Lattimore, R., *Themes in Greek and Latin Epitaphs*. University of Illinois Press, 1942.

Lecouteux, C., *The Return of the Dead: Ghosts, Ancestors, and the Transparent Veil of the Pagan Mind*. Inner Traditions, 2009.

Le Goff, J., *The Birth of Purgatory*. University of Chicago Press, 1986.

Lichtheim, M., *Ancient Egyptian Literature*, 3 volumes. University of California Press, 1975, 1976, 1980.

Linderski, J., Mommsen and Syme: Law and Power in the Principate of Augustus. In *Between Republic and Empire: Interpretations of Augustus and his Principate*, eds. K.A. Raaflaub and M. Toher (University of California Press, 1993): 42-53.

Locke, J., *An Essay Concerning Human Understanding*. Penguin Classics, 1997.

Loffler, C.M., *The Voyage to the Otherworld Island in Early Irish Literature*. University of Salzburg, 1983.

Lopez, D.S., Jr., Buddhism in practice. In *Asian Religions in Practice: An Introduction*, ed. D.S. Lopez, Jr. (Princeton University Press, 1999): 56-87.

Luxenberg, C., *The Syro-Aramaic Reading of the Koran: A Contribution to the Decoding of the Language of the Koran*. Hans Schiler Publishers, 2007.

Lyons, D., *Gender and Immortality: Heroines in Ancient Greek Myth and Cult*. Princeton University Press, 1997.

MacGregor, G., *Reincarnation in Christianity: A New Vision of the Role of Rebirth in Christian Thought*. Quest Books, 1978.

MacGregor, G., *Images of Afterlife: Beliefs from Antiquity to Modern Times*. Paragon House, 1992.

MacGregor, R., *Indiana Jones and the Last Crusade*. Ballantine Books, 1989.

Magee, B., *The Philosophy of Schopenhauer*, revised edition. Clarendon Press, 1997.

Malinowski, B., Baloma: the Spirits of the Dead in the Trobriand Islands. In *Magic, Science, and Religion and Other Essays*, by B. Malinowski (1916; reprint Beacon Press, 1948): 125-227.

Malinowski, B., *The Sexual Life of Savages in North-Western Melanesia*. Routledge, 1929.

Malory, Sir T., *Le Morte Darthur*, in four volumes. J.M. Dent and Co., 1898.

Martin, R. and Barresi, J., *The Rise and Fall of Soul and Self: An Intellectual History of Personal Identity*. Columbia University Press, 2006.

Mascaró, J. (translator), *The Upanishads*. Penguin Books, 1965.

Matt, D.C., *The Essential Kabbalah: The Heart of Jewish Mysticism*. Castle Books, 1998.

Matthews, C., *The Elements of the Celtic Tradition*. Element Books, 1989.

Matthews, C., *The Celtic Book of the Dead*. The Aquarian Press, 1992.

Matthews, G.B., *Augustine*. Wiley-Blackwell, 2005.

Mautner, T., *The Penguin Dictionary of Philosophy*. Penguin, 2000.

McClelland, N.C., *Encyclopedia of Reincarnation and Karma*. McFarland and Co., 2010.

McDannell, C. and Lang, B., *Heaven: A History*. Vintage Books, 1990.

McGinn, B., *Visions of the End: Apocalyptic Traditions in the Middle Ages*, revised edition. Columbia University Press, 1998.

McGinn, C., Can we solve the mind-body problem? In *Philosophy of Mind: A Guide and Anthology*, ed. J. Heil (Oxford University Press, 2004): 781-97 (reprinted from *Mind* 98, 1989).

McGinn, C., *Character of Mind*. Oxford University Press, 1997

Mettinger, T.N.D., *The Riddle of Resurrection: 'Dying and Rising' Gods in the Ancient Near East*. Almqvist & Wiksell International, 2001.

Midgley, D. (ed.), *The Essential Mary Midgley*. Routledge, 2005.

Midgley, M., *Science as Salvation: A Modern Myth and its Meaning*. Routledge, 1996.

Midgley, M., *The Myths We Live By*. Routledge, 2003.

Midgley, M., *Are You An Illusion?* Routledge, 2014.

Miller, L., *Heaven: Our Enduring Fascination with the Afterlife*. HarperCollins, 2010.

Mills, A. and Slobodin, R. (eds.), *Amerindian Rebirth: Reincarnation Belief Among North American Indians and Inuit*. University of Toronto Press, 1994.

Milton, J., *Paradise Lost*. Oxford University Press, 2008.

Mitchell, S. (translator), *Gilgamesh*. Profile Books, 2004.

Moen, O.M., The case for cryonics. *Journal of Medical Ethics* 41:8 (2015): 493-503. http://dx.doi.org/10.1136/medethics-2015-102715

Moore, R.I., *The War on Heresy: Faith and Power in Medieval Europe.* Profile Books, 2014.

Moreira, I., *Heaven's Purge: Purgatory in Late Antiquity.* Oxford University Press, 2010.

Moreira, I. and Toscano, M. (eds.), *Hell and its Afterlife: Historical and Contemporary Perspectives.* Ashgate, 2010.

Morphy, H., *Ancestral Connections: Art and an Aboriginal System of Knowledge.* University of Chicago Press, 1991.

Moss, R., *The Life After Death in Oceania and the Malay Archipelago.* Oxford University Press, 1925.

Mulhall, S., *Heidegger and* Being and Time. Routledge, 1996.

Nagel, T., Panpsychism. In *Mortal Questions* (Cambridge University Press, 1979): 181-95.

Nagel, T., *Secular Philosophy and the Religious Temperament.* Oxford University Press, 2010.

Nagel, T., *Mind and Cosmos: Why the Materialist Neo-Darwinian Conception of Nature is Almost Certainly False.* Oxford University Press, 2012.

Nelson, P. and Masel, J., Intercellular competition and the inevitability of multicellular aging. *Proceedings of the National Academy of Sciences* 114 no. 49 (2017). www.pnas.org/cgi/doi/10.1073/pnas.1618854114

Newell, W.H. (ed.), *Ancestors.* Mouton Publishers, 1976.

Niem, D. von, *De schismate... libri III.* Johann Petreius, Nürnberg, 1532.

Nozick, R., *Invariances: The Structure of the Objective World.* The Belknap Press of Harvard University Press, 2001.

Nussbaum, M.C., *Love's Knowledge: Essays on Philosophy and Literature.* Oxford University Press, 1990.

Obeyesekere, G., *Imagining Karma: Ethical Transformation in Amerindian, Buddhist, and Greek Rebirth.* University of

California Press, 2002.

Obeyesekere, G., *Karma and Rebirth: A Cross-Cultural Study*. Motilal Banarsadass, 2005.

O'Connell, M., *To Be A Machine: Adventures Among Cyborgs, Utopians, Hackers, and the Futurists Solving the Modest Problem of Death*. Granta, 2017.

Ogren, B., *Renaissance and Rebirth: Reincarnation in Early Modern Italian Kabbalah*. Brill, 2009.

Olupona, J. (ed.), *African Spirituality: Forms, Meanings and Expressions*. Crossroad Press, 2000.

Onyewuenyi, I.C., *African Belief in Reincarnation: A Philosophical Reappraisal*. Snaap Press, 1996.

Orlin, E. (ed.), *The Routledge Encyclopedia of Ancient Mediterranean Religions*. Routledge, 2016.

Osborne, C., *Dumb Beasts and Dead Philosophers*. Oxford University Press, 2007.

Ovid, *Metamorphoses*, translated by M.M. Innes. Penguin Books, 1955.

Parrinder, E.G., Varieties of belief in reincarnation. *Hibbert Journal* 55/2 (1956): 260-67.

Pearsall, P., *The Heart's Code: Tapping the Wisdom and Power of Our Heart Energy*. Broadway Books, 1999.

Pearsall, P., Schwartz, G.E. and Russek, L.G.S., Changes in Heart Transplant Recipients That Parallel the Personalities of Their Donors. *Journal of Near-Death Studies* 20:3 (2002): 191-206.

Pérez-Remón, J., *Self and Non-Self in Early Buddhism*. Mouton Publishers, 1980.

Peters, F.E., *A Reader of Classical Islam*. Princeton University Press, 1994.

Pew Research Center, Many Americans Mix Multiple Faiths. 9 December 2009.

Pew Research Center, U.S. Public Becoming Less Religious. 3 November 2015.

Phelps, E.S., *The Gates Ajar*. Milner and Company, 1890.

Phelps, E.S., *Chapters from a Life*. Houghton Mifflin, 1896.

Pico della Mirandola, G., *On the Dignity of Man; On Being and the One; Heptaplus*, translated by C. Wallis, P. Miller and D. Carmichael. Bobbs-Merrill, 1965.

Pikirayi, I., 'The living dead': Shona worldview around death and burial and implications for archaeology. In *Global Ancestors: Understanding the Shared Humanity of our Ancestors*, eds. M. Clegg, R. Redfern, J. Bekvalac and H. Bonnet (Oxbow Books, 2013): 134-45.

Plato, *The Last Days of Socrates (Euthyphro, The Apology, Crito, Phaedo)*, translated by H. Tredennick. Penguin, 1969.

Plato, *The Republic*, translated by D. Lee. Penguin, 1974.

Plato, *Symposium*, translated by R. Waterfield. Oxford University Press, 1994.

Plato, *Gorgias*, translated by R. Waterfield. Oxford University Press, 2008.

Pliny the Younger, *The Letters of the Younger Pliny*, translated by B. Radice. Penguin Classics, 1969.

Poe, E.A., *Selected Tales*, edited by K. Graham. Oxford University Press, 1967.

Popper, K.R., *Objective Knowledge: An Evolutionary Approach*. Oxford University Press, 1972.

Powell, A. (ed.), *Roman Poetry and Propaganda in the Age of Augustus*. Bristol Classical Press, 2013.

Price, S. and Kearns, E. (eds.), *The Oxford Dictionary of Classical Myth and Religion*. Oxford University Press, 2003.

Pritchard, J.B. (ed.), *Ancient Near Eastern Texts Relating to the Old Testament*, third edition with supplement. Princeton University Press, 1969.

Pyszczynski, T., Solomon, S. and Greenberg, J., *In the Wake of 9/11: The Psychology of Terror*. American Psychological Association, 2002.

Quinet, E., *Merlin l'Enchanteur*. Michel Levy Frères, 1860.

Quinet, E., *The Enchanter Merlin*, adapted by B. Stableford.

Hollywood Comics, 2014.

Quirke, S., *Ancient Egyptian Religion*. Dover Publications, 1992.

Radhakrishnan, S., *Principal Upanishads*. Harper and Row, 1953.

Raphael, S.P., *Jewish Views of the Afterlife*, second edition. Rowman and Littlefield Publishers, 2009.

Raudive, K., *Breakthrough: An Amazing Experiment in Electronic Communication with the Dead*. Taplinger, 1971.

Restall Orr, E., *The Wakeful World: Animism, Mind and the Self in Nature*. Moon Books, 2012.

Robineau, D., Ageing Britain: two-fifths of NHS budget is spent on over-65s. *The Guardian*, 1 February 2016.

Robinson, H. (ed.), *Objections to Physicalism*. Clarendon Press, 1993.

Rodda, M.A., L'*Inno Omerico ad Afrodite* (V) e la cronologia relativa dell'epica greca arcaica. In *Comincio a cantare: contribute allo studio degli* Inni Omerici, ed. R. Di Donato (Edizioni ETS, 2016): 82-101.

Rooke, B.E. (ed.), *The Collected Works of Samuel Taylor Coleridge: The Friend, Volume 4* (in two volumes). Routledge & Kegan Paul/Princeton University Press, 1969.

Roy, O., *Jihad and Death: The Global Appeal of Islamic State*, translated by C. Schoch. Hurst and Company, 2017.

Runes, D.D. (ed.), *Treasury of Philosophy*. Philosophical Library, 1955.

Russell, J.B., *A History of Heaven: The Singing Silence*. Princeton University Press, 1997.

Rustomji, N., *The Garden and the Fire: Heaven and Hell in Islamic Culture*. Columbia University Press, 2009.

Sandars, N.K. (translator), *The Epic of Gilgamesh*. Penguin Classics, 1960.

Sasson, J.M. (ed.), *Civilizations of the Ancient Near East*, 4 volumes. Charles Scribner's Sons, 1995.

Scarre, G., *Death*. Acumen, 2007.

Schibli, H.S., *Pherekydes of Syros*. Clarendon Press, 1998.

Schmidt, B.B., *Israel's Beneficent Dead: Ancestor Cult and Necromancy in Ancient Israelite Religion and Tradition*. Eisenbrauns, 1996.

Schumacher, S. and Woerner, G. (eds.), *The Rider Encyclopedia of Eastern Philosophy and Religion*. Rider, 1989.

Seabrook, W.B., *The Magic Island*. George G. Harrap and Co. Ltd., 1929.

Seachris, J.W. (ed.), *Exploring the Meaning of Life: Anthology and Guide*. Wiley-Blackwell, 2013.

Seager, W., Consciousness, information, and panpsychism. *Journal of Consciousness Studies* 2:3 (1995): 272-88.

Segal, A.F., *Life After Death: A History of the Afterlife in Western Religion*. Doubleday, 2004.

Severin, T., *The Brendan Voyage*. Gill and Macmillan Ltd, 2005.

Sharma, C., *A Critical Survey of Indian Philosophy*. Motilal Banarsidass, 1987.

Shaw, G.B., *Back to Methuselah*. Penguin, 1987.

Shaw, I. and Nicholson, P., *The British Museum Dictionary of Ancient Egypt*. British Museum Press, 1995.

Silverberg, R., *Recalled to Life*. Panther, 1975.

Sima Qian, *The First Emperor: Selections from the* Historical Records, translated by R. Dawson. Oxford University Press, 2007.

Simpson, M.A., *Death, Dying, and Grief: A Critically Annotated Bibliography and Source Book of Thanatology and Terminal Care*. Plenum, 1979.

Skrbina, D., *Panpsychism in the West*. MIT Press, 2005.

Slusser, G., Westfahl, G. and Rabkin, E.S. (eds.), *Immortal Engines: Life Extension and Immortality in Science Fiction and Fantasy*. University of Georgia Press, 1996.

Smith, J.I. and Haddad, Y.Y., *The Islamic Understanding of Death and Resurrection*, new edition. Oxford University Press, 2002.

Smith, J.Z., *Drudgery Divine: On the Comparison of Christianities and the Religions of Late Antiquity*. Routledge, 1990.

Smith, M., Democratization of the Afterlife. In *UCLA Encyclopedia of Egyptology*, eds. J. Dieleman and W. Wendrich, 2009. http://digital2.library.ucla.edu/viewItem.do?ark=21198/zz001nf62b

Solomon, S., Greenberg, J. and Pyszczynski, T., *The Worm at the Core: On the Role of Death in Life*. Random House, 2015.

Sophocles, *Antigone*, translated by R. Fagles. Penguin, 2015.

Sparks, H.F.D. (ed.), *The Apocryphal Old Testament*. Clarendon Press, 1984.

Spencer, B. and Gillen, F.J., *The Northern Tribes of Central Australia*. Macmillan and Co., 1904.

Sperling, H. and Simon, M. (translators), *The Zohar*, 5 volumes. Second edition. Soncino Press, 1934.

Stahl, H.-P., *Poetry Underpinning Power – Vergil's* Aeneid: *The Epic for Emperor Augustus*. Classical Press of Wales, 2016.

Statius, *Thebaid Books 8-12, Achilleid*, translated by J.H. Mozley. Loeb Classical Library. Heinemann, 1928.

Steiner, R.C., *Disembodied Souls: The* Nefesh *in Israel and Kindred Spirits in the Ancient Near East*. Society for Biblical Literature, 2015.

Stevenson, I., *Twenty Cases of the Reincarnation Type*. University of Virginia Press, 1974.

Stevenson, I., *Cases of the Reincarnation Type: Vol. 1 – Ten Cases in India*. University of Virginia Press, 1975.

Stevenson, I., *Children Who Remember Previous Lives: A Question of Reincarnation*. University of Virginia Press, 1987.

Strawson, G., Realistic monism: why physicalism entails panpsychism. *Journal of Consciousness Studies* 13:10-11 (2006): 3-31.

Stump, E., *Aquinas*. Routledge, 2005.

Sturluson, S., *The Prose Edda: Prologue and Gylfaginning – Tales from Norse Mythology*, translated by A. Faulkes. Clarendon Press, 1982.

Suy, R., Philip Verheyen (1648-1710) and his *Corporis Humani Anatomiae*. *Acta chirurgica Belgica* 107 (2007): 343-54.

Swain, T., *A Place for Strangers: Towards a History of Australian*

Aboriginal Being. Cambridge University Press, 1996.

Swain, T. and Trompf, G., *The Religions of Oceania*. Routledge, 1995.

Swedenborg, E., *Heaven and Hell*, translated by G.F. Dole. Swedenborg Foundation, 2009.

Swift, J., *Gulliver's Travels*. Macmillan and Co., 1932 [1726].

Taylor, A.K., *The History of Hell*. Robert Hale Ltd, 1996.

Tennyson, A., *The Works of Alfred Lord Tennyson: Poet Laureate*. Macmillan and Co., 1894.

Tenzing, T., Karma and Rebirth in Buddhism. *Bulletin of Tibetology* 1 (1996): 13-20.

Tertullian, *On the Resurrection of the Flesh*, translated by P. Holmes. In Volume 3 of *The Ante-Nicene Fathers: The Writings of the Fathers Down to A.D. 325*, eds. A. Roberts, J. Donaldson and A. Cleveland Coxe. Christian Literature Company, 1885.

Thucydides, *History of the Peloponnesian War*, translated by R. Crawley. J.M. Dent, 1910.

Tigay, J.H., *The Evolution of the Gilgamesh Epic*, second edition. Bolchazy-Carducci Publishers, 2002.

Tononi, G., *Phi: A Voyage from the Brain to the Soul*. Pantheon, 2012.

Tononi, G. and Koch, C., Consciousness: here, there and everywhere? *Philosophical Transactions of the Royal Society London B* (2015). DOI: 10.1098/rstb.2014.0167.

Toynbee, J.M.C., *Death and Burial in the Roman World*. Thames and Hudson, 1971.

Tvardovsky, A., *Tyorkin and the Stovemakers: Poetry and Prose by Alexander Tvardovsky*, translated by A. Rudolf. Carcanet Press, 1974.

Twain, M., *Extract from Captain Stormfield's Visit to Heaven*. Harper and Bros, 1909.

Tylor, E., *Primitive Culture*. John Murray, 1913.

Tzamalikos, P., *Origen: Philosophy of History and Eschatology*. Brill, 2007.

Uchendu, V., *The Igbo of Southeast Nigeria*. Holt, Rinehart and Winston, 1965.

Ucko, P.J., Ethnography and archaeological interpretation of funerary remains. *World Archaeology* 1 (2) (1969): 262-80.

United Nations, *World Population Prospects: The 2017 Revision*. United Nations, 2017.

Velmans, M., *Understanding Consciousness*, second edition. Routledge, 2009.

Vetter, T., *The Ideas and Meditative Practices of Early Buddhism*. Brill, 1980.

Virgil, *The Aeneid*, translated by R. Fagles. Penguin, 2006.

Voth, H.R., The traditions of the Hopi. *Field Columbian Museum Publication 96. Anthropological Series 8*, 1932.

Walker, S., *Memorials to the Roman Dead*. British Museum Publications, 1985.

Warren, H.C., *Buddhism in Translations*. Harvard Oriental Series, 1909.

Weon, B.M. and Je, J.H., Theoretical estimation of maximum human lifespan. *Biogerontology* 10 (2009): 65–71. DOI:10.1007/s10522-008-9156-4.

West, M.L., *The Orphic Poems*. Clarendon Press, 1983.

Whitbread, L.G. (translator), *Fulgentius the Mythographer*. Ohio State University Press, 1971.

Whitehead, A.N., *Process and Reality*. Free Press, 1979.

Willerslev, R., *Soul Hunters: Hunting, Animism, and Personhood among the Siberian Yukaghirs*. University of California Press, 2007.

Williams, B., The Makropulos case: reflections on the tedium of immortality. In *Problems of the Self: Philosophical Papers 1956-1972* (Cambridge University Press, 1973): 82-100.

Wilson, I., *Mind Out of Time: Reincarnation Investigated*. Gollancz, 1981.

Wolfram von Eschenbach, *Parzival* and *Titurel*, translated by C. Edwards. Oxford University Press, 2006.

Wood, J., *The Holy Grail: History and Legend*. University of Wales Press, 2012.

Wright, J.E., *The Early History of Heaven*. Oxford University Press, 2000.

Wright, N.T., *The Resurrection of the Son of God*. SPCK, 2003.

Zaleski, C., *Otherworld Journeys: Accounts of Near-Death Experiences in Medieval and Modern Times*. Oxford University Press, 1987.

Zaleski, C. and Zaleski, P. (eds.), *The Book of Heaven: An Anthology of Writings from Ancient to Modern Times*. Oxford University Press, 2000.

Zanker, P., *The Power of Images in the Age of Augustus*, translated by A. Shapiro. University Press of Michigan, 1988.

Ziolkowski, T., *Gilgamesh Among Us: Modern Encounters With the Ancient Epic*. Cornell University Press, 2011.

Select Index

BOOKS

SPIRITUALITY

O is a symbol of the world, of oneness and unity; this eye represents knowledge and insight. We publish titles on general spirituality and living a spiritual life. We aim to inform and help you on your own journey in this life.

If you have enjoyed this book, why not tell other readers by posting a review on your preferred book site?

The Holy Spirit's Interpretation of the New Testament
A Course in Understanding and Acceptance
Regina Dawn Akers
Following on from the strength of *A Course In Miracles*, NTI
teaches us how to experience the love and oneness of God.
Paperback: 978-1-84694-085-9 ebook: 978-1-78099-083-5

The Message of A Course In Miracles
A translation of the Text in plain language
Elizabeth A. Cronkhite
A translation of *A Course in Miracles* into plain, everyday
language for anyone seeking inner peace. The companion
volume, *Practicing A Course In Miracles*, offers practical lessons
and mentoring.
Paperback: 978-1-84694-319-5 ebook: 978-1-84694-642-4

Thinker's Guide to God
Peter Vardy
An introduction to key issues in the philosophy of religion.
Paperback: 978-1-90381-622-6

Your Simple Path
Find Happiness in every step
Ian Tucker
A guide to helping us reconnect with what is really important in
our lives.
Paperback: 978-1-78279-349-6 ebook: 978-1-78279-348-9

365 Days of Wisdom
Daily Messages To Inspire You Through The Year
Dadi Janki
Daily messages which cool the mind, warm the heart and guide
you along your journey.
Paperback: 978-1-84694-863-3 ebook: 978-1-84694-864-0

Body of Wisdom
Women's Spiritual Power and How it Serves
Hilary Hart
Bringing together the dreams and experiences of women across
the world with today's most visionary spiritual teachers.
Paperback: 978-1-78099-696-7 ebook: 978-1-78099-695-0

Dying to Be Free
From Enforced Secrecy to Near Death to True Transformation
Hannah Robinson
After an unexpected accident and near-death experience, Hannah
Robinson found herself radically transforming her life, while a
remarkable new insight altered her relationship with her father, a
practising Catholic priest.
Paperback: 978-1-78535-254-6 ebook: 978-1-78535-255-3

The Ecology of the Soul
A Manual of Peace, Power and Personal Growth for Real People
in the Real World
Aidan Walker
Balance your own inner Ecology of the Soul to regain your
natural state of peace, power and wellbeing.
Paperback: 978-1-78279-850-7 ebook: 978-1-78279-849-1

Not I, Not other than I
The Life and Teachings of Russel Williams
Steve Taylor, Russel Williams
The miraculous life and inspiring teachings of one of the World's
greatest living Sages.
Paperback: 978-1-78279-729-6 ebook: 978-1-78279-728-9

On the Other Side of Love
A woman's unconventional journey towards wisdom
Muriel Maufroy
When life has lost all meaning, what do you do?
Paperback: 978-1-78535-281-2 ebook: 978-1-78535-282-9

Practicing A Course In Miracles
A translation of the Workbook in plain language, with mentor's notes
Elizabeth A. Cronkhite
The practical second and third volumes of The Plain-Language *A Course In Miracles*.
Paperback: 978-1-84694-403-1 ebook: 978-1-78099-072-9

Quantum Bliss
The Quantum Mechanics of Happiness, Abundance, and Health
George S. Mentz
Quantum Bliss is the breakthrough summary of success and spirituality secrets that customers have been waiting for.
Paperback: 978-1-78535-203-4 ebook: 978-1-78535-204-1

The Upside Down Mountain
Mags MacKean
A must-read for anyone weary of chasing success and happiness – one woman's inspirational journey swapping the uphill slog for the downhill slope.
Paperback: 978-1-78535-171-6 ebook: 978-1-78535-172-3

Your Personal Tuning Fork
The Endocrine System
Deborah Bates
Discover your body's health secret, the endocrine system, and 'twang' your way to sustainable health!
Paperback: 978-1-84694-503-8 ebook: 978-1-78099-697-4

Readers of ebooks can buy or view any of these bestsellers by clicking on the live link in the title. Most titles are published in paperback and as an ebook. Paperbacks are available in traditional bookshops. Both print and ebook formats are available online.

Find more titles and sign up to our readers' newsletter at http://www.johnhuntpublishing.com/mind-body-spirit

Follow us on Facebook at https://www.facebook.com/OBooks/ and Twitter at https://twitter.com/obooks